Still Improving:
Becoming the World's Most
Experienced 747 Captain
by
Nick Eades
ISBN: 978-1-914933-12-7

Copyright 2021
All rights reserved. No part of this publication may be reproduced, stored in a retrieval system or transmitted in any form or by any means, electronic, mechanical, photocopy, recording org otherwise, without prior written consent of the copyright owner. Nor can it be circulated in any form of binding or cover other than that in which it is published and without similar condition including this condition being imposed on a subsequent purchaser.

The right of Nick Eades to be identified as the author of this work has been asserted in accordance with the Copyright Designs and Patents Act 1988.

A copy of this book is deposited with the British Library.

Published By: -

i2i
PUBLISHING

i2i Publishing. Manchester.
www.i2i.publishing.co.uk

This book is dedicated to all those young pilots striving to achieve a career in aviation. The world in 2021 is a world in crisis and the airline industry has been one of the hardest hit.

One of the major casualties from the collapse of international air travel is the new generation of pilots. The majority of them will have huge training debts to repay, with little prospect of immediate employment.

Hopefully, this book and its predecessor, *The Self-Improver*, will remind them that even in the darkest hour, there is always hope.

4

Acknowledgements

Once again, my heartfelt thanks to everyone mentioned in this book. They have, for many and varied reasons, made my career unforgettable.

Following on from my first book, *The Self-Improver*, writing this sequel reminds me that the years have literally flown by and without the help and support of my family, I could never have remained airborne for nearly fifty years.

Once again, special thanks go to my publisher, Lionel Ross, and his chief editor, Mark Cripps. Without their help and support, neither book may have made it to print.

Also, special thanks to my son, Rob, who once again, designed the book covers and has provided invaluable support with his copy writing and technical skills. I now know how to turn my computer on and off; the rest I leave to Rob. My eldest son, James wisely moved to New York before either book was written. Luckily for me, James made time from his successful film company to help proofread the book. To both of my sons and my wife Liz, thank you for your enthusiasm and support.

Sally Pitiakoydis, again helped with her editing, and Mike McCarthy, again provided the illustrations.

Thank you all, my family and friends.

Contents

Prologue	Two Worlds About to Collide	9
Chapter 1	The End of an Era	11
Chapter 2	Nearly a Tragic End	19
Chapter 3	No Going Back Now	27
Chapter 4	Having My Cake and Eating it	45
Chapter 5	A Jumbo Beginning	51
Chapter 6	Look Out World – Here I Come	69
Chapter 7	Unhappy Times	75
Chapter 8	A Very Welcome Return To Gatwick	83
Chapter 9	A Tragic Christmas	91
Chapter 10	A Silent Night Miracle	97
Chapter 11	Unexpected Consequences	107
Chapter 12	A Day Out To Remember	115
Chapter 13	Meeting the Mujahideen	125
Chapter 14	A Merger, and a New Start	133
Chapter 15	The Kalahari Canoe Club	141
Chapter 16	Nyumbani and the Old Oak Tree	151
Chapter 17	Characters	161

Chapter 18	The Youngest BA 747 Captain	169
Chapter 19	The Beach Fleet	177
Chapter 20	The Day the World Stopped	189
Chapter 21	A New World; A New Aircraft	197
Chapter 22	Sad Times	211
Chapter 23	A Time To Reflect	221
Chapter 24	Singapore Sling	229
Chapter 25	Send Three and Fourpence	237
Chapter 26	Unexpected Consequences	245
Chapter 27	Busy Going Nowhere	253
Chapter 28	Life Changes Forever	265
Chapter 29	They Think It's All Over	271
Chapter 30	Thank You and Good Night	279
Epilogue	Pathway for the Modern Pilot	295
Photo Gallery	Life with the 747	299

Prologue

Two Worlds About to Collide

Choose a job you love, and you will never have to work a day in your life --- Confucius

The world breaks everyone, and afterward many are strong at the broken places --- Ernest Hemingway

Following on from *The Self-Improver*, the next stage of my career beckons. From the world of small aircraft, I make a leap of faith into the world of the major international airlines. These institutions had never before considered the self-taught pilot, instead preferring their own students or pilots from the Armed Forces.

The two worlds were about to collide, the results were totally unpredictable.

Chapter 1

The End of an Era

I had, up until this point in my flying career, been a relatively large fish in a very small pond. I had managed this, not through any sense of achievement; I had simply stayed within a very small sector of the aviation world and had not ventured into the infinitely larger world of airline flying.

The year was 1987, and after a long and winding road, I had managed to beg, steal and borrow my way into becoming a professional pilot. This path has been duly recorded in the first part of my memoirs, *The Self-Improver*. From very humble beginnings, I had managed to work my way up from being the proud owner of a private pilot's license. I had served my time as a flying instructor, and more by luck than judgement, had ended up running an executive jet company. Now, at the age of thirty, I had a life-defining decision to make: Do I stay put and enjoy the fruits of my labour or start from scratch and apply to join the airlines?

Unlike other professional careers, the life of a typical airline pilot is inextricably tied to one or two airlines by the binding thread of the all-important seniority system. No other profession ties a pilot to an employer quite like the airline industry. A banker or solicitor may leave one firm and move to another, taking their seniority and experience with them. A

Queen's Counsel can move from one chamber to another and still expect to be a Queen's Counsel. A highly experienced surgeon may move from one hospital to another and still expect to be recognised as a senior surgeon. Neither professional would accept that such a move would necessitate them starting their careers all over again. Our QC would not accept becoming an articled clerk and our surgeon would not accept the position of a junior doctor. They had both earned the right to be respected for the skill and experience they had gained over many decades.

Unfortunately, this luxury is not afforded to the professional pilot. Should a senior captain decide to move from one airline to another, then he goes from the top of one pile to the very bottom of another. With very few exceptions, usually restricted to pilot managers only, a senior pilot of one company will find himself the most junior co-pilot of another company. Like the disgraced army officers of the past where their uniform decorations were cut off by a sword, our captain would suffer the same fate, although swords are now rarely used. Instead, the hard-earned four stripes on the cuff and shoulder would be replaced by a mere two stripes, indicating that the wearer was now the lowest of the low. A two-striper could be on his first flight and would be treated accordingly. Decades of piloting flights and all the related experience would be discounted at a stroke and careers would have to start from the beginning once again.

Why then, would anyone in their right mind subject themselves to this perceived and sometimes actual humiliation? The answer is that the majority of pilots do their very best to avoid this reversal in their careers. Some may, after a few years in the smaller airlines, decide that returning to the bottom of the career ladder was a price worth paying to fly with one of the major airlines. Other pilots suffer the trauma of being made redundant from failing or failed airlines. They have to accept that starting all over again is the only way to restart their career.

Very few pilots move between airlines through choice unless they decide to fly for a foreign carrier.

So why then, does the airline industry continue to treat pilots in this seemingly inhumane fashion? The answer lies simply in one word - seniority. Seniority is something you are given on the day you join an airline. It starts as a very high number, if there are two thousand pilots already in the airline then you become number two thousand and one Each year or so, pilots at the top of the seniority list retire and you subsequently move one place up the ladder. If the airline is expanding and employs another fifty pilots the day after you join, then once again, you move up the ladder by fifty places. This process continues until you become senior enough to start a command or a captain course. If you are fortunate enough to pass this course, then you move from the top of the co-pilot's seniority list, which allows you to have control over your work pattern, to the bottom of the captain's list, which means you fly the trips that more senior pilots do not want to operate. An airline pilot's life is controlled by this seniority system, from the first to the very last flight. The most important number in a pilot's life is their seniority number. And if you change airlines, then it matters not if you are the most senior captain or most junior co-pilot; both of you will start all over again at the very bottom.

Would this seemingly draconian system be tolerated in other industries? If not, why do the airlines continue to employ such a process? To try to understand why this system continues to control a pilot's career, you have to look beyond the harshness of the procedure and to try to make sense of the seemingly senseless.

As an airline passenger, you have the right to expect that the people flying your aircraft are all highly trained and skilled. If you employ a lawyer, you can research who is most qualified to represent you. If you are fortunate enough to have private medical insurance, then you can choose which surgeon is most qualified to treat your condition. One thing you are unable to choose is the pilot who is going to fly your aircraft, unless of course, you are wealthy enough to own your aircraft.

"Let's go to Spain next month," your partner suddenly announces. You immediately start to look at the availability and cost of flights. One thing you will not and could not do is look for a flight with the best or safest pilots. Imagine a conversation along the following lines.

"Darling, let's go to Barbados."

"That's a wonderful idea. Let me just check which flights have the safest pilots."

Whilst this is possible when choosing a physician or lawyer, it is most certainly not possible to choose a pilot. Herein lies the problem, airlines cannot promote based on ability. All pilots must achieve and maintain the highest of standards. This level of ability is scrutinized and checked to a degree unequalled in any other profession. Twice a year, every pilot is put in a simulator for eight hours. Every possible emergency is thrown at them and their reactions are analysed in great detail. Any shortcomings are immediately addressed and if these highest of required standards are not met and maintained, then a pilot's career is over. No other career subjects its workforce to such continual and judicious assessment.

So, if airlines cannot promote ability, what criteria can be applied to decide when to promote pilot and which pilots are deserving of such a promotion? This is how the seniority system came into being. As ability is a prerequisite, pilots are promoted according to their length of service. Whilst not a perfect system by any means, it does ensure that each pilot is offered a chance of promotion and the airlines do not suffer the high cost of pilots moving between employers regularly.

This then was the choice I was facing in early 1987. Did I stay where I was, the chief pilot of a company I had set up, or give up all I had worked so hard for and become a very junior co-pilot in one of the airlines? I was turning thirty. I was no longer the young and upcoming pilot who was going to change the face of aviation. Well in truth, I was never going to be that; the ambitions of youth slowly dim with time.

Our small company was doing well. We had built a solid reputation within the small world of executive aviation. We operated a variety of aircraft and sub-chartered aircraft as and when we needed them. The HS 125 executive jet, a ten-seater aircraft we had used to great effect, was our main aircraft. From flying royalty to the famous U2 Irish band, I loved to fly this superb aircraft. Our holding company had bought the aircraft outright and we needed to keep it flying to cover the enormous operating costs. So far, we had managed to achieve this. However, every day presented an opportunity for us to fall behind on our projected flying programme.

Every aircraft has to be maintained to a strict maintenance schedule. From daily to weekly, monthly and annual checks, each aircraft is subjected to the same rigorous examinations as the pilots who fly them. It was time for our aircraft to undergo one of its major checks. This had to be completed at Southampton, a twenty-minute flight away from our home base. I taxied our aircraft out to the runway at London Gatwick for the short flight to Southampton on the south coast. The mood onboard was celebratory; I had invited members of the cricket club I played for, along for the ride. The weather was beautiful. We flew a sightseeing trip around the Isle of White before self-positioning for a visual approach into Southampton. Parking our aircraft outside of the maintenance hangar, a noisy and slightly worse for wear cricket team poured itself from the aircraft for a photo session before boarding the bus back to Gatwick. I secured the aircraft and handed all of the maintenance manuals to the waiting engineers. I would pick the aircraft up in a week after its major check. With hardly a backward glance I left my pride and joy sitting outside the hangar. Had I known at the time that I would never set eyes on this wonderful aircraft again, then I would have given it the send-off it so richly deserved. Instead, I turned my back on my flying friend and accepted the first of many beers on the drive home. As she sat there awaiting her fate, I hoped that the fading laughter from the team bus as it drove away did not offend her majestic dignity.

Two days after leaving our aircraft alone outside the maintenance hangar, I received the worst possible news an aircraft owner could get. Our beautiful aircraft had a crack in the tail spar. Well, I thought to myself, that does not sound too serious. A bit of welding here and there, a bit of filler, a new paint job, and away we go. I fell silent as the chief mechanic carefully explained the full extent and seriousness of the problem. A tear rolled down my face as he finally made it clear that the cost of repairing the aircraft exceeded its current value. The entire back section of the aircraft would have to be removed and a new tail section fitted. The aircraft in its current state was unflyable and the aircraft was now only worth the parts that could be salvaged and fitted to other aircraft. For a moment, my aviation world stopped dead in its tracks. I slowly replaced the telephone and simply sat there staring straight ahead; I have no idea how long I remained in this position. Eventually, however, I was brought back to reality as the telephone sprung back into life. It was an enquiry as to the availability of our now permanently grounded aircraft. After politely informing the customer that unfortunately, we had no spare capacity, I did what I normally do in times of crisis, I collected my belongings and went to the pub.

Two hours later, Pete Brown, my business partner, found me still sitting at the bar. Luckily, I had taken the ill-fated call at the end of the working day, and even more luckily, the pub was not a pub but a social club two doors down from our office in the Beehive Building at Gatwick. We were fortunate to have our office in this art deco building which had originally been the main terminal at Gatwick. There was a convivial atmosphere about the building, and at the end of each day, you would always find the occupants of other offices meeting in the bar to exchange war stories.

Today, I had a rather major war story to tell. After relating the extent of our problem to Pete, he joined me at the bar. We rarely drank heavily; the beer was usually just a backdrop that allowed us to relax and work through the problems of the day. We both decided that this was indeed a huge problem which no amount of beer could resolve. Our glasses sat untouched as we tried to figure out how to make the best of a bad situation. Hours later, the problem still unresolved, we finally drained our glasses and called for a taxi to take us home. I knew in my heart that I had reached a turning point in my career, from now on life would be very different.

Chapter 2

Nearly a Tragic End

With our executive jet now history, our priority was finding a replacement aircraft for our holding company, Foodbrokers. The company itself had begun to downsize and had moved its main base to Portsmouth on the south coast. As its markets began to change, the company had different requirements for its aircraft. The cost of the jet had been very high, and it had been a struggle to justify its upkeep. The decision was made to return to the world of the turboprop. After looking at several contenders, we finally settled on the Cessna Conquest. This was a big step down as far as I was concerned. However, it did fulfil the Foodbrokers requirement. The Conquest was an eight-seater aircraft, reasonably fast, and it had an acceptable range. I found it very difficult to work up any great enthusiasm to fly the plane. Everything up to this point had been a leap forward in terms of size and performance, and this was the first time we had gone backwards. To be fair to the aircraft, it did a good job for the company and kept our executives moving around the UK and Europe. Our problem was that we were again flying at eighteen thousand feet. Also, at two hundred and fifty knots, we were once again staring enviously at the airliners, quickly overtaking us at least twenty thousand feet above us. It began to dawn on me that with another thirty years flying ahead of me, this was not what I wanted to do anymore.

Being an executive jet pilot has many advantages. You are your own boss. But even before your passengers arrive at the aircraft, you are a jack of all trades. Once a flight has been booked, it is up to the pilot, and with the Cessna, there was only one pilot, to organise everything. Flight planning could take hours, as permissions were sought for landing, airway, and parking slots. Fuel had to be ordered and paid for. Catering had to be ordered, collected, and placed in the aircraft. When the passengers eventually arrived at the airport, they had to be met and escorted through the terminal and out to the aircraft. And finally, when the aircraft door was shut, you had to fly the plane to its destination. The flying of the trip was sometimes the easiest part of the job. These extra duties could be endured as an eager young pilot desperate to accumulate experience and flying hours. For me, at this point in my career, I had experienced the highs of flying an executive jet with two pilots and an air hostess. I had also flown an airliner with one hundred passengers and three cabin crew members. Various departments had looked after all the ancillary ground duties instead of doing them myself. I recognised that I had experienced the high life and was reluctant to go backward.

However, I could not simply apply to the airlines and walk away from the company that Pete and I had set up. I had also had a taste of flying charter flights for Dan-Air to gain experience flying larger jets. Although I had thoroughly enjoyed flying with this airline the summer before, the idea of short-haul trips back and forth to Europe for the next thirty years also held no great appeal. I had reached a crossroads in my career, and I was struggling to see which direction I wanted to go next. Our HS 125 had sadly departed. Unhappily, as a consequence, I had to authorise a number of the pilots who flew with us to also leave. This was very hard, both for them and for me personally. With the arrival of the Cessna, only one extra pilot was needed to fly the aircraft when I was unavailable. This would be a very part-time position and probably suit a retired pilot who still enjoyed the occasional trip.

My father had been a Boeing 707 captain with British Caledonian based at Gatwick. British Caledonian would later merge with British Airways. After retiring, I had managed to persuade him to join the company flying the HS 125. Luckily, I was a fully qualified instructor and examiner. I had personally trained him on the aircraft. He had been reluctant at first; luckily, the sheer pleasure of flying the jet had lured him out of retirement. Could I possibly perform a similar feat with our new Cessna Conquest? I very much doubted it; however, as they say, nothing ventured, nothing gained.

To my great surprise, after an afternoon of getting to know the aircraft, my father agreed to continue with the company as a stand-in pilot. The only condition stipulated was that he insisted on having a co-pilot with him at all times. Whilst this increased costs, as legally we did not require two pilots, a compromise was agreed that we would have a pilot's assistant in the co-pilot's seat. Although not commercially qualified pilots, these assistants would hold a private pilot's twin-engine rating and be capable of assisting the pilot. As they were not commercial pilots, we could not pay them for flying. However, we could pay all expenses, and in return, they could log flying hours on the sectors that had no commercial passengers. It turned out to be a win-win situation for both the company and the pilot assistants.

So it was, that on one very grey day in the winter of 1986, our Cessna Conquest was taxiing out for a return flight from Edinburgh in Scotland to Shoreham Airport. In command and in the left-hand seat was my father. His assistant that night was none other than my friend and co-owner of the company, Peter Brown. Sitting comfortably in the back enjoying a well-earned aperitif and meal were four weary executives. The flight to Edinburgh had been completed without incident, and the aircraft touched down ahead of schedule. Although the weather was challenging with numerous storm clouds along the route, the considerable experience of the captain ensured that the passengers had a mainly smooth flight.

The aircraft sat on the ground for five hours as the executives attended their meetings. After a full Scottish breakfast, including the all-important black pudding, the two pilots whiled the hours away exploring the facilities at the airport. They visited the local flying club for a leisurely lunch. Take-off was scheduled for five o'clock that afternoon, which meant a night flight back to Shoreham. The enroute weather forecast for the return flight was carefully considered. Due to the forecast of thunderstorms, a higher than usual cruising altitude was selected to fly above the weather. This was close to the aircraft's performance capability. Hopefully, it would ensure a smoother flight above the gathering storm clouds. Both pilots realised that this was going to be a challenging flight. However, the level of experience in the cockpit that night meant that the atmosphere on the flight deck was calm, as the Cessna left the runway and climbed into the stormy skies.

The aircraft climbed steadily and reached its cruising altitude of twenty-two thousand feet, thirty minutes after departure. The aircraft was still flying in the cloud, and full use had to be made of the aircraft's de-icing system. A warning light suddenly illuminated, indicating the presence of ice. The rubber leading edges of both wings were then expanded and retracted to loosen and break away the layers of ice accumulating on the wings. Suddenly, both the windshield and engine ice warning lights illuminated. The aircraft was in severe icing conditions, and a change of attitude was immediately required. A radio call was made to request this descent; climbing was not an option due to the limitations of the aircraft's performance. The propeller de-icing was then selected after another warning light illuminated the glare shield. Still, the atmosphere was calm and professional, both pilots carrying out their duties steadily and meticulously. Then, in an instant, everything changed. Ice had begun to break away from the propellers causing vibration throughout the aircraft. The vibrations continued for another thirty seconds, not an unusual occurrence as the propellers shed their ice. Suddenly, there was a deafening bang, and the pilots lost control of the aircraft.

The Cessna Conquest had a chequered history, with several unexplained aircraft losses. These had occurred mainly during the cruise, which is highly unusual. Aircraft accidents typically occur during the take-off or landing phase of flight. This is when the aircraft is most exposed to the elements; flying straight and level at height is generally without incident. For an aeroplane to fall from the sky is thankfully a very rare event. However, this is precisely what had happened to several Conquests in the past. History was now repeating itself.

Pete stared out of the windscreen, unable to believe what he was seeing. Through an ice-caked window, he saw a large piece of the aircraft flapping against the nose and windscreen of the aircraft. The noise was deafening, making communication between the pilots impossible. The noise also made contact with air traffic control impossible.

The Cessna Conquest has a very large and long nose. On either side of this nose were two cargo or baggage doors, which gave access to the nose compartment. These were large doors and had to be securely closed before take-off. Unbelievably, one of these doors had opened in flight and was now thrashing itself against the aircraft's nose and windscreen. Even more dangerously, the large access hole had increased the drag on the aircraft to the point that the aircraft had simply become unflyable. In this state, there was no way the aircraft could remain airborne. The open baggage door was dragging the aircraft and its occupants to certain destruction. Pete watched, horrified, as the aircraft began its inevitable drop towards the ground below.

Suddenly, the cargo door closed itself, a seemingly impossible feat. Control of the aircraft was once again possible, and the wings began to level themselves. Slowly, the aircraft regained its proper flight path. Pete looked around for an explanation as to what miracle had just occurred. With the door no longer hitting the aircraft, communication between the pilots was again possible. Using as few expletives as he could, Pete asked my father what had just happened and how the hell had the door closed itself? There were no checklists to cover this scenario. Pete was asked to declare an emergency. A request was made for a diversion into the nearest airport, London Gatwick. With the aircraft back under control, there was now time to try to establish what had happened. The moment the door had flown open, my father realised that the aircraft was in mortal danger.

There was no possibility of a safe outcome with the door open. Therefore, they either had to close the door or lose the aircraft. The door started to destroy itself against the aircraft. By luck, instinct, or just great skill, my father applied full opposite rudder. The rudder is the large vertical control surface attached to the tail of the aircraft. Its purpose is to balance the aircraft in turns by moving the nose from side to side. On multi-engine aircraft, it also balanced the aircraft if one engine failed. By applying this full rudder, the aircraft's nose immediately swung sideways and pulled the nose door shut. The plane was now flying almost sideways with the air pressure holding the door closed. If this lateral pressure was released, even for a moment, the door would reopen, and the aircraft would once again become uncontrollable. The autopilot could not cope with this abuse of the aircraft and had given up and sulked somewhere behind the instrument panel. Down through the storm clouds, the Cessna made its sideways progress towards the safety of Gatwick's main runway. Apart from keeping the aircraft flying with crossed controls, the wings could only be kept level by turning the control column in the opposite direction to the rudder. Somehow, this action had to be reversed before the aircraft could land safely.

As Pete recalls, "We came out of the low cloud base, and I looked ahead for the runway; there was nothing ahead but a black hole. Still, we descended, and still no runway. I looked across at Phil and was about to mention the lack of runway when I saw him looking out of the side window. To my complete and utter surprise, there was the runway. Of course, it would only be visible from the side window as we were flying sideways. As we crossed the runway threshold at fifty feet, the rudder pedal was suddenly released, and the control column was used to keep the aircraft straight. As the sideways force was reduced, the nose door flew open and struck the windscreen. Fortunately, we were now safely on the runway, and it could do no more damage. As the aircraft slowed, the door lost its momentum and gently fluttered down into its correct position. We taxied slowly to the terminal and shut the aircraft down." Four very shaken passengers were taken to their awaiting cars as the pilots examined the damage to the aircraft.

The following day, we contacted the Civil Aviation Authority to inform them of the incident. All the Cessna Conquests were immediately grounded until a new and improved door locking system could be fitted. I, of course, have no idea how or why the other Conquests were lost, but I am not sure that I would have the skill and forethought to regain control of that aircraft and bring it safely back to earth. I had always had a problematic relationship with my father, one that would eventually break down completely. However, when I think back to that night, I always feel a deep admiration for a man who was so skilled and dedicated to his profession. He saved six lives that night, and as one of them was my best friend, I will always be deeply in his debt for that. I just wish that I had had an opportunity to tell him that before he died. Unbelievably, in the years ahead, he was to become my greatest enemy. For the last few years of his life, we never communicated, except through lawyers. Our feud would have extraordinary consequences. For the first time in the six hundred years of English law, a barrister would be jailed for his actions in court. That story will be told later in this book; however, my father was still my friend at this point in time.

Chapter 3

No Going Back Now

At the beginning of 1987, thoughts of what to do now were at the forefront of my mind. I knew that my time in executive aviation was coming to an end. I also knew that I did not want to fly around Europe for the rest of my career. I desperately wanted to fly around the world. However, I had no idea how or where I should go to achieve this goal. So, as a start, I went to the local newsagent and bought a copy of *Flight* magazine. Readers of my first book will remember that I had a love-hate relationship with this publication. At the beginning of my flying career, I studied this magazine every week, always starting at the back where advertisements for job vacancies were published. Despite spending a small fortune, I had never managed to secure a flying job through the magazine's advertisements. It was, therefore, with very few expectations, that I opened it for the first time in many years. True to form, I skipped the many articles and stories and went straight to the back pages, to the classified advertisement section. There, to my surprise, were two full-page advertisements for pilots to join two of the largest UK airlines.

The first one was for Britannia Airways, at that time, the largest airline in the leisure market. They flew the Boeing 767 to far-flung exotic destinations, which excited me. I felt my heart rate increase as I immediately wrote a letter requesting an application form. I had the flying experience they required. I felt wildly optimistic as I rushed to the post box to ensure that my application would be one of the first to reach the airline.

Returning home, I continued to turn the pages of the magazine. There, to my utmost surprise, was the second full-page advertisement. However, this time, the advert read like a wish list of aircraft any pilot would climb over hot coals to fly. There were pictures of Concorde, Tri-stars, and the Boeing 747. I was starstruck, and I could not believe that British Airways were advertising to recruit pilots for the first time in its history. In the past, the airline had regularly trained its new pilots. From the very first day until retirement, British Airways had always been a closed shop. Never before had they considered employing a qualified pilot from outside of the airline. Of course, they had to invent a new name for these pilots to differentiate them from the homegrown pilot. The abbreviation DEP, which stood for Direct Entry Pilot, was decided upon.

Every pilot in the country must have been tempted to apply. The lure of eventually flying Concorde or the Boeing 747 compelled pilots to ignore the dreaded seniority system and apply to join the world's favourite airline. I sat staring at the page, not quite believing what I was reading. Visions of being seated at the controls of Concorde or a jumbo jet swam in front of my eyes until reality hit home and snatched my dreams away. There was no way British Airways was going to employ a self-improver. A DEP was one thing, but a pilot who had taught himself to fly would never get past the security guard at the gate, let alone be allowed to fly for one of the most prestigious airlines in the world. I was, of course, the epitome of a self-improver, having never attended any recognised pilot training school. Although I had all my flying licenses, I had achieved them by borrowing textbooks and cleaning aircraft in return for a few minutes of flight time. I had no proven pedigree and no traceable training history. In other words, I had no chance of being employed by British Airways. As reality dampened my mood, I slowly filled out the application form. I retraced my steps to the post box to send off my second application of the day. I consoled myself with the thought that I may have an outside chance of a job with Britannia Airways. With both applications posted, I returned to my world of flying the Cessna and put my dreams of long haul flying firmly back where they belonged, at the back of my mind.

Two weeks later, I received an invitation from Britannia to attend a one-day ground course. If that was successful, I would be invited to return for a simulator assessment. This would determine if I was capable of operating the Boeing 767. I was delighted. This could be the start of the second phase of my career. My next few flights on the Cessna were a more joyous affair as there was now a chance to go back to what I loved the most, flying jet aircraft.

The date was set for my interview. Surprisingly, Britannia wanted to see me the following week. I had thought that the process would take much longer. Seven days later, I arrived at Britannia's training school with a certain amount of trepidation. This was a huge step up from what I had been used to. Everything looked incredibly professional, and I was awe-inspired by the facilities. From the classroom to the simulator, it was impressive, to say the least. The day quickly sped by as our group of would-be Britannia pilots were quizzed on our knowledge, experience, and desire to fly with the airline. The whole affair seemed to be run on a military-type premise. At times, I was even tempted to salute the instructors and assessors. I had to admit that my desire to join Britannia had waned at the end of the day. Maybe, after all, airline flying was not for me.

On the drive home, I reflected that I probably would not fit into the regimented set-up at Britannia. I was unlikely to be asked back for a simulator assessment. I needed to rethink my career goals, and my mood darkened as I pulled up in front of my house that night. Opening the front door, I was bowled over by my canine friend, Roffey. At least, someone was pleased to see me. Stepping into the kitchen, I noticed a wet soggy envelope on the floor, slightly worse for wear after obviously losing a fight with Roffey. Before I could retrieve this letter, I had to feed Roffey and take him for a well-deserved walk. By the time I returned, made a simple supper, and settled myself in front of the television, I had forgotten entirely about the partially destroyed letter. Only later, when I was washing up, again, I noticed the soggy mass on the table. As I bent down to retrieve it, my Golden Retriever saw an excellent opportunity for a game. He immediately snatched the letter away and set off for a run around the house. Following him, I could appreciate his amusement at this new adventure. However, I was tired and not really in the mood for a rough and tumble with an excited dog. Roffey, being Roffey, quickly realised that my heart was not in the game, and he released the letter and trotted off to find new mischief to occupy him.

Bending down to pick the letter up, I noticed a livery on the envelope that I immediately recognised. It was the famous British Airways logo. I immediately assumed that it was a letter of rejection. I quietly thanked my faithful hound for giving it the treatment it so richly deserved. Putting the soggy mess back together, I finally managed to read its contents. This was not, after all, a rejection. It was an invitation to attend a selection day at the Holiday Inn hotel at Heathrow in a week's time. The very last line instructed me to bring this letter along to the interview with me. I looked at the bits of chewed-up letter plastered on the table in front of me. How was I going to explain this away? I started a new game with Roffey, but this time, I chased him, waving bits of the letter. Luckily for him, he was faster and more agile than me, so I gave up and went to bed, followed by a very excited dog a few moments later. Maybe, he thought that it would be a good idea to attack the post more often if it meant a good chase before bedtime.

A week later, I found myself in a queue waiting to enrol in the British Airways assessment day. There must have been at least fifty candidates lined up ahead of me, awaiting the chance to present their letters of invitation. I stood in the queue and watched each candidate take their letters out of the envelope and show them to the adjudicators. Each letter was carefully unfolded and checked off against a list. This process was repeated until it was my turn to produce the all-important letter. Of course, I had no envelope that had passed through my dog's digestive system many days previously. Instead, I produced a crumpled piece of paper that I had inexpertly tried to Sellotape together. I placed this offering in front of the adjudicator and stood back to await the inevitable questions. Luckily, I had a plan, and after the adjudicator looked up in astonishment, I gently placed a picture of Roffey looking his most adorable next to the destroyed letter. I stepped back and shrugged my shoulders and hoped for the best. Luckily, I had chosen the queue in front of a fellow dog lover. I received a broad smile and a knowing wink. She then showed my letter and picture of Roffey to everyone around her. There were many laughs from the assessors and candidates alike. Although my pride had been badly dented, at least I had managed to get over the first hurdle, and I was allowed into the assessment room.

The day itself was very different from my experience with Britannia. The atmosphere was much more friendly. We were treated as professional pilots, not as new recruits, which had very much been the case with Britannia. Finally, we came to the last assessment. The room of fifty candidates was divided up into teams of ten people. We were led out of the main hall into smaller anterooms. We entered the smaller room and were seated at a round table. A large box of children's building materials was then emptied onto the table. With three assessors looking on, we were told to pick a leader. This leader would then have to organise the construction of a farm together with animals and outbuildings. We had thirty minutes to complete the project. The assessors withdrew to the sides of the room. A whistle was sounded to announce the start of the project.

We all sat and stared at the assortment of Lego, straws, and Meccano in front of us. Nobody wanted to make the first move or suggestion for fear of making a fool of themselves. After what seemed an eternity, I decided that looking like a fool was preferable to looking like a statue, and so I asked if anyone fancied being the leader. Two hands shot up, and their owners put forward the reasons which would make them the best choice. Seven anxious faces then turned to me, and I realised they were waiting to see who I would choose. One candidate was far more qualified than the other as he had been a keen model maker as a child. I, therefore, chose this candidate as the primary leader and pacified the other candidate with the task of the animal maker. I asked them to choose who they would like to assist them with their tasks. After the teams were chosen, unsurprisingly, I was not asked to join either group. I retired to watch their endeavours. I had no skill at model making, so I was quietly relieved at my exclusion. Thirty minutes later, a small farmhouse sat in the middle of the table surrounded by animals made out of the straws. It was quite an achievement and everybody, except me, looked very pleased with themselves. We were then thanked for our efforts and attendance at the selection day, and with that, we were dismissed. The majority of us, sadly, were never to be seen again. I had a powerful feeling that I would be one of them.

Three days later, I received a letter asking me to attend a simulator check ride. I should have been excited beyond belief, but sadly the invitation had come from Britannia, not British Airways. It was, therefore, a rather reserved pilot that sat in a Boeing 767 simulator. The briefing before entering the simulator had been long and detailed. There were no reassuring smiles from the instructors. They were not here to help us but to chop the ones they did not like.

Consequently, the atmosphere was unpleasant, it was a case of us against them, and sadly they held all the cards. The check ride itself went reasonably well. The aircraft was a delight to fly, much more manageable in fact than the ones I had been flying. This was new technology, and it took a lot of the hard work out of the actual flying. At the end of the four-hour session, we were thanked for our time and dismissed with an instruction to call next week to find out if we had been successful. Now, I am sure that working for Britannia would be an outstanding achievement. It was a first-class airline with an excellent reputation. However, I felt unsure if I would fit in with the military-style of their operation. I was then and have always been a very relaxed pilot. I tried to achieve and maintain a high standard not through dogmatically following procedures to the letter but through understanding what was required and achieving a successful outcome through applying a mixture of knowledge, ability, and teamwork. I am also a great believer in the adage, if there is nothing to do, do nothing. Sometimes, sitting on one's hands and not rushing into a hasty decision was the best way to achieve a safe outcome. This approach seemed at odds with the approach expected at Britannia and I surmised that we were not a match made in heaven. Once again, I was reticent and reflective on the drive home from Britannia's training facility. I was not sure if I wanted to fly for the airline after all and to be fair, I thought they would probably not want me to fly for them either.

And so, it was back to the flying I knew best: the executive charter world. I decided to put all my efforts into revitalising our company and exploring new and exciting contracts. With Pete running the commercial side of the business, I made sure that the operational side remained competitive and our Operators' Licence remained valid.

We had been operating out of London Gatwick for over three years now. Despite losing our jet aircraft, we still mainly operated our Cessna out of Gatwick due to the airport being open all day and night. We often returned from a day trip late in the evening when the smaller airfields had long since closed. This added to our costs, but they could be offset by advertising us as a 24-7 company. This was invaluable, especially if we had a last-minute request for a medical emergency flight or to fly spares to an aircraft stranded abroad. Aviation was expanding rapidly at this time, and the major airports were approaching their maximum capacity. New airlines and executive jet companies were applying to fly into Gatwick. This situation could not go on for much longer. There are only so many operators that could be based at Gatwick.

I was in our office at the Beehive sorting through our regular pile of mail. There were no emails in those days. My attention was drawn to a very official-looking letter from the British Airports Authority, the operators of Gatwick Airport. With some trepidation, I opened the letter, wondering if, being such a small operator, we would be asked to move from Gatwick. Rumours had been circulating that a system of 'slots' was going to be introduced. This would entail each company bidding against each other to buy a slot of time to use the runway. There was absolutely no way we could afford to bid against the major airlines. We were expecting to be asked to leave Gatwick once these slots had been distributed amongst the big boys. This letter would no doubt confirm what we had been expecting and would probably signal the beginning of the end of our company.

I read the letter slowly and carefully. The devil was always in the detail. Instead of being asked to vacate the airport, we had been given 'Grandfather' rights. Not only could we remain as an operator, but we'd also been invited to attend the official meeting to bid in this new slot system. Well, this was indeed a delightful surprise. Although we could not possibly afford to buy slots, we could remain as a Gatwick operator. Still, it would be interesting to watch the major operators at work. And so, I accepted the invitation to attend the auction. I put this firmly to the back of my mind as I concentrated on finding new avenues for the company to explore.

Whilst all this was going on, I had all but forgotten about joining the airlines. I had yet to call Britannia to enquire if I had passed the simulator check. Unsurprisingly, British Airways had not sent me a letter begging me to join their illustrious ranks. Maybe, just maybe, I should stay where I was and try to make the most of our new status as a confirmed Gatwick operator. Airlines were queuing up to fly from Gatwick, and here we were, already a Gatwick company. I could see a possible commercial advantage in our new position. I had picked up my mail as I had rushed out of the front door that morning, at the same time trying to eat the last of my bacon sandwich. I now retrieved my slightly greasy mail and went through the variety of bills and advertisements. At the bottom of the pile, I again noticed an envelope with the British Airways logo. Ignoring everything else, I snatched the letter up and tore it open. At least this time, Roffey had not managed to get there first, so I did not have to reconstruct the letter to read it. My heart rate soared as I read, then re-read the letter. Instead of being rejected, I was being asked to attend a check ride in a simulator. I could hardly believe what I was seeing. How on earth had I managed to get through the assessment day? Especially as I had not even participated in the building exercise.

Still, I was not complaining, although, after the initial excitement, the memory of the Britannia simulator ride quickly brought me back to earth. If Britannia were that regimented, what on earth would British Airways be like? Still, that was a problem I would have to face at a later date. For now, I needed to prepare for our future at Gatwick. As for Britannia, I decided that I did not want to fly for them. I never made that telephone call to find out the result of my simulator check. It was not that I did not want to know. It was the complete opposite. In the unlikely event, they offered me a job, then I was pretty sure that I would accept their offer. Sometimes it's best not to know and that way you do not have to make a difficult decision.

A week later, Pete and I attended the Gatwick runway slot meeting. Although we looked the part, dressed in our finest executive suits, we knew that we were frauds. We had barely enough money to buy a meal at lunchtime, let alone afford a landing slot at Gatwick. True to form, as the meeting adjourned for lunch, whilst the rest of the participants went to the various local restaurants, Pete and I made our way to a local fast-food outlet for a beef burger and chips. This pretty much summed up our existence at that time, and we both chuckled at the thought of the other participants seeing us now. We returned after our 'executive' meal. We spent the rest of the day watching the prime-time slots being distributed around our fellow operators. By the time we were thinking of leaving, empty-handed, there were only a few other people left in the room. All the significant slots had been sold. There was nothing left except for two weekly take-off and landing slots at two o'clock in the morning. The large airlines were not interested as a ban on jet aircraft would apply at this time of night. Nobody else was interested, and so these slots would remain unsold. Pete and I looked at each other, we had saved a considerable amount of money on our lunch, so should we spend the money on these slots instead? We knew that the chances of us using these slots were remote, to say the least. However, we both had a gut feeling that this could be an opportunity that was too good to miss. Being a Gatwick operator with slots just sounded a whole lot better than being one without a slot to their name. We bought both for around the cost of a second-hand car, probably the best business decision either of us would ever make. However, at the time, we each blamed the other for making such a stupid mistake. What on earth would we do with these unflyable slots? It was a quiet drive home that night.

Whilst all this was going on, the date for my British Airways simulator check drew closer. Bolstered by the new impetus in our company, for we had managed to secure a lucrative contract, the desire I had felt for flying for an airline had diminished. I was enjoying a new wave of enthusiasm for my present position. Maybe, I should just stay where I was, after all. Then again, this was an invite to fly a British Airways simulator. It would perhaps be a Concorde or a Boeing 747. Just to fly either simulator would be an experience I could not afford to turn down. The outcome was not as important as the chance to fly something so extraordinary. This was the reason I had accepted the offer in the first place. Two weeks later, I found myself parking outside Cranebank, the British Airways training centre at Heathrow.

This complex was on a different scale than anything I had seen before. It was more than a training facility. It was more like a university. I was more than a little intimidated as I approached the main reception hall. After the registration process, I was shown into a waiting room clutching my temporary pass as if my life depended on it. Without this pass, we would be unable to access the vast simulator block, which stood proudly on the opposite side of the campus. There were about twenty of us sitting nervously in this small room. We had no idea who our simulator partner would be or which type of simulator we would be flying or attempting to fly. I found out later that this was a deliberate tactic to prevent candidates from getting an unfair advantage by practising on a simulator ahead of the assessment.

Names were called in pairs, and two victims would duly stand up, heads slightly bowed, and shuffle off to meet their fate. For almost everyone in the room, this was a life-defining moment. Never again would they get a chance to fly for one of the world's great airlines. This was the pinnacle of most pilots' careers, and we were all within touching distance of achieving our dream. I looked around at the anxious faces. I do not recall ever having seen so much apprehension manifest itself in one room. I calmed my nerves by reckoning that I was undoubtedly the only one here to have wasted a lot of money on two useless landing slots.

Suddenly, I heard my name called and I immediately returned to the matter at hand. Who was going to be my partner? And what simulator would we be flying? We were led by an assistant past several briefing rooms with names of aircraft I had only ever dreamed of flying in as a passenger, let alone as a pilot. We passed the Tristar rooms, the Boeing 757 and 767 rooms, we slowed down as we approached the Boeing 747 simulators. Surely, we were not going to be this lucky. We were asked to wait outside the 747 briefing rooms, and the assistant left us there. We looked at each other in sheer wonderment. We were going to fly a jumbo, a 747. A huge grin spread across both our faces. A moment later, our examiner appeared and beckoned us to follow him. Whatever the final outcome, this was going to be an experience never to be forgotten.

The examiner set off at quite a pace, and we hurried to keep up with him. To our confusion, he carried on past the 747 simulators and began walking down a wooden ramp into a wooden shed. This made no sense at all. He had obviously mistaken us for some other candidates, maybe engineering or cabin crew? As he asked us to take our seats in this wooden hut, I thought I had better point his mistake out to him before he wasted any more of his and our time. I politely explained that we were awaiting a 747 pilot to test our flying skills as we were pilots, not ground staff. He looked at me with a mixture of amusement and sympathy. Looking at his clipboard, he read out our names and asked us to confirm that we were indeed who he thought we were. I was tempted to deny my identity and just walk out; such was my embarrassment. Luckily for me, he saw the funny side and explained that we were in temporary accommodation due to the current expansion of a new simulator block. He also informed us that we would be flying a British Aircraft Company (BAC) 1-11 aircraft and not a Boeing 747. I could see the disappointment on my partner's face, and I tried to mimic his expression. I was, in fact, incredibly relieved that we were going to fly the 1-11. I had flown this aircraft before and was actually an authorised examiner on it. Still, best keep this little fact to myself, I thought, can't give away all my secrets too early on.

After a comprehensive briefing about what we could expect from the simulator check and how to fly the 1-11, we were asked if we had any questions. I had assumed that we would be asked if either of us had flown the 1-11 before. I did not know that, just as we were not told which simulator we would be flying, the examiners were not informed about our previous flying experience. In this way, an unbiased evaluation could be made. I would not have felt so smug at being able to maintain my secret had I known this. However, true to form, I would soon reveal my secret, albeit inadvertently.

We were asked if we had a preference to sit in the captain's seat on the left or co-pilot's seat on the right. Almost exclusively, all the candidates were co-pilots from other airlines. Very few captains changed seats to fly for a rival airline. I was happy to operate from either seat. An examiner has to be able to fly in both seats. Magnanimously, I offered my partner the choice. He immediately chose the right-hand seat, the one he was used to flying from. This decided, we were invited to take our seats; the examiner would sit behind us to assess our abilities. We both duly strapped ourselves in whilst the examiner turned around to close the door. As he turned around to face us once again, he looked at us both with an expression of confusion. In the right-hand seat sat a pilot struggling to find the three levers that would position his seat at the correct height and distance from the controls. Whilst in the left seat, the pilot, me, had miraculously not only found the levers but had fully adjusted himself and had started to carry out the pre-flight scan of the instruments.

I felt a heavy hand land on my right shoulder, and, as I looked around, I was met by a stern face asking why I had not informed him that I had flown this type of aircraft before. I was astonished that he had discovered my secret so quickly. I had rather hoped that he may have asked that question after a dazzling display of aviation perfection. However, I had not even started and had obviously given myself away already. I reluctantly had to admit that I may have once or twice had the pleasure of flying the 1-11. I also could not help but ask him how he knew my secret, what had given me away. Looking across at the pilot in the right-hand seat, still pulling and pushing seat levers, he informed me that only a qualified 1-11 pilot knew the secret of the seat adjustment. Damn! I thought that would teach me a lesson, especially as I was now informed that I would be judged as a current 1-11 pilot and not a general candidate. The whole exercise was made a lot more difficult for the occupant of the captain's seat.

At the end of the day, we were given the usual thanks for attending and told that they would be in touch with our results. At least, this time, we did not have to call them; they would write to us. The one thing we were all asked is what aircraft would we accept if we were offered a position with the airline. The majority of candidates were not concerned about the type of aircraft. They just wanted a job. Others were already flying short-haul aircraft and were only willing to accept a position on long-haul aircraft. As always, I wanted to be different. In reflection, it was a ridiculous request borne out of my ignorance and arrogance. Before I could stop myself, I announced that I would only accept a position on the Boeing 747. Astonished faces turned to look at this upstart trying to dictate terms to the world's favourite airline. I was offered the opportunity to change my mind and expand my choice, which would increase my chances of being accepted. Unbelievably, I declined this offer, and the official duly wrote down that I would only consider accepting a job if it meant I would fly the 747. With my British Airways career seemingly over before it had begun, we were all sent on our way. Almost immediately, I regretted being so stupid and stubborn but consoled myself with the fact that I had two worthless landing slots at Gatwick. British Airways obviously did not know who they were dealing with.

A week later, the third letter arrived. This one, I actually managed to open at home and without Roffey being able to intercept it. I already had guessed the outcome of my application before I opened the letter. As I started to read the words, 'we are sorry to inform you ...' I was not in the least surprised at its contents. I put the letter down and went to make myself a coffee.

Returning to read the letter in full, I skimmed through the rest of the paragraph, sipping my hot drink reflectively as the disappointment really began to strike home. I had been busy trying to convince myself that I really was not too bothered about working for British Airways. After all, I still had a job and a company that most people would envy. Deep down, though, I ached to be able to fly for this terrific airline. I had thrown it all away with this ridiculous request to only accept a position on the 747. What on earth had I been thinking?

I began to re-read the letter. After the first sentence, I had only skimmed through what remained, not really noticing what was written. It was not until I had read the letter for the third time that I understood what was on offer. I was being turned down as a pilot on the 747, and they regretted that. However, they offered me a position as a first officer on the much smaller Boeing 737 based at Heathrow. I could not believe that I was being offered a job at all. The ultimate self-improver was being offered an appointment with the leading airline. Unbelievable! A dream had come true. All my ships had come in at once. All those doubters who had written me off, most especially, my father, could now eat their words. My initial failed medical, all of it, all the doubters. I was now vindicated. So, what did I do? I turned British Airways down, of course. To this day, I am not really sure what I was thinking when I wrote a very polite reply thanking them for the offer of a job. I explained that, as I had indicated at the interviews, I would only be interested in a position on the 747, and sadly I was not interested in the 737. Therefore, I would not be attending the induction course starting in March, a few weeks away. Roffey and I walked to the post box, and I ended my chances of ever flying for British Airways with the simple act of dropping my letter into the mouth of the box. There was a feeling of finality when Roffey cocked his leg on the post box, and with that, we both made our way home. Back to what I knew best, those slots had better be worth something now, I had put all my eggs into one basket.

Three days later, British Airways rang me. It was early morning, I was due to fly to Paris later that day, and I was enjoying a quiet breakfast before setting off. I found myself apparently speaking to the head of recruitment. This charming chap just wanted to talk to the first person who had ever turned down a chance to fly for British Airways. The novelty factor obviously amused him, although I could tell that he was also interested in why I had made my decision. I explained that I wanted to fly the 747 and made it clear that I would only accept that aircraft. I could hear him rustling through some papers. Eventually, he informed me that they were not offering any positions directly onto the jumbo. It simply was not possible that I had been offered that choice. I very politely informed him that the 747 was, in fact, one of the options I had been offered at the interview. With a heavy dose of scepticism, he informed me that he would check this and get back to me.

An hour later, the call came that changed my life. I was indeed correct that the option had been made available, a mistake on their behalf. There were no 747 courses available at the moment, so I had three choices. I could accept the 737 course that would start in two weeks, decline to work for British Airways, or start on a 747 course on the ninth of September. He was wrong; there was no decision to be made. I grabbed my 747 course before he changed his mind. Neither of us could possibly have imagined at the time that this would be the start of a career that would eventually result in me becoming the longest-serving pilot on the Boeing 747. I was about to start my journey and my next thirty-four years on that beautiful aircraft. There was indeed no turning back now.

Chapter 4

Having My Cake and Eating it

I now had six months to prepare for my departure from the world I had known, to a totally new phase of my working life. Although this gave me some breathing space, there was still much work to do before starting my 747 course. Handing over the running of the company to a new chief pilot was my main concern. This was not a conventional position. It required a delicate balance between flying with Foodbrokers, the holding company, and operating charter flights. Flying with Foodbrokers typically involved the company chairman, who held a private pilot's licence, flying the aircraft from the captain's seat. Whilst the chairman could fly the plane to a good standard, the other pilot needed to ensure that the operation was safe, especially in poor weather. This required a delicate balance of both patience and diplomacy. Knowing when to take over was the key to a safe outcome. On charter flights, we operated with two pilots, a much more straightforward system. The new chief pilot would have to metaphorically wear two hats, not an easy task. In the meantime, I had the difficult task of preparing the company for a new future, something I was not looking forward to. Once I started my course, I realised that I would have little or no spare time or capacity to help Pete run the company.

At least there was one pilot I could ask to help out with flying the Cessna. Could I possibly persuade my ageing father to fly with the equally senior chairman of Foodbrokers? To my total amazement, he readily agreed. We had two pilots flying together within a few weeks with a combined age of over one hundred and twenty years, probably another record. My father flew on the Conquest for another year. This allowed me both the time and space to finish my training and return to flying the Cessna and the 747. However, that was in the distant future. In the meanwhile, there were a lot of changes to come over the next few months.

Pete and I began to look closely at our Gatwick operation. It was expensive to maintain our Gatwick office. The charter work from the Cessna did not justify this continued expense. We began to seriously consider moving our aircraft down to Shoreham and taking it off the commercial register. This would mean that we would only fly our own employees and not allow the aircraft to be chartered. Initially, I was very reluctant to do this. It had taken years of hard work to obtain and maintain our Air Operator's Certificate. Without it, Air Services Limited would become virtually worthless, a terrible waste. The only other option would be to sell the company as a going concern and allow another operator to take over the business. The only problem with this was that we could not sell the aircraft along with the company. Foodbrokers owned the aircraft and still needed it to move their executives around. What other assets could we possibly offer a buyer? And that was when the penny dropped. We owned runway slots.

Airlines were queuing up to establish a base at Gatwick. Without any of these all-important slots, they were unable to get a foothold. Could we possibly sell our company to one of these airlines? The prospect was exciting as well as daunting. Ultimately, we made the difficult decision to move our aircraft back to Shoreham and use it exclusively for company flying. From now on, we would be returning to where it had all started.

It felt like a huge setback. We had failed to take the company forward. Instead, we had gone backwards. All we had to do now was decide what to do with the Air Services itself. Although we had no aircraft, we still held a valid operator's licence and a foothold at Gatwick. Surely that must be of interest to someone?

We placed an advertisement in the *Financial Times* inviting offers for our company, together with our newly acquired runway slots. There was an airline based in Manchester which we had heard rumours was very keen to expand into Gatwick. Could we possibly interest them in our small enterprise? It was unlikely; however, we hoped that they would respond to our advertisement. We never got that far. Before we had a chance to approach this airline, we were approached from a very unexpected direction. The Greeks had arrived. Apparently, they wanted to get a foothold in the British aviation market.

This was the time before the low-cost carriers had begun to take over the short-haul market. There was, at this point in time, no EasyJet. Ryan Air was still in its infancy and had yet to establish itself in the UK market. The office phone rang, and a foreign-accented voice asked if we would like to meet up and discuss a possible business proposition. With a hefty dose of scepticism, we cautiously agreed to a meeting the following week. We had very few expectations. After all, how could a Greek company possibly operate aircraft out of Gatwick? The idea was definitely incredible. We put the idea out of our minds and concentrated on proper work.

A week later, we welcomed two very smartly dressed Greek businessmen into our Gatwick office. Now what I would like to say is that this was a particular Greek gentleman who went on to start EasyJet from the ashes of our company, but sadly, it was not. This was another businessman named George who, together with his partner, had built up a very successful telephone sales company and now wanted to move into aviation. After this initial meeting, it quickly became apparent that their hopes and expectations needed to be modified. There was, however, a possibility that we could do business together, and a date for another meeting was agreed.

We then received another telephone call from a Nigerian businessman. He wanted to operate a freighter aircraft between London and Lagos. We arranged a meeting, and at the appointed hour, this gentleman turned up at our office. He explained his idea and asked if our company could operate this freighter service. As the meeting progressed, his ambitions became more unrealistic. We politely advised him that although what he was suggesting was possible, there was a lot of work to be done before he could operate this aircraft. Unfortunately, he believed that he could simply buy our company and start flying the next day. At this point, he lifted the large suitcase he had brought with him and placed it on the desk. With a flourish, he opened the case. There, unbelievably, lay bundles of banknotes. Pete and I looked at each other in astonishment. Things like this did not happen in real life. There was a lot, and I mean a lot of money in that suitcase. Ignoring the money on offer, he continued to describe his vision for our company. Eventually, his presentation came to an end. He got up to leave the office, leaving the case with the money still sitting on our desk. We pointed this oversight out, and he hesitated before returning to his money and closing the lid. We promised to get back to him by the end of the week with our answer to his offer.

Pete and I looked at each other after we closed the door behind our departing visitor. The one thing we had not asked - I think we were both afraid to know - was just how much had been in that suitcase. There was a chance that he was a legitimate businessman. There was also the chance that we had nearly been involved in a money-laundering scheme. We decided that we could use this proposition as leverage in our negotiations with the Greek contingent. We rang George and informed him of this new development. Two hours later, a Rolls Royce pulled up outside our office. For the second time that day, a foreign businessman entered our premises carrying a large amount of cash and this time we accepted. Three weeks later, we sold our company to this new consortium, with two crucial provisions; Pete would remain in his position and I would continue to oversee the operational side until they could appoint their own chief pilot.

At the same time, our new partners started a package holiday company. They then combined the two enterprises into one large holiday airline. Over the next few months, we looked at various aircraft that would meet their requirements. Negotiations were held to purchase such aircraft as the Boeing 737 and my old favourite, the BAC 1-11. We would spend a great deal of time and money putting together a prospective sale. Time and again, we would arrive at an acceptable stage in the negotiations only to have the carpet pulled from under our feet. When the time came for the money to be put on the table, our Greek friends would suddenly make an excuse and withdraw.

We were losing all our hard-earned respectability with the aviation market as each deal simply faded away. Companies with whom we had dealt successfully over the years now became very wary of us. We were getting a reputation for wasting everyone's time. Businesses began to realise that we did not have the financial muscle to complete a deal.

I finally realised that this new venture would never get off the ground. I was embarrassed that all the hard work in negotiating aircraft purchases were all in vain. Our company, which we had passionately built up over the years, was becoming a laughingstock. I could no longer be part of this new venture, and I resigned as chief pilot. My career in this section of the aviation industry was at an end. While I would ultimately continue my involvement with the company later on, at this stage, it seemed like a sad way to finish off my time in the executive aviation world. However, I had little time to reflect as my new career was literally about to take off.

Chapter 5

A Jumbo Beginning

I sat in classroom number six at Cranebank, the training establishment of British Airways. There were five of us in the room. The clock ticked onto ten minutes past nine. There should have been six of us starting that Monday morning in September 1987. The lecturer's patience had finally run out as he announced that the course would begin without our absent colleague.

From previous experiences, I was a firm believer that there will usually be three types of candidates on any course. A standout performer, a middle group, and inevitably there would be an idiot. The trick was to discover as quickly as possible just who was who. I knew that I would never be the stand-out performer. It was far more critical to decide who would be the weakest link, the one most likely to fail. Once this unfortunate candidate was identified, everyone else could relax. The spotlight would be on this person and leave the rest of us to quietly get on with the course. The problems really started if you could not identify this weakest link. If you could not spot them, then there was an excellent chance that you were the idiot in the room.

We had to stand up one by one and introduce ourselves, together with our full backgrounds and which aviation college we had attended. I was the last to speak. The other four people in that room announced that they had been through an approved training course. The majority were from Oxford. Sadly, they all looked and sounded incredibly confident and competent. All eyes fell upon me as I stood up and was about to admit that I was basically an aircraft cleaner, and I had cut up a few pieces of cardboard to make a screen to complete my instrument rating. I was the ultimate self-improver. I had never attended an approved lesson, let alone been through a two-year pilot training course. My face began to blush as I cleared my throat and was about to launch into my personal history. The four other candidates looked on with a flood of relief coursing through their veins, the weakest link was about to reveal himself. Sighs of relief echoed around the room as each pilot realised that it would not be them.

I had got as far as my name when suddenly the room was filled with the noise of screeching car tyres. Suspecting a serious accident had occurred, we all rushed to stare out of the windows. Our classroom was on the ground floor and overlooked the car park. There was a blue cloud of burnt rubber arising from a red car in the centre of the parking area. The scene was a mixture of *Back to the Future* and *The Spy Who Loved Me* as the cloud slowly settled to reveal a Lotus Esprit. The driver's door slowly opened, and a tall leather-clad figure slowly uncurled itself from the constraints of the small sports car. Stretching himself out and flicking back his long hair, the figure adjusted his aviator sunglasses. It was a cold, cloudy day, so sunglasses were an interesting choice. He strode towards our building. Moments later, the door burst open and in came our missing colleague. I let out a massive sigh of relief. I was no longer the prime candidate for failure.

My relief was short-lived as this new arrival confirmed that he had not only been on an approved course but had graduated with the highest possible score and had won the pilot of the year award, or whatever it was called. So that confirmed it! I was the only self-improver there. Despite this, my instincts, fortunately, turned out to be correct. As the course progressed, the spotlight became firmly fixed on just one character. Our late arrival sadly failed the course. If he was the pilot of the year, god knows what the rest were like!

The introductory part of our course lasted two weeks, and it included everything British Airways. We were indoctrinated and submerged into the history and culture of the company and what was expected of us. We even spent two days practising how to make the welcome announcements to the passengers. I had spent less time than that on learning how to fly a new aeroplane. Still, they were paying me, so I did my best to hide those thoughts and just tried to keep my head down and get through the course. After the introductory part, we finally got down to the serious part, learning everything there was to know about the Boeing 747.

The first jumbo flew in the sixties, and this was known as the 747-100. This was the first generation of the 747. When I started to fly the aircraft, British Airways operated the 747-100 and the 747-200 series. This later aircraft had the much more powerful Rolls Royce engines. We would initially fly the earlier version and then do a short difference course to enable us to fly both versions. It would be a few more years before the vastly updated version, the 747-400, would enter service with British Airways, and it would be over a decade later that I would finally have a chance to fly this new version.

All of that was in the future. For now, I had three weeks of classroom tuition and a series of written examinations to pass before I would be allowed anywhere near a simulator, let alone the real aircraft. The ground school phase was very demanding. We would start at eight in the morning, a short break for lunch, and then back to the classroom for an entire afternoon's study. There were no computers to help us in those days. Instead, we used a system known as carrels. This was basically two chairs situated in front of a life-size photographic reproduction of the flight deck. We were divided into pairs and given a carrel to sit in. We then wore a pair of headphones through which we listened to a pre-recorded description of each of the aircraft's systems, how it was designed, how it worked, and what to do if it did not work. The main problem I found was that everyone has a different optimal learning speed. Mine was slow, very slow; whilst my partner was fast, very fast. This meant that he rarely needed to watch any lesson twice, whilst I rarely needed to watch it less than three times before it began to make any sense. As we were paired together, we could not move on to the next lesson before both pupils were satisfied that they fully understood the current lesson. My partner was incredibly patient and only rarely let out an audible sigh of frustration as I hit the replay button again and again. We were falling behind the other two pairs. As the day of the written examinations approached, I could feel the tension between us increase. At the rate we were going, we would struggle to finish the course before the date set aside for the exams.

Several instructors were overseeing this basic self-study system, and I decided that I needed their help. These instructors were usually from an engineering background and knew the aircraft inside out. A few minutes of discussion usually clarified my queries. Had it not been for their help and patience, I seriously doubted I would have finished the course successfully. This was the first time I had experienced this carrel method of learning. In previous classes, we had the traditional 'chalk and talk' where an instructor would stand in front of a blackboard and teach us how things worked. For me, this worked really well. If I did not understand anything, which was a common occurrence, I simply raised my hand. I could then have it explained to me before we moved on. With the carrel method, I could not stop and ask questions and instead had to try to remember what I didn't understand and then seek out an instructor for clarification. I had a feeling that these instructors attempted to disappear whenever they saw me coming with a puzzled look on my face.

We were also given a cassette tape of each lesson and advised to listen to this at home and when we were driving in each morning. I'm not sure if I made any friends amongst the instructors when I thanked them for the cassettes and asked when the cassette player would be fitted to my car. It was a genuine question as I drove an old car with nothing but an ancient valve radio. I was abruptly advised to buy my own cassette player.

Despite all these setbacks, I stoically managed to finish the course the day before the exams, leaving very little time for revision. Some of the subjects I had not seen for two or three weeks at this point, and I'd forgotten most of what I had learned. This was not how I had imagined my career with British Airways ending, falling at the first hurdle. This first hurdle was set very high, almost too high for me to see beyond it. History repeated itself, and after my usual arduous night of last-minute studying, I managed to get through the gruelling examination the next day, probably more by luck than judgement.

Ground school over, it was time for the dreaded simulator course. This was where all that theory was going to be put into practice. Ahead of us, we had twelve details, each lasting four hours. The first eight details would be training, the last four details would be checking, a tall order which stood like an intimidating mountain in front of me.

The original 747s were operated with three crew, two pilots, and a flight engineer. The systems on the aircraft were very basic, and the flight deck resembled a Second World War bomber rather than a modern airliner. There were dials and gauges everywhere, in front of the pilots, above the pilots, to the side of the pilots, and most difficult of all, behind the pilots. Whilst we could just about manage those in front, to the side, and above, the gauges behind us were a gauge too far. The aircraft was designed and built in an era when human intervention was essential for the safe operation of the aircraft. There were no computers to monitor the aircraft's performance or flight path. Everything had to be done manually. There were too many complex systems on the 747 to entrust monitoring them to us, the mere pilots. Enter the flight engineer, nearly always the most experienced and capable member of the crew. To me, this was a fantastic way in which to operate an aircraft. It was like taking your car in for a major check and then having the garage engineer sit in the back seat just to make sure all went well. Although I could drive the vehicle perfectly well, the mechanic knew precisely how it was built and how it worked. Should I be on the motorway and the car started to make a strange noise, how wonderful it would be to have the mechanic sitting behind you to tell you exactly what was wrong and even better what to do about it. This is precisely what we had on the original jumbos. Welcome to the world of flying with a flight engineer. The other benefit was that they always knew where the best bars were around the world.

It became immediately apparent that this three-crew operation was the way to go. We had an onboard flying encyclopaedia, someone who actually knew how everything worked and what to do about it when it didn't. Once we had mastered the actual flying of the aircraft, then operating it became relatively straightforward. The main difficulty with flying the 747 was the sheer size of the aircraft. With smaller aircraft, you could make sizable changes to the aircraft's flight path, and the plane would react almost instantly. Try that on a jumbo, and the aircraft would take an eternity to respond. By the time the aircraft finally responds, you probably wanted it to do something different anyway. Think of a supersized oil tanker trying to navigate a few bends in the River Thames and you will get the idea. The other problem with the aircraft was that you were seventy feet above the ground in the pilot's seat. It was a little like trying to land a block of flats from the seventh floor, not an easy task. However, once these issues were overcome, the seamless system of operating this remarkable aircraft became apparent. When you had a problem, very rare on this aircraft, each crew member knew precisely what to do. The co-pilot would fly the aircraft. The flight engineer would produce the checklist and fix everything. The captain would peer over the top of his newspaper to ask when his first-class meal would be ready. This system worked very well for everyone, especially for me, when eventually I became the captain.

Therefore, all I really had to concentrate on was the actual flying of the aircraft. Technical problems could be safely left to the walking encyclopaedia sitting behind me. For such a large aircraft, the 747 flew beautifully; she had no vices. I always felt that the plane was on my side, treat her with respect, and she will repay you with a smooth flight and gentle landing. I quickly learned that to fly the aircraft accurately, you had to literally fly by numbers. On take-off, you raised the nose to twelve degrees above the horizon. To level off, you lowered the nose to five degrees. To descend, you lowered it to two and a half degrees, the 747 descended with her majestic nose still pointing skywards. You also had to learn the power setting that went with the varying weights of the aircraft. Once these figures were memorised, you had pretty much mastered the art of flying a 747. On landing, the flight engineer would call out the aircraft's height, and when he got to thirty, you raised the nose a bit or flared to give it the correct name, and the aircraft would settle gently onto the runway. At this point, the captain had usually finished the crossword puzzle, and everyone went home happy.

This simulator training lasted for twelve sessions. In the end, we were slightly dizzy with all this new knowledge buzzing around in our heads. The original group of six had been reduced to five. Our late arrival had been taken off the course and was now probably burning rubber in another car park. For the rest of us, we could look forward to actually flying the real aircraft. The simulators we had been learning to fly on were the first generation of modern simulators. Although we could practise general flying and emergency procedures, the simulators were not advanced enough to teach us how to land the aircraft. The main problem was the visual presentation or the graphics. Looking out of the front screens of the simulator, all you could see was a night presentation. It was a little like looking at an old black and white movie. It was adequate for practising landings once you were qualified. It was not sufficient for a newly converted pilot. Today's generation of simulators has incredible natural scenery. Terminal buildings, maintenance vehicles, taxiway routes, and runways are all perfectly represented to the pilot. You can learn to fly an aircraft solely by using the simulator. This is known as Zero Flight Time. As the term suggests, a pilot can now operate an aircraft carrying passengers after having literally no first-hand flight time in the real aircraft. The first time I flew a Boeing 777 was the first time I had actually been on a Boeing 777. Quite impressive when you think about it.

However, back in 1987, we had to fly the real aircraft and perform several take-offs and landings before letting loose on the general public. This phase of our training was known as base training. Basically, each pilot had to fly a series of take-offs and landings with a training pilot in the other seat. Obviously, we could not do this at a busy airport such as London Heathrow. So it was, that five fresh-faced pilots reported early one morning for a flight to Shannon in Ireland, for a series of circuits and bumps. A pilot was selected to fly the aircraft to Shannon, and another was chosen to fly it back later that day. I made sure that I took a toilet break whilst this process of choosing was completed. There was no point in exposing myself to more scrutiny than was absolutely necessary. And so, with one poor chap residing in the co-pilot's seat, we set off on our adventure. Whilst he sweated away, we relaxed on the upper deck, helping ourselves to the drinks and food that had been supplied. We were all very jolly, except for the poor guy in the hot seat, and thoroughly enjoying ourselves. We had all seemingly forgotten that it would be our turn soon. The weather in Shannon was beautiful, sunny skies, gentle wind, and unlimited visibility. We made our first approach. There were three operating crew and five eager faces peering through an open flight deck door.

Our colleague did an outstanding job of flying the approach. It was going so well until the last fifty feet. What happened next, nobody was quite sure. All we knew was that we had hit the runway quite hard and had bounced back into the sky. Many hands were moving very quickly. We were suddenly flying away from the ground with all four engines screaming away at full power. The party mood was most definitely over, and we quickly made our way back to our seats and strapped in very tightly. We could feel the power reducing as the aircraft levelled off at one thousand five hundred feet. The aircraft then began to reposition for another approach. We could all feel the tension in the air. Our heart rates increased as we felt the giant aircraft begin another descent towards what we dreaded was to become another collision with the ground. Looking out of the window, I saw the runway rushing up to meet us. I braced myself for the imminent impact. To our collective amazement, we felt the aircraft touchdown in a gentle manner. A few seconds later, those four massive engines once again accelerated to full power. We shot back into the sky; a manoeuvre known as a touch-and-go. This training technique allowed a pilot to land and then take off again without stopping and taxing back for another take-off. Each of us would need to demonstrate three successive take-off and landings before we could be signed off to fly with passengers.

After the successful second attempt, our mood reverted back to a more light-hearted affair, and we all cheered at each good landing and groaned at each poor one. We ensured that the poor pilot performing these landings could hear us and know we were supporting them. After the first three victims had been put through their paces, we stopped for lunch. Parking our 747 in front of the terminal building, we made our way down the steps that had been positioned at the side of the aircraft. Just walking down these steps reinforced just how big this aircraft was. We had entered the aircraft by an airbridge at Heathrow, which disguised the sheer size of the aircraft. Now we could stand at the bottom of the stairs and just look up and marvel at this beautiful aircraft. Our contemplations were rudely interrupted by a grumpy flight engineer complaining that he was starving and why were we wasting his lunchtime by staring at the aircraft. We turned and obediently followed him to the staff canteen.

The plan for the afternoon was to finish off testing the three remaining pilots and then fly the aircraft back to Heathrow that evening. A phone call from the operational department soon changed that. We were told that now they did not need the aircraft back until lunchtime the next day. There was apparently a shortage of parking at Heathrow. The aircraft was not required until the following evening for a flight to India. And so, a new plan was formulated over a now very leisurely lunch. We could take our time. We were then booked into a local hotel. The training captain and flight engineer had the experience and foresight to bring a night stop bag, just in case one of the students broke the aircraft! The five of us, of course, had much greater faith in our abilities and so found ourselves having to buy the bare necessities at the airport terminal building. I never made the same mistake again. From that day forward, I always carried enough to see me through an unexpected night stop.

The current plan was to check out two pilots that afternoon and the third and final pilot on the way back to London the next day. Of course, none of us wanted to be the pilot chosen to fly back to London. Instead, we would prefer to complete our training that afternoon and enjoy a glass or two of Guinness that night. The only fair way to decide who would fly home was to draw lots. Guess who lost. And so, I sat on the upper deck that afternoon and watched the others complete their checkouts. The weather was beautiful, calm wind prevailed, and everyone enjoyed themselves. We finished the flying programme early and set off for the hotel. As the training captain knew the local area well, he suggested that we all meet up in the hotel lobby for a short walk to an excellent local pub, Dirty Nellies. As promised, the food was terrific, and apparently, the Guinness was superb. I say apparently, as I thought it would be unwise to partake the night before my final check. No such constraints applied to my colleagues, and pint after pint disappeared, as if by magic. The captain and engineer were flying with me and duly departed for the hotel after the meal. I was persuaded to stay, although I continued to sip lemonade rather than Guinness.

It was a noisy and happy group that staggered back to the hotel that night, only to find that the establishment had closed for the night. We knocked at the front door, we knocked on the windows, nothing, no one was home, well no-one who would open the door. This was a disaster for me. Whilst the others laughed, I was unhappily aware that I had my final check in the morning and nowhere to sleep that night. I then spotted a small notice informing us that there was a night porter's entrance at the rear of the hotel. Feeling colossal relief, we all made our way around the back of the hotel to seek this entrance. Now, I am sure that we have all seen and used a peephole in a door before. It allows you to see who is at your door before opening it, a sound and safe idea. We rang the bell at the porter's door and waited to be let in. Eventually, he arrived at the fully transparent, glass, yes glass door.

In the middle of this door was a peephole, probably the most useless spy hole in the history of spy holes. And yet the porter walked up to this spy hole and loudly asked who we were and what did we want? We were all taken aback. Why was he using the spy hole when he could clearly see us, and equally, we could clearly see him. He again loudly demanded why we were ringing the bell. We replied that we were staying at the hotel and would like to be let in, especially since it had now started to rain quite heavily. He asked to see some form of identification, so we obediently fumbled around and held up our room keys. He then asked us to hold up the keys to the spy hole so that he could see them properly. We looked at each other in confusion. Surely, if we could see him, he could see us. Still, he demanded that we hold up our keys to the spy hole if we wanted to be let in. Each of us obeyed his demand, and we were finally allowed back into the hotel. Dripping wet, we looked back at the glass door. We could clearly see outside right through it. Turning to confront the porter, we found that we were talking to an empty space. He had disappeared, and we began to wonder if he had existed at all. Cold, wet and confused, we made our way to our rooms.

Checking out of the hotel the following day, four of us with severe hangovers, the captain, asked us how our night had gone. We described our difficulty in getting back into the hotel and the spy-hole episode. Both he and the engineer burst out laughing as they turned to leave the hotel. We followed them, and as we left the hotel, our phantom night porter was standing there laughing with the captain. The final words we heard, confirming that they had created the situation to have a gentle laugh at our expense, went something along the lines that these new pilots were so gullible. It was a quiet journey back to the airport, which made the noise of distant thunder even more noticeable. A slight shudder of apprehension trickled down my spine. Where had the beautiful weather of yesterday gone? Sure enough, by the time we had reached the airport, the heavens had opened. None of us had any suitable clothing, and by the time I was settling myself into the pilot's seat, I was thoroughly soaked. A steady trickle of water had joined the apprehension, slowly making its way down my spine.

I had to complete three take-offs and landings. The plan was to do two of these at Shannon and the last at Heathrow. There was only one precision instrument approach at Shannon, and that was on the westerly runway. That morning, there was a strong easterly wind which meant that we could not use the instrument runway for landing. Well, that was the theory anyway. After a long discussion, it was decided, obviously not by me, that we could use the westerly runway with a fifteen knot, or twenty miles an hour tailwind. Usually, an aircraft will try to take off and land into a headwind, allowing the aircraft to use the wind for extra performance and lift. If you take off or land with a tailwind, you will use a lot more runway. We decided to take off on the easterly runway and then position ourselves to make two approaches and landings onto the westerly runway, using the precision approach to guide us down. We could not fly a visual approach as the base of the cloud was around five hundred feet, and it was still raining heavily. I was very apprehensive about the whole idea. I suggested that we just fly back to London and I could do my training another day. The captain was having none of it and insisted that we could complete my training. He was not a man to be deterred by a bit of rain, turbulence, and tailwinds. I, on the other hand, was precisely the sort of man who could be deterred by inclement weather.

And so, I found myself damp, miserable, and very apprehensive taxiing this massive aircraft for the first time. The noise of the rain battering the plane meant that we had to put the headphones over both ears to make sure we could hear each other. We usually flew one earpiece on and one-off. The windscreen wipers did their best to repel the rain as we cautiously entered the runway and stopped on the centreline. On take-off, it is standard practice to slightly increase the power on the engines and then wait for a few moments to make sure that all the engines are producing the same amount of thrust. Suppose you applied full power and one or more engines were slow to accelerate. In that case, you could suddenly find yourself facing sideways due to the uneven thrust.

Once you were happy that all the engines were working normally, you set the required take-off thrust. The amount of power required varied according to the aircraft's weight, the runway's length and the air temperature. Rarely was full power needed or used. One exception was when the wind was gusting, known as wind shear. If there was a possibility of this, then you had to use full power. On that day, there was a possibility of wind shear, so we had no choice but to apply full thrust. This allowed us to climb away from any possible wind shear and turbulence. In the simulator, we had been using reduced power for the vast majority of our take-offs. The only time we had used full power was when we practised a heavyweight departure. On this occasion, we had a very light aircraft, just seven people on board and only twenty tonnes of fuel, instead of one hundred and twenty tonnes on a heavy take-off. In other words, we were using full power on a very light aircraft.

I pushed all four thrust levers fully forward, and the aircraft leapt forward at an astonishing rate. Even the rain hitting the windscreen was taken by surprise and soon began to merge into little streams before being blown away by the aircraft's speed. We literally leapt into the air as we reached our take-off speed in approximately half the time it usually took. The jumbo felt more like a bucking bronco than an airliner. The nose pointed skywards, and all four engines were producing full power. It was as challenging to control as an angry bull. I was meant to level off at one thousand five hundred feet. However, we were climbing at over five thousand feet a minute. As I pushed the aircraft's nose forward to stop the climb, at the same time pulling back the thrust levers, all seven of us were only held in our seats by the seatbelts. Had we not been securely strapped in, then we would certainly have hit our heads on the cabin roof. This felt more like I was undertaking my first solo flight rather than a conversion course. Eventually, I managed to regain some form of control over this excitable aircraft. We settled down at more or less the correct height and speed, and then it all went very wrong.

We were flying in thick cloud cover and moderate turbulence. We were positioning to land on the opposite runway from the one we had taken off on. That was the only runway with an available approach aid. I was fighting to keep the aircraft at the correct height and speed, which was not an easy task in these conditions. Throw in the after-take-off checklist, the before descent checklist, and the approach checklist, and it would be fair to say that I had my hands full. Finally, we were lined up with the correct runway, and I started my final descent. Gently reducing power, I lowered the nose to the correct two and a half degrees and waited for the aircraft to slow down and go down as I called for the landing flaps. As I have mentioned, the plane is a fly-by-numbers aircraft; set the correct numbers, and it performs accordingly. Well, that is the theory anyway. With the correct power and pitch set, the aircraft only wanted to go down or slow down. It stubbornly refused to do both at the same time. I lowered the nose to keep the aircraft descending, which of course, it did quite happily. The only problem was that it started to accelerate at the same time. The next moment, I heard the flight engineer shout in my ear as we approached our maximum speed for our flap setting. Instinctively, I closed the thrust levers and raised the nose to help us to reduce our speed. We were now slowing down but not going down. What the hell was going on?

Suddenly, the captain shouted that I was getting too high. I lowered the nose again to increase my descent rate, only for the flight engineer to shout in my other ear that we were now going too fast. Well, this was not going very well, I thought to myself. Trying to please two people at the same time was not working. All the time we were being rocked by ever-increasing turbulence; I have had better days at work, I thought to myself as the faint smell of vomit and stale Guinness permeated the flight deck. I guess my hungover colleagues were having about as much fun as I was. Finally, at five hundred feet, the captain realised that we were not in a position to land safely and called for a go-around. Obediently, and gratefully, I raised the nose of the aircraft and applied full power. The jumbo also thought this was a good idea. She suddenly started behaving as she was meant to as she climbed gracefully away and back into her natural environment.

Flight engineers are generally not known for their shy and retiring nature. They tend to speak their minds loudly and forcibly. Our engineer was most certainly a chip off the old engineering block. A torrent of abuse flowed over me and the captain. Our colleague, quite rightly in my humble opinion, enquired what the hell we were doing trying to make an approach and landing with a forty knot, or fifty miles an hour tailwind. Didn't we know that the aircraft was not designed for that? This was news to both of us pilots. I was too busy trying to make the aircraft do something it didn't want to do whilst the captain was busy watching me making a mess of the approach. The ground controller was only reporting a fifteen-knot tailwind. We were loudly informed that the flight engineer really didn't care what the controller had said as he had a current wind readout right in front of him. He also told us that this was why the aircraft had behaved as it had on the approach. The captain looked at me, and I looked at him. We quickly decided to head straight back to London. Those passengers hoping to go to India that night would not thank us if we bent their aircraft. It was time to go home.

Forty-five minutes later, I made a successful approach and a passable landing into a headwind at Heathrow. This time, the aircraft flew precisely on the numbers. Unfortunately for me, I had now only completed one of the three required landings. And so, a week later, I found myself on another aircraft heading back to Shannon with a different crew and trainees. There were eight of us this time, so we were scheduled to stay the night at the same hotel. I made sure I was the first pilot to complete three landings. I was finally qualified to fly a Boeing 747. That night in the pub, it was my turn to devour Guinness after Guinness. Of course, we were late back to the hotel, and once again, I found myself ringing the bell on the night porter's glass door. Again, he asked each of us to hold up our keys to the spy hole. This time, however, he could see nothing at all through his peephole. Eventually, he gave up trying and opened the door. Somebody had applied a coat of Tippex on the spy hole rendering it useless. I had got my own back and felt a certain sense of satisfaction as we climbed away from Shannon the following day.

I did not know it at the time, but I would be returning to Shannon in the not-too-distant future, and this time, my arrival would make headline news throughout the world. My picture made the front pages of the national and international newspapers. Oh, how I regret that eighties moustache now. However, I was pleased just to sit back and enjoy the flight home for the time being.

Chapter 6

Look Out World – Here I Come

The last part of my conversion course was known as line training. I had to complete twelve flights with a training captain before I was finally released on an unsuspecting travelling public.

My first flight was to Nairobi, Kenya. The trip lasted for five days which meant we had two clear days in Nairobi to enjoy some winter sunshine. It was late autumn in England, the nights were closing in fast and temperatures were struggling to get above freezing. I was certainly looking forward to some sunshine. First, though, I had to actually get to Africa, and as I was operating this flight there was a lot of hard work ahead before I could relax and enjoy the warmer weather. Leaving my car in a cavernous multi-storey car park, I wondered to myself how I was ever going to find it again. I made my way to a windowless waiting room, where I sat with about twenty other pilots and flight engineers all sitting silently on chairs placed around the room. It was reminiscent of a dentist waiting room and all those sitting around looked like they were about to have root canal treatment. I gave a cheery hello as I entered the room and took my seat. Not one bowed head moved in acknowledgement of my greeting. I took my seat and put on my best 'at the dentists' face. Now and then, a bus driver would put their head around the door and call out a flight number, nothing else, no greeting, no smile, just a flight number. Three people would stand up and without even acknowledging each other, quietly follow the driver to his bus. This all seemed surreal. If you were about to spend up to two weeks with another two people why not introduce yourselves when you had the opportunity? With this thought in mind, I turned to the chap on my left and politely asked where he was going. Everyone in the room immediately looked at me as if I had just committed some horrible crime. I had broken the sacred silence twice in as many minutes. This was like taking an oath of silence at the monastery, I thought miserably to myself. At that precise moment, another driver called out a flight number and another obviously relieved team of pilots and an engineer left the room as quickly as possible. The rest just stared at me for another few moments and then resumed their previous stances. I was tempted to tell a joke or two, anything to lighten this atmosphere. Luckily for me, a driver called out my flight number and I followed two of the grumpier looking individuals towards the waiting bus. This was not the start I had been hoping for; it was going to be a long five days, I thought to myself, as we boarded the bus.

From one windowless room, we soon found ourselves in another much larger room, again not a window in sight. On the bus journey, the captain asked me to confirm my name and produce my pilot's licence. This was checked and returned without comment. These were the only words spoken on the entire journey. Our flight number was once again called out, this time, by a man standing behind a vast counter. The three of us made our way over to be briefed on our flight. The briefing officer produced three flight plans, one for each of us. There was also a large pile of papers that contained all the operational information we needed for the eight-hour flight. As I was the operating pilot, it was my responsibility to read all these notices, check that everything was in order, and finally, make a decision as to how much fuel we required. I could feel the captain's eyes burn into the back of my head as I tried to make sense of all the information in front of me. After about thirty seconds of pretending to understand what was expected of me, I turned to the flight engineer and said I thought everything looked good and I was happy with the fuel figure on the flight plan. The captain immediately interrupted and asked how I could possibly know how much fuel we needed if I had not looked at the weather map. Damn, I thought. I hadn't even seen a weather map, which was not surprising as the meteorology officer had not produced one. On cue, he stood in front of us and handed me a weather map of our entire route. Placing this map in front of the three of us, I studied the squiggles and arrows with great concentration. Finally, I stood back stroking my chin and with suitable authority, announced that I was satisfied with the weather. The captain gave me a very sceptical look and asked how I could be so sure? Before I could reply, he took a step forward and slowly turned the map the correct way up. With what remained of my dignity - I had made a similar mistake on my first cross country flight many years before - again, I looked at the map. Sadly, it made as much sense to me the right way up as it had previously. Instead of making another decision regarding the fuel, I sheepishly turned to ask the captain how much fuel we should load. To my chagrin, all I could see was his back as he disappeared towards the waiting bus. Turning back to the briefing officer, I asked for the fuel on the flight plan. Smiling, he informed me that the captain had already ordered ten tonnes of extra fuel due to the thunderstorms expected on our route. I beat a hasty retreat and jumped on the bus as it made its way to our aircraft. This was definitely going to be a very long five days.

There were eighteen cabin crew members on the aircraft, which meant together with the three of us, there were twenty-one individuals, almost double the number of passengers my beloved executive jet could carry. I offered a cheery hello as I climbed the circular stairway to the upper deck and flight deck. Again, my greetings were met with a look of surprise and occasionally, even a look of hostility. What on earth was going on? Surely, we should all be looking forward to the trip. I could not understand the underlying tension between the cabin and flight crew. We were all there together to do a job so why was there such a barrier between us?

Anyway, I had no more time to consider this as I began to prepare for my first take-off with passengers. Eventually, everyone was on board, the doors were closed and we were given permission to push back and start our engines. Twenty minutes later, we were climbing away from London and what was to be my thirty-four years of flying the 747 had finally begun. The flight itself went well, no dramas and we landed on time with a very passable landing. The captain grunted something about beginner's luck, and the flight engineer actually patted me on the shoulder, such a simple gesture, yet it meant so much. It made me feel that I was accepted; I was really part of the crew.

That night, the three of us met in the bar to discuss the possibility of a game of golf the following day. There was no sight of our cabin crew members, and my inquiry as to their whereabouts was met with a shrug of the shoulders. I was beginning to realise that there were deep divisions between the flight deck members and our cabin crew colleagues. Over the coming months and years, I came to accept that the two groups rarely socialised together and just about tolerated each other on the aircraft. The good news was that I was finally getting to know the captain a little better. Away from the aircraft, he was much more approachable and became virtually amiable as we finalised plans for the next day. At the end of the evening, he looked at me in an almost fatherly way; the alcohol, by this time, had mellowed the old chap. With all the gravity he could muster, and only slightly slurring his words, he informed me that he would like to give me two pieces of advice if I wanted to have a successful career in British Airways. There were two golden rules that must never be broken. The first was to look after the Ray-Ban sunglasses I had been issued with on joining the company. He proudly informed me that his sunglasses were nearly thirty years old and were still in the same condition as the day he had received them. The second piece of advice was even more important. He took a deep breath and his expression became even more serious as he looked directly into my eyes.

"Make sure, young man, that on the day you retire, nobody knows your name."

Asking why this was so important, he looked at me as if I was intellectually subnormal.

"Because young man, only the pilots who have made mistakes become known. The good pilots remain anonymous."

And with those two pieces of advice delivered, he made his way unsteadily towards the lifts. We had booked an early tee time for golf in the morning.

The next day, heeding his advice, I carefully took my sunglasses off and laid them next to me before hitting my first shot of the day. The drive, unusually for me, soared straight and true, perfectly bisecting the narrow fairway. I cannot remember ever hitting such a magnificent shot before. Excitedly, I turned to receive the congratulations of my playing partners. Unfortunately, in my moment of euphoria, I forgot that I had placed my sunglasses on the ground behind me. There was a sickening crunch as my precious Ray-Bans disintegrated beneath my size eleven feet. The captain regarded me with a look of sadness and resignation. I could see that as far as he was concerned, I would have a very short career in front of me. I have no idea what he might have thought a few months later, when he sat down at his breakfast table, opened his newspaper only to see my face smiling back at him. Luckily for me, our paths never crossed again; I doubt he would have passed me after I broke both of his golden rules.

The remainder of the route training went reasonably well. We flew to India, South Africa, North America, and the Middle and the Far East. The world really was becoming my oyster.

On a subsequent training flight, we were taxiing out from Dubai for the return sector to London. As we started to move, the visibility started to deteriorate. Incredibly, within the space of two minutes, we were enveloped in a thick, dense fog. It was as if a white towel had been thrown over the aircraft. All reference to the outside world was lost; we could not even see the ground from the flight deck. I stopped the aircraft and set the parking brake; we were going nowhere fast. We sat there for over thirty minutes until finally the fictional white towel was whisked away as quickly as it had arrived. Never before or since had I experienced such conditions; all three of us were astounded by the power and unpredictability of mother nature.

The remaining flights went without incident and I was finally signed off to fly the line just before Christmas 1987. This was the start of a very long and passionate affair with one of the most iconic aircraft ever built. For the next four decades, this remarkable aircraft would transport me and my passengers to just about every corner of the world. I was officially a 747 pilot, the self-improver now had little to prove, or so I thought.

Chapter 7

Unhappy Times

I was now flying from London Heathrow as a very junior first officer. My four gold shiny stripes, which had indicated my status as a captain, had now been replaced with a mere two silver bars. My neighbours, no doubt, wondered what terrible crime I had committed to justify this demotion. The destinations I had enjoyed during my training were now only distant memories. The seniority system made sure of that. The senior co-pilots enjoyed the sunshine whilst I picked up the destinations that nobody else wanted. I became a regular visitor to such places as Lagos in Nigeria and Riyadh in the Middle East. The east coast of the United States also became my playground. The flights were difficult due to the complexity of the American air traffic control system. The unpredictable nature of the weather, especially during the winter months, also added to our workload. Some of the east coast snowstorms had to be seen to be believed. On one memorable flight to Chicago in late autumn, we landed on a warm sunny afternoon. The temperature was so mild that I walked to the local bar in shorts and a T-shirt. I even had my Caribbean flip flops on. Two hours later, I stepped out into a snowstorm. A cold front had swept down from Canada, and across the great lakes. This resulted in the infamous lake-effect snow as the cold air picked up moisture from the lakes. The twenty-minute walk back to the hotel was the coldest and most embarrassing walk of my life.

Despite the destinations and weather, I very happily accepted all of this. The sheer pleasure of flying this remarkable aircraft more than made up for the not so enticing route structure. The main problem I had was that I was simply not enjoying my new career. The attitude and behaviour of some of the crew I flew with were starting to make me feel uncomfortable. For the first time in my career, I found myself not looking forward to going to work. Some of the older captains treated me with disdain as if I had only just learned to fly. One captain would only communicate with me through the flight engineer. Not only was this extremely irritating, but I also thought it totally unprofessional. I had been flying for six months on the 747, and each trip seemed to deliver a new humiliation for me. I began to dread sitting in that windowless room waiting to meet my next captain.

To be fair to the crews, British Airways had not actively recruited for many years. As direct entry pilots, we were the first pilots employed that British Airways had not trained themselves for a long time. Understandably, there was a certain apprehension felt at the arrival of these new and unknown pilots. Invariably, the first question a captain would ask me as he studied my two stripes would be, "are you a DEP?" meaning a Direct Entry Pilot. It was more like an accusation than a question. I could feel the tension rising as this typically meant I was in for a tough time on that trip. I was often tempted to reply that it was better than being a Hamster, the term used for those pilots trained by British Airways at Hamble. Still, I never did work up the courage. Some things are best left unsaid.

Things finally came to a head on a flight to New York. The trip started as usual, with the three of us meeting as we left that dreaded windowless room. I tried to introduce myself to the captain on the bus, only to be ignored as he struck up a conversation with the flight engineer. At the briefing, he ignored me as he discussed the route with the engineer and the flight planners. During the entire flight to New York, I was again only addressed through the flight engineer. Not a word was spoken directly to me. He flew the aircraft; the flight engineer moved the switches and I simply moved the landing gear and flaps when instructed to do so.

Oh well, I thought, it's his aircraft and if he wants to play it that way, I really don't care. I probably would never fly with him again anyway. After clearing customs, we made our way to find our transport to the hotel. In those days, the flight crew usually stayed in different hotels to the cabin crew, and we had our own vehicle. In New York, we had a minivan with a sliding door on the side to gain access to the passenger seats. As I was the first to reach the van, I placed my bag in the rear compartment and used the side door to make my way to the seats at the very back of the vehicle. It was very hierarchical, the junior at the back and the captain at the front.

As I made myself as comfortable as possible, the engineer popped his head into the van. He informed me that the captain wanted me to exit the van and enter again through the back doors. Laughing, I told the engineer that I was not that gullible. He looked at me straight and reiterated that the side door was for the captain and junior ranks were to use the back door. It slowly dawned on me that he was being serious. I was expected to get out, go to the back and climb over the suitcases to get to the seat I was currently occupying. Of course, I refused, and the engineer went to inform the captain. He quickly returned with the captain, who was now standing beside the van. I was tersely told that we were not going anywhere until I got out and entered by the correct door. It was a cold, wet day. I was sitting comfortably inside the warm van. The captain was standing in the wind and rain. I told the engineer that was fine with me. This ridiculous scene went on until I was finally told that the captain would refuse to talk to me for the remainder of the trip if I did not get out. Well, that just made me laugh. He had not spoken one word directly to me since we left London. At this point, I think he realised that this co-pilot was not for moving, and so a wet and cold captain finally entered the van, and we set off for the hotel.

Although this was probably the worst experience I had with a captain, it was sadly not unusual to be treated in such a derisory fashion. It would probably take me another twenty years to achieve my own command. Could I suffer this sort of treatment for such a long period? I decided on that trip that this was not the way I wanted to spend my career. Dignity at work, or anywhere else for that matter, is a human right, and I was simply not prepared to be treated like this. I made an appointment to see the chief pilot when I returned to London. I decided to go back to my previous job. I was going to resign.

The moment I made that decision, I could literally feel a great weight lift from my shoulders. I would be free to enjoy my flying once more. I hated the idea of leaving the 747. However, I hated the idea of being treated in this manner even more. I was happy with my decision. The flight home went precisely as expected. The captain refused to talk to me; well, no change there, I thought to myself. We flew silently throughout the night. The only break was when I gave the regular progress reports as we made our way across the Atlantic. We had to use the High Frequency or HF long-range radio, which always involved a bit of shouting. It was a very old-fashioned and unreliable way to talk to air traffic control. It was also a very welcome break from the otherwise stony silence on the flight deck. After landing, the captain merely collected his bags and walked away, the flight engineer following in his wake. I simply sat in my seat and looked around the flight deck. I would seriously miss this aircraft. It was, however, a price I was prepared to pay to avoid another miserable trip like this one.

My appointment with management was not until nine o'clock. We had landed at six in the morning. I had three hours to spare and maybe to change my mind. I dropped my bags off at the luggage storage room and made my way to the myriad of offices hidden in a rabbit run of corridors. I had never been in this part of the building before, and having seen it once, I immediately had no desire ever to return. The corridors were long and dark. Just the occasional bare lightbulb lit my way. There was no natural light anywhere to be seen. The whole area resembled a Second World War government bunker rather than the headquarters of a national airline. I felt very sorry for the people who had to work in a place like this. Maybe, I was not so badly off after all. With time to kill, I decided to explore this world a little more closely. The offices were set above the multi-storey car park we used when at work. I had barely given them any thought. There were hundreds of people hidden away in these dark labyrinths. As I made my way around, a few people stopped to stare at me. Obviously, pilots rarely made an appearance. Eventually, I found a small area with a coffee machine and made myself at home. I now had just over an hour before my appointment. As it was so early, few people were around, the main offices would not open until nine.

I had an hour now to make what was probably one of the most important decisions of my life. If I did resign, which I fully intended to do until a few moments ago, I would be returning to an uncertain future. Although I was still running the Cessna Conquest operation, I could not imagine doing that or something similar for the next thirty years. On the other hand, I could not bear to think of spending the next few decades flying with people who refused to speak to me. As these thoughts were making their way around my head, I suddenly heard a cheery, "Good Morning."

Looking up, I was met by a friendly face looking down on me. I returned his greeting as he sat next to me and began enquiring about where I had just been or where I was just off to. We eventually started to discuss why I was waiting in the offices after being up all night. I was hesitant to give too much away. I had no idea who this pleasant chap was, and so I mumbled something about wanting to change fleets. I informed him that I was currently flying the 747. He looked at me with astonishment. Why would anyone want to fly anything else he enquired unless, of course, it was Concorde? Now that's a good idea, I thought to myself. However, you cannot change aircraft types until you have completed three years on your current aircraft. Anyway, the chance of flying Concorde was beyond the bounds of possibility for a junior pilot. We continued to chat and he did give me his name although sadly, I have long forgotten it. I would love to have thanked him personally all these years later.

He explained why he was here. It was to finalise a new base at Gatwick. He cheerily informed me that British Airways was starting a base with initially just one 747, flying to the Caribbean. The company was going to be operated by the charter arm, British Airtours. Why not apply to fly from Gatwick were his parting words as he set off for his meeting. Realising the time, I hurried off to find the chief pilot's office, this time with a new plan formulating in my head. I bumped into streams of office workers, leaving the bright sunlight outside to disappear into this dark and unwelcoming place for the next eight hours. Finally, working out the numbering system, I found myself in the waiting room of the great man's office. I was not offered tea or any biscuits, and I could tell from his secretary's expression that I was an unwelcome intruder. I remained standing for the next twenty minutes until I was finally called through into the main office.

I had thought that this would be a quick meeting. I would simply say that I had made a mistake joining the company and would like to hand in my notice, which should not have taken more than a few minutes.

As I entered the room, the chief pilot looked up at me. He remained seated and abruptly asked what I wanted. My brain was about to make my resignation speech. Instead, my mouth asked if I could possibly be transferred to Gatwick and fly for

British Airtours. Luckily for me, my mouth won the day. He inquired how I knew about the upcoming operation at Gatwick? Apparently, it was a well-guarded secret. I gave a very non-committal reply which seemed to satisfy him. My request was granted, and with that, I was abruptly dismissed. So, instead of resigning, I had applied for and got a new job with a subsidiary company. As I made my way back to the car park, I really did not know whether to celebrate or commiserate. Fortunately, I had plenty of time to ponder this as it took me nearly an hour to find my car.

Chapter 8

A Very Welcome Return To Gatwick

The year was 1988. There are years in all our lives that, in retrospect, turn out to be far more significant than we realised at the time. For me, 1988 was such a year. On a whim, I had left British Airways and joined British Airtours. Unbeknownst and very luckily for me, the two companies shared a joint seniority list, so in effect, I was still on the British Airways master list. This meant that I could move between the two companies and still retain that all-important seniority number.

On the domestic front, I had asked Liz to marry me at Christmas. Surprisingly, she agreed. As soon as the festivities were over, we began making arrangements for the upcoming wedding in May. I was still heavily involved in the Cessna Conquest operation at Shoreham. I spent a lot of my spare time flying for Foodbrokers and Desmond Cracknell. Now that I was happily flying the 747, I could relax and really enjoy the luxury of flying both aircraft types. The main problem was remembering which aircraft I was in when I began the flare. Trying to flare the Cessna at seventy feet or the jumbo at ten feet would result in a dramatic outcome. We had also moved into our first home together. As always, with a new house, there was a lot of work to be done. Liz was still flying long haul for British Caledonian on the DC-10 and 747 aircraft.

All in all, we both had our hands very full. There was precious little spare time for either of us. That's when we found out that our first son, James, had decided to book an appearance for later that year. Liz was pregnant. We were delighted and, to be honest, a little daunted at this news. We were both so busy that the little time we had together was spent with Roffey or visiting family and friends. How could we possibly have time to look after a baby? Still, it was a bit late for such thoughts. James was on his way. Plans for the wedding intensified. I was about to start my new job with British Airtours, and life was running at full throttle.

I would often return from a trip and drive down to Shoreham Airport to fly the Foodbrokers aircraft the next day. When we spoke to air traffic control, our standard call sign was 'Food 125'. I totally embarrassed myself one winter's evening returning to Gatwick on the Conquest. It had been a long day visiting a major client, Baxter's Soups, up to Inverness in Scotland. It was too late to land at Shoreham by the time we set off southwards for the return flight. They closed at eight o'clock. On the approach to Gatwick, struggling to stay awake, I called up the approach controller with the call sign 'Speedbird 125'. All British Airways aircraft have the call sign, 'Speedbird' followed by the flight number. The poor controller was expecting a light twin, not a British Airways scheduled flight. Twice he asked me to confirm who exactly I was. I could not understand why he was asking until I actually got it right on the third request. It was a quiet time of night, and luckily, he saw the funny side of my mistake. Had I done that on an approach into New York, I would very quickly find myself with a fighter escort? I realise that I am biased, but British air traffic controllers are simply the best in the world. I wish the same could be said of some of its pilots.

One of the advantages of flying is that you cannot do it if you are pregnant. This meant that Liz had to stop flying for the following year. Happily, we were now able to see a lot more of each other. Before the pregnancy, we were like ships in the night. I could be returning from a five-day trip the same day Liz left for a seven-day one. We could go for weeks without seeing each other. Now at least, one of us could start to live a more normal life. The one thing we were both determined about was that the new arrival would have to fit into our lifestyle and not vice versa. James would have to adapt quickly, and it's fair to say that he more than lived up to his side of the bargain. Not many babies make headline news as James was destined to do.

The day arrived for my first flight from Gatwick. To say I was a little nervous would be an understatement. I was going to be a father, I now had real responsibilities, and I could no longer choose to leave an airline on a whim. I needed to grow up quickly. Therefore, I had to make this job work, no excuses, no blaming anyone else. Whatever the circumstances, I had to commit to this new position. The first advantage of working from Gatwick was my commute was reduced from two, or sometimes three hours to a mere twenty minutes. No more worrying about queues on the M25 motorway. The only traffic I now had to worry about were a few farm tractors that sometimes trundled along the narrow country lanes. The car park at Gatwick was next to my office in the Beehive, so I could now pop in on the way to work or home. So far, so good, it only remained to find out if the captains at Gatwick would actually speak to me.

The bus from the car park to the operations building took five minutes. Instead of stony silence, there was the welcome sound of happy voices and laughter. People even said hello to me. Well, this was a definite change for the better. I made my way to the check-in counter, where I was warmly greeted and welcomed by the operational staff. On enquiring where I would meet the captain and flight engineer, I was told they would find me soon enough. I then asked if there was a windowless room where I could sit in silence and await my fate. As were the majority of my jokes, this attempt at humour was met by a blank stare. Things were obviously done very differently here, and it was very much to my liking so far.

As I could find neither the captain nor the engineer, I thought that I would get ahead of the game and go in search of the paperwork for the flight. After a few false starts, I managed to get all the required documents, and I spread them across the counter for the captain to peruse when he arrived. Still waiting, I thought I would go a step further. So, I produced my yellow marker pen and began highlighting all the relevant information. That completed, I again looked around to find my colleagues. Still, there was no sign. And so, I carried on and thoroughly checked the flight plan and all the weather en route. I even made sure the map was the correct way up. Everything seemed to be in order, and it looked like it would be a smooth flight all the way to Barbados. I was still standing there alone. The report time had long since come and gone. Finally, I began to wonder if it was me. Had I arrived a day early or a day late?

I could no longer simply stand there, and so I set off in search of my crew. Returning to the ops desk, I thought I would go and meet the cabin crew to let them know that there would be a delay as I was the only flight crew member there. I was given the room number where our crew would be briefing. Wandering down unfamiliar corridors, I eventually found the correct room. I gently knocked and entered. At Heathrow, we only met the cabin crew when we were on the aircraft. Once onboard, the captain would proceed with a formal briefing, occasionally asking a technical question resulting in that crew member being offloaded if answered incorrectly. Therefore, the atmosphere was always formal and slightly threatening, not a pleasant experience. This was probably one of the reasons that there was such a vast divide between flight and cabin crew.

As I entered the room at Gatwick, I was expecting a similar bleak reception to the one I was used to at Heathrow. Instead, as I entered, all faces turned towards me with welcoming smiles and greetings. There was laughter reverberating around the room and searching for the source. I saw the captain doing a decent impersonation of a well-known celebrity, ably supported by the flight engineer. Well, this was undoubtedly a very different way to brief the cabin crew. There are no tricky questions, no formal briefing, and, most importantly, no divide between flight and cabin crew. Not quite knowing what to do or say, I meekly offered the captain the paperwork for the flight.

Wiping tears of laughter from his eyes, he asked if I was happy with everything and did we need any extra fuel? Again, this was very different from the way things were done at Heathrow. Assuring him that I could see no reason for more fuel, he simply handed back the paperwork. He asked me to order whatever fuel I felt was reasonable, and with that, he continued with another impersonation. Returning to the ops desk, I ordered the fuel, feeling slightly uneasy that I was the only one who had checked the figures. I felt a whole lot better when the operations officer winked at me and said the captain had checked all the paperwork an hour ago. Apparently, he always arrived very early to make time to get to know the rest of the crew. It was a lesson well learned and a practice I regularly used from that day onwards. One of the beautiful things about aviation is that there is something new to discover on every flight. The day you stop learning is the day you retire. Over the coming years, I learnt so much from the captains I flew with. I knew how not to treat people if you want the best out of them. Equally, like today, I learnt how to get the best out of a crew. The rest of the trip went much the same way. Everyone had already bonded before we had even reached the aircraft. Another lesson I learned that day; a happy crew nearly always resulted in happy passengers.

On arrival into Barbados, the whole crew piled into a rickety bus which banged and clattered its way around the narrow, uneven roads. The moment we left the airport behind, bottles of rum punch miraculously appeared, and glasses of this potent brew was passed around at great speed. There were no barriers between the cabin and flight crew. We were simply one crew. Arriving at the hotel, we unloaded ourselves to check in at a thatched cottage on the hotel grounds. From there, golf buggies were lined up to take us to our rooms or, more accurately, cottages.

There was bad news, our rooms would not be ready for another two hours. It had been a long day, and we were all tired. Quite a few of the crew had already had a couple of rum punches too many. The hotel staff knew how to appease a tired team. More rum punches were placed in front of us. Knowing that it would be rude to refuse, we sat drinking for another two hours. Eventually, our rooms were declared ready. This was just as well as it was now late at night. The captain, the engineer and I poured ourselves into one of the golf buggies to be whisked away to our cottages. Personally, I was feeling more than a little worse for wear. I have never been a spirit drinker. I preferred beer and wine. The rum had definitely gone to my head, and I was a little unsteady on my feet as I climbed the steps to my room. Our three cottages were next to each other, and I called out a drunken goodnight as I struggled to open the door. Whichever way I tried to fit my key into the lock, I had absolutely no success opening the damn thing. In my inebriated state, I thought the best thing would be to sit down and work out why my key would not fit the lock.

I woke up some hours later as a bright Caribbean sun rose above the trees behind me. It took me a few moments to realise where I was. I was highly embarrassed and prayed that the other two had not seen me asleep in front of my room. I stood up only to notice two feet sticking out from a bush next to me. I hurriedly made my way over to check on the well-being of the owner of these feet. There, in the bush, snoring loudly, was the flight engineer. It appeared that the task of gaining access to his room had also proved beyond him. If the captain saw either of us in this state, there could be trouble ahead. As I turned around to ensure his door was closed, I noticed an arm apparently attached to his door handle. On closer inspection, this arm belonged to our captain. The rest of him lay in an untidy heap at the bottom of the door. Fortunately for me, it appeared that I was the least affected by the rum punches.

Eventually, all three of us were awake. Again, we tried to open our doors, again without success. We began the steep ascent towards the reception hut. Each step painfully reminded me just how delicate my state was. Finally, we staggered into the reception room. We must have looked a sight. People just stopped and stared at us. Thank goodness we had the foresight the previous evening to change into shorts and a T-shirt. It transpired that we had been given the wrong keys. It was a ten-minute walk up very steep steps to reception. We now knew how difficult this was. We had little chance of making it back to the reception hut without serious injury if we attempted this in the dark. Our drunken fates were sealed the moment the golf buggy drove off.

If this was a typical Gatwick trip, I knew I would be happy at my new base and my new airline, British Airtours. I felt at home.

Chapter 9

A Tragic Christmas

In December 1988, I was celebrating having completed my first full year of flying the Boeing 747. Our first child James had arrived in October, and we were planning our first Christmas as a family. Unfortunately, as I was a very junior pilot, I had to work that Christmas. There would be no family celebrations at our new home. Instead, I was rostered to be away for five days over the festive period, landing back in England on Boxing Day. The trip was to Barbados and back to Manchester, landing on Boxing Day. We were then rostered to position home on the twenty-seventh. So not much chance of a White Christmas this year. Also, sadly, there would be no Santa Claus coming down the chimney for James's first Christmas. Still, he was only a few months old and hopefully, I would be at home next year.

This, of course, was not welcome news for the brand new Eades family. I really could not face being parted from Liz and our two-month-old baby for our first Christmas. Luckily, where there is a will, there is sometimes a way. After a lot of red tape, I secured tickets for Liz and James to join me on the trip. Even better, I managed to get permission to make my own way home from Manchester instead of flying back to Gatwick with my crew on the twenty-seventh of December. Liz had been brought up on the Wirral. Her parents and the house she grew up in were only a forty-minute drive from Manchester Airport. The plan was made, Christmas in the Caribbean followed by Boxing Day with my new in-laws, who I adored. The only downside was that we would be spending Christmas night on a 747. Still, it was a price we were prepared to pay to be together.

The day before we were due to fly to Barbados, we had everything packed and ready to go. Travelling light with a new baby is just about impossible, especially as we were both very new to the parenting game. As Liz finally appeared satisfied that everything was in order, I looked at the enormous case and the pile of baby paraphernalia. How could such a tiny human being require such a large amount of equipment? I mentioned this to Liz, which was probably a mistake in hindsight as I rubbed my arm to reduce the pain of a well-placed punch. I was relieved that we had an estate car and a jumbo jet. We would need all the space we could find. All that remained was to say farewell to friends and get an early night. Tomorrow promised to be a long day, especially for Liz with a new baby to look after.

With everything finally stowed, packed, checked, and double-checked, we sat down for a quick supper. We would not be returning until the New Year, so we emptied the house of food and locked everything away. All we had to do now was get a good night's sleep, although, with a newborn, that is actually an impossible dream. We set our alarm for six o'clock in the morning. James set his alarm for four o'clock.

Whilst this routine family scene was being played out, a sinister and deadly plot was being put into action. A Pan Am 747 had just taken off from Frankfurt on its way to London. From London, it was due to continue its journey to New York. A suitcase had been loaded at Frankfurt that had no right to be there. After a routine stop in London, the 747 climbed away and headed for Scotland where it was scheduled to start its Atlantic crossing. It never made it that far.

Turning on the television, supper on our laps, our programme was interrupted with the tragic news that a Pan Am Boeing 747 had crashed into a small town in Scotland, Lockerbie.

Along with the rest of the world, we were shocked into silence. Even the baby seemed to sense that something was wrong and lay quietly at our side.

We sat there for what seemed an age as news filtered through of the extent of the tragedy. We were due to fly in the next twelve hours on precisely the same type of aircraft. There was no news about how and why the Pan Am aircraft had fallen out of the sky. We only knew that we were about to take our eight-week-old child on a similar aircraft the following day. Looking at each other and then at James, we had to decide about our flight in the morning. Of course, I would still have to go unless the initial findings of the crash grounded all Boeing 747s. However, was it still wise to take my family with me if there was even the slightest hint of danger? It was a decision that I could really only leave to Liz. She had to feel safe and comfortable if she and our baby were to join me. As much as I wanted them both to be with me, I knew that the choice was hers alone to make.

It was impossible to imagine that her decision that night would result in all three of us making headline news. Only a few days later, our little family would become famous. Our fate was sealed. Liz had made the brave decision to accompany me to Barbados. Decision made: We tried to have an early night, like that would happen with an eight-week-old baby who had very different plans for us.

The eight-hour flight the following day went very smoothly. We even managed to get all our luggage onto the aircraft, which came as a pleasant surprise. The mood on board the aircraft was very sombre. The news that a bomb explosion had downed the Pan Am aircraft had reached us before departure. The whole tragedy was appalling. The only slight comfort for us was that the cause of the crash had quickly been identified, and thankfully, there were no inherent problems with the 747 itself.

The trip itself was enjoyable in the sense that the three of us were together and enjoying some winter sunshine. James proudly wore his 'Santa's Little Helper' T-shirt on the beach each day. His presence helped us and a lot of the crew to put the tragedy of Lockerbie to the back of our minds, at least for a while.

Christmas Day 1988 was not the usual opening of presents. We had both agreed that we had enough luggage without bringing gifts. Besides, we would have turkey and all the trimmings tomorrow, Boxing Day, at Liz's parent's house. Instead, we gave James some more swimming lessons in the warm Caribbean Sea.

Departure that night was scheduled for eight o'clock in the evening. The flight, unsurprisingly, was almost empty. Not many people wanted to spend Christmas night on an aircraft, and who could blame them? Liz decided to sit on the upper deck directly behind the flight deck. I think this was to ensure that if the baby cried all night, both of us would have to be awake. Liz vehemently still denies this.

There were only twenty-five other passengers on the aircraft that night. We had eighteen cabin crew members, plus the three of us on the flight deck. It was a pretty even match between passengers and crew. We were all looking forward to a peaceful night after the events of the past few days.

I left the flight deck as we reached our cruising height of thirty-three thousand feet. I went to check on Liz and the baby; both were resting peacefully. I made my way down the spiral stairs and checked that all was well with the crew and passengers. The cavernous interior of the aircraft was extenuated by the lack of people. In the twilight, it was difficult to make out the dim shapes of passengers sleeping or crew working. We were all suspended in mid-air over the Atlantic Ocean on the holiest of nights. I quietly made my way back to my seat, not wanting to disturb this silent and peaceful world. What could possibly go wrong on such a silent night? As the aircraft steadily droned on through the night sky, we were about to find out.

Chapter 10

A Silent Night Miracle

Three hours into the flight and it appeared we were the only aircraft in the sky. There was nothing but the Atlantic Ocean between us and our departure and destination airports. All we could hear on our headsets was the occasional crackle of static from faraway thunderstorms. There were no other aircraft within a hundred miles of us, and apart from checking in with air traffic control every hour, there was little for the three of us on the flight deck to do. The engineer monitored all of the aircraft's complicated systems, carried out routine fuel checks, and tried to stay awake. The captain was on his scheduled rest period and had his seat pushed back, a gentle snore the only indication that he was still with us.

Liz would occasionally pop her head into the flight deck to make sure that at least two of us were awake. When it was my break, I would take over baby duties to allow Liz to get some rest. The whole scene was almost surreal as the 747 continued to power its way on through what remained of Christmas night. I stared out of the window at the stars trying to work out which one had guided the three wise men all those centuries ago. All was peaceful, all was quiet, but not for much longer.

The first sign that all was not well was when a little blue light illuminated the overhead panel accompanied by a muffled bell. This meant that one of the crew was calling us from the cabin. Whilst this in itself was not an indication that something was wrong. Usually, the crew came into the flight deck if they needed to speak to us. If there was a problem in the cabin, such as an unruly passenger, the crew would use the interphone system to keep us updated. I was not unduly concerned if that was the case tonight as we pretty much had the passengers outnumbered. Let them try anything if they dared was my idle thinking as I answered the phone.

Being young and relatively immature, I would often answer a call to the flight deck with the following greeting:

"Thank you for calling the flight deck. Your call is very important to us. I'm sorry there is no one here at the moment to take your call, but if you leave your name and number, we will get back to you."

Well, it amused me, and believe it or not, a few of the crew actually did begin to leave a message before I could no longer contain my laughter. Tonight, was not a good night for such frolics. "Don't be so bloody stupid" got my immediate attention, and I realised that this was not a social call after all.

I sat upright and listened intently. The Cabin Service Director, Elaine Stadniki, the head of the cabin crew, was fast asleep in the crew bunks. Her deputy explained precisely what was taking place. A young Irish couple had boarded the aircraft in Barbados, the wife clearly pregnant. There is a rule that a pregnant woman usually is not allowed to fly after thirty-two weeks due to the risks to her and her unborn baby. The couple confirmed that the wife was within the permitted time frame, so they had been allowed to board the aircraft. The purser explained that this lady was now showing early signs that the baby had decided that Christmas night would be an excellent night to make an appearance. Nobody then would ever have an excuse for forgetting their birthday. I could see the baby's point of view.

We were now in the middle of the Atlantic. Barbados was three hours behind us, and Ireland was another three hours in front of us. There was nothing else but the ocean in between. I was a new father. I had been at my own son's birth just a few weeks earlier. So, I knew a thing or two about babies being born, why I was nearly an expert at the whole business, or so I imagined. I did know for sure that the entire process, from first contractions to the actual birth, takes ages and ages. Days and days if you are really unlucky. With this reassuring knowledge to hand, I relayed the words of perceived wisdom to the purser. She was not entirely convinced and asked if one of us could come down to reassure the expectant mother as she was beginning to panic. No problem, I thought to myself, a few wise words from me should do the trick. I informed her that I would be down in a minute. Before I could leave the flight deck, I had a captain to wake up.

As I was about to find out, captains do not like being woken during their rest period. After a couple of gentle shakes of his shoulders, one eye suddenly opened wide, the mouth moved, and I was greeted with the words.

"This had better be bloody important."

I hoped that a pregnant woman apparently going into premature labour made it onto his list of essential things. Luckily for me, it did.

Our captain belonged to the generation of fathers who, at the first signs of anything to do with the arrival of their offspring, would literally hop off somewhere, anywhere else. I, however, was made of much sterner stuff. I had accompanied my wife to as many prenatal clinics as I could manage, well, to be fair, as many as I could not avoid. I had learned what to do and what not to do at the actual birth. The most important things I took away from the lectures were not fainting and not getting in the way. I had indeed been at my wife's side for the whole long-drawn-out procedure. I knew from my first-hand experience that these things took time, a lot of time. With this knowledge firmly at the forefront of my mind, I set off to reassure our soon-to-be mum.

I thought before going downstairs I would see how my own offspring was doing, and of course, to check up on my wife, Liz. Both looked very relaxed and James, bless him, was asleep in his mother's arms. Best not disturb them, I thought. I set off in search of a passenger with a big tummy. As there were only twenty-five passengers to choose from, this did not take me long. My main difficulty was finding any passengers at all. The 747 is a large aircraft, and with so few people on board, we could have all played hide and seek without anyone winning. Luckily one of the crew guided me through the semi-darkness to the very back of the aircraft, where I found a very anxious couple.

The strange thing about being in uniform, especially a pilot's uniform, is that everybody immediately listens to you. They generally accept whatever you have to say without question. Had I been in jeans and a T-shirt, I would not have been given the time of day. At one of the most stressful times of their lives, the couple were looking at me and hanging on to every word I said. I realised that I definitely needed to choose my words very carefully.

I gently explained that we could not land immediately, which would involve us all getting very wet. I went on to explain that we were over three hours from any airport. I reassured them that this presented no problem as if labour had started, we would be on the ground in plenty of time to get to a hospital in time for the birth. I remembered to ask them to time the contractions and let the cabin crew know if there was any change in her condition. Fortunately for all involved, one of the crew had previously been a nurse and volunteered to look after the couple. I reassured them that we would monitor the situation and increase the aircraft's speed if we needed to get anywhere quickly. The young couple relaxed, and the situation suddenly seemed a lot less stressful for all concerned.

Now, it's not often that I have a good idea, and when one eventually does come along, it's precious and needs to be cherished. Tonight, I had a good idea. The couple were sitting in the economy section of the aircraft with limited space, even with a near-empty aircraft. I, therefore, suggested that we all move to the front of the aircraft, where there were empty beds. The couple could then lie down and sleep for the remainder of the flight. I returned to the flight deck with that organised, intending to let the old one-eyed sleepyhead return to the land of nod. I felt satisfied that I had handled the whole situation very well. After another quick stop to check on Liz and James, I returned to staring at the stars listening once again to the gentle snoring from the other seat.

Another twenty minutes passed quietly. I made our hourly call to Piarco Radio, checked our fuel, and settled down as Christmas Day slowly drew to a close. I was idly reflecting on our first Christmas with James and how we would never forget this trip; how right I was. The tranquillity was shattered once again as the little blue light and chimes brought me back to our present predicament. With a healthy amount of trepidation, I answered the call, no silly phone messages this time. The purser informed me that the passenger was now lying on the floor. She was by one of the doors and was in extreme pain. Could I please come down immediately?

There was no gentle shaking of the captain's shoulder this time. He was rudely awakened by a very heavy-handed engineer. After a quick update, the captain asked me to assess the situation whilst preparing for a possible diversion to the nearest, suitable airfield. I felt the power increase on our four giant Rolls Royce engines as I left the flight deck. Wherever we were going, we were going there in a hurry.

Entering the upper deck cabin, I saw that Liz was awake and chatting to one of the crew. James was also awake and doing his best to keep them amused with his antics. Remembering that Liz had also been present at James's birth, I had another of my light bulb moments. Asking the crew member if she could look after James for a short time, I grabbed Liz's hand and asked her to help with a small problem downstairs. Poor Liz's Christmas was about to take a turn for the worse.

We both descended the circular staircase. At the bottom, we found a scene that more resembled a hospital than an aircraft. Our poor pregnant passenger was lying down covered by a blanket in obvious distress and great pain. Her husband was in total panic, and the crew surrounding them were doing their best to calm him down. I turned to Liz and asked her to please sort this out and tell me when all was well. With that, I turned around and went back to the flight deck.

Well, that was my first instinct. Instead, I thought I had better assess the situation and see how long we had before the baby arrived. Our nurse was doing a great job of calming the passenger, who had now turned into our patient. After a quick discussion, we discovered that I was the only one who had actually been at the business end of a birth. So, I volunteered to assist in that department. Liz began to time the contractions, and the nurse went off to collect the aircraft's medical kit.

Now without going into graphic detail, I had closely monitored James's birth, and the midwife had been kind enough to talk me through the whole delivery. I had always been fascinated by all things medical. Indeed, if I had been better at Latin and a lot more intelligent, I would have loved to have gone into medicine as a career. Instead, all I could offer this poor woman was a very nervous pilot to help deliver her baby.

I did know that the cervix had to be fully dilated to allow the baby to be born. During James's birth, this process had taken a few hours. I had been shown how to check the process of dilation. We needed to know how much time we had before the baby arrived. The aircraft was still two hours away from any airport. Making sure that the soon-to-be mum and dad were happy for me to intervene, I took the plunge and began my very amateurish diagnosis. At least I could pass the latest information back to the captain, enabling him to make a more informed decision as to where we would need to divert.

Gently lifting the blanket, with Liz at my side, I began to reassure the patient. I had expected to see no more than the very beginning of the birth process. The nurse had now returned and counted the contractions, advising the mum not to push. It was far too early for that.

As I looked down, I could not quite believe what I was seeing. I immediately forgot about dilation, counting the contractions, or any other of the procedures I had witnessed only weeks earlier. Instead, I was met with a baby's head about to make its entrance into the world. I could hear the nurse telling the mum not to push. I popped my head from under the blanket with the words "No, please push, push." The nurse gave me a quizzical look, then seeing my expression, she quickly changed her advice and began asking mum to push.

A few moments later, I was holding the smallest baby I had ever seen in the palms of my hands. Liz was next to me, helping as best she could. Drawing on my limited experience in these matters, I immediately realised that all was not as it should be. When James had made his arrival, he did it with aplomb, announcing his introduction into the world with a very healthy pair of lungs. After his birth, the doctor tied and cut the umbilical cord and delivered the placenta, all very clinical and straightforward.

I had a tiny human in my hands that showed absolutely no interest in her surroundings. There was no crying, no movement, and instead of a healthy pink, her colour was a pale blue. This was the worst possible scenario. The baby was deprived of oxygen. We had a very short timeframe to act, or the consequences would be devastating for mother and baby. The nurse wanted to cut the umbilical cord, as is standard practice. I'm not sure what warned us, but we thought that this would not be a good idea. This cord had been supplying the baby with oxygen for the past seven months. Maybe there was a chance it was still providing even the smallest amount. Rightly or wrongly, we decided to leave mother and baby attached.

The next and most pressing problem was that the baby was not only quiet, but her mouth was not open. Again, remembering the antenatal classes, I asked the nurse if a mucus extractor was in the medical kit. Good old British Airways, of course, there was, and it was produced. This device fits into the baby's mouth and clears the airways of anything that should not be there with gentle suction. Unfortunately, there was still no response from the baby. Turning her over on her tummy, I gently rubbed and tapped her back just in case anything was obstructing her airway, still nothing. The only other procedure we could think of was Cardiopulmonary Resuscitation or CPR.

As part of our initial training in British Airways, we had to attend an entire medical course. We learned how to perform CPR, recognise and treat heart attacks, and many other medical emergencies. Our knowledge and practical skills were checked every year. That training saved the baby's life that night. Sadly, Flight Crew no longer receive this training. It is reserved for the Cabin Crew only. This, in my humble opinion, was a great mistake. The accountants in the company should hang their heads in shame.

Luckily for all concerned, we were thoroughly trained in CPR, although I had only practised on an adult-sized dummy. Still, what could be so different, I thought. Using just a finger instead of both hands, I gently pressed on the baby's chest. Every few moments, I used the mucus extractor to gently breathe air into her lungs. In the classroom, after a minute or two, the instructor would declare Annie, as we all affectionately called the dummy, had recovered. In real life, things went very differently. After two minutes, there was no miraculous recovery. The baby still showed no signs of life. Her colour was still a pale blue, and she was still not breathing unaided.

However, the baby had other ideas. It was still Christmas Day, well on Barbados time it was, and a Christmas miracle was about to happen before our very eyes.

The first thing I noticed was that Shannon's colour began to change from a very pale blue to very pale pink. The colour then began to deepen until I was holding a very pink baby. Oxygen was finally getting into her bloodstream, an excellent sign. Continuing the CPR, I saw that Shannon was trying to breathe by herself, taking in small gulps of air between my breaths. She then began to wriggle, slowly at first, then became more pronounced with each breath in her movements. Suddenly she started the most enormous wailing. Even James would have been proud of that volume. Her eyes opened, and the crying became even louder. No doubt, seeing such an ugly face in front of her did not help. The baby had truly arrived. I laid her on her mother's tummy, and her father returned to complete the scene. We decided to leave the umbilical cord attached, hopefully it could do no harm. We thought mother and baby had been through enough for one night. Liz stayed with the crew looking after the new family. We were now in the latter stages of our approach into Shannon and I hurriedly mounted the stairs to return to the flight deck. I briefly stopped to check on James. True to form, he had been behaving perfectly and had charmed his carer. As new parents, we could not have been more proud of him. Thirty-three years later, we still feel exactly the same.

After a perfect touchdown, carried out by the captain, we were very quickly taxying onto the stand. Amidst a sea of blue flashing lights Liz stood by the now open door as the paramedics and a midwife rushed to check on our newest passenger. Luckily mother and baby were doing well after the umbilical cord was finally cut. Five minutes later mother, father and baby were being driven away to the local hospital. There was an air of celebration as we stood and watched the last of the red taillights of the ambulances disappear into the glorious sunrise.

Chapter 11

Unexpected Consequences

Returning to the flight deck, I explained to the captain and Engineer what had taken place literally just below their feet. Although mother and baby seemed to be doing well, we obviously needed to get them to a hospital as quickly as possible.

Our nearest airport was now Shannon in Ireland, a place I knew well from my training and night stops just a year earlier. Decision made; we pointed the aircraft directly towards our new destination after a new clearance from Air Traffic Control. We had previously increased our speed and maintaining this, we raced across the night sky, hoping our new and unexpected passenger remained stable for the next few hours.

Shortly before we began our high-speed descent, I went downstairs to check on the new family. Everyone seemed very calm, and the baby was fast asleep in her mother's arms. Quietly, I returned upstairs and prepared for our arrival, noticing as I passed, that Liz and James were also sleeping. As we still had forty minutes to run, I left them to enjoy a well-earned rest.

The captain made one of the smoothest landings I had experienced in a 747, and very shortly afterwards, we were opening the aircraft's doors. As we had called ahead, an ambulance waited for our arrival with a proper midwife and doctor to take over. I explained what had happened and why I had left the umbilical cord attached. After a comprehensive examination, both the doctor and midwife were satisfied that the baby was doing well. However, she needed to get into an incubator as soon as possible. And with that, mother, father and baby were whisked away in a haze of flashing blue lights.

Excitement over, we now had to decide what to do with a Boeing 747, its passengers and crew. It was now the early hours of Boxing Day morning, and we were in Shannon instead of Manchester. Before making any hasty decisions, we rang our operations control in London to ask them where they wanted the aircraft. Unfortunately for Liz and me, we were asked to bring the plane directly back to Gatwick. It was needed later that day for a flight to Orlando, Florida. Any passengers who wanted to go to Manchester were booked onto other flights later that morning.

So, off we set, my sector this time, for the short flight to Gatwick. We landed late in the morning and said our goodbyes to the crew, who were delighted to be home a day early. Of course, Liz and I had made arrangements to be picked up at Manchester. After such a long night, I could not drive the four-and-a-half-hour journey without having some rest, and so we went home to a cold and empty house.

The three of us were exhausted, just about managing to struggle up the stairs to get some well-deserved sleep. There was absolutely no food in the house. After all, we had not expected to return until after the New Year. Of course, we had a mountain of baby food with us. At least James was not going to go hungry. We all climbed into one bed to keep warm. The house was like an icebox. The central heating would take hours to warm everything up.

As I shut my eyes, I thought I heard a knocking at the door. At the same time, the telephone began ringing. Of course, this was many years before mobile phones were in regular use; otherwise, I'm sure that would have rung as well. Nobody knew that we were home. Friends and family thought we were away.

Naturally, the first thing we had done when we landed was to call Liz's parents to let them know that we would be driving up later that day, so it would not be them calling or knocking at our front door. Swearing under my breath, I climbed out of bed to see what was going on.

I'm sure that the writers of the movie *Notting Hill*, had got their inspiration from the scene at my front door that morning. I wandered downstairs in a pair of old running shorts and a cut-off vest. I knew how to dress to impress in bed. Opening the door, I expected that maybe one of our neighbours was checking why we were home so early. They had both kindly offered to keep an eye on the house until the New Year. Instead, I was met by a group of people holding note pads and microphones, all talking over each other shouting questions at me. I was totally bemused. What on earth was going on? What on earth had I done to arouse this sort of attention. My blood ran cold, actually what had I done? This must all be some horrible mistake. I was a law-abiding citizen, for goodness sake. Well, I used to pinch the odd packet of crisps when I was a barman, but I was sure I'd always get away with that.

All at once, I heard the words, "Baby," and "Aircraft." The mystery was solved. My life of crime as a crisp thief was not about to be revealed. Unlike in the movie, I did not wander outside in my pants. I did what any sensible person would do. I closed the door and went to get dressed. The phone was still ringing, and so I stopped to answer it. This time, the *Daily Mail* asked if I was the pilot who had delivered the Christmas baby. I put the phone down. I returned to bed to give Liz the good news. We were famous. If looks could kill, I would not be here today. The knocking on the door continued, and the phone rang constantly. For goodness sake, it was Boxing Day. Did these people not have a home to go to?

We sat up in bed and tried to make a plan. It seemed evident that we would eventually have to face the press. Just where and when was the question. It suddenly became apparent that there was only one way the press could have found out my name, phone number, and address so quickly. British Airways must have given the press my personal details.

I was upset and furious. Why would the company do such a thing, especially without my permission? Boxing Day or no Boxing Day, I rang the company to have a good old moan. Of course, there was nobody there except the operational departments. I had a number to use in case of emergency, and so I rang that. A fleet manager was on duty every day of the year, and he answered on the second ring. Yes, he had heard of last night's drama, and no, he had not given out my home number. Instead, he suggested I call the press office at BA; apparently, they also work on bank holidays. This time, it took a little longer for the phone to be answered. Eventually, I spoke to a very excited journalist who informed me that he was very busy with a story and could I call back later? Asking the story, he quickly explained that a baby had been born on one of our 747s last night, and guess what? One of the pilots had delivered the baby. Before I could interrupt him, he went on to explain that just under a week ago, the world had been stunned by Lockerbie, and now there was a good news story involving a 747, and it was a British Airways 747. He had to go as he was trying to contact the pilot to ask him to speak to the press. I just managed to get his attention before he put the phone down.

After a long conversation and after expressing my displeasure at having my details given away without my consent, we eventually came to a solution. I would agree to be interviewed by one newspaper only, *The Times*, which would have to take place at my house. I also reluctantly acquiesced to his plea for a photoshoot as long as Liz and James were included. Liz had after all been fully involved, James not quite as much, but he was darn cute and very photogenic. The deal was struck, and the interview and photos took place a few hours later.

Finally, we were left in peace. The press had got their pound of flesh, and at last, we could get ready for the drive to the Wirral and the start of our Christmas. Well, that was the idea until the phone rang one more time. Oh, how I wish I had never answered that call.

Instead of walking away from the telephone, I stopped and looked at it. The reason I paused was on account of an awful system known as forced draft. Until recently, British Airways were allowed to ring any pilot, even on their days off, and demand that they fly. While we did not have to sit by a phone awaiting a call, known as home standby, we could be forced to work if we answered the phone. Once again, these were the days before mobile phones. The house phone was all we had to communicate with the world.

This ridiculous system meant that we were permanently afraid to answer our own telephone. Pilots employed many tricks to try to avoid being caught out in this way. Some would ensure their partners always answered the phone, informing the company that the pilot was away, usually on a boat in the mid-Atlantic. Others would put on a phoney accent and pretend to be someone else. Eventually, the company would find someone who, in an unguarded moment, simply answered their own house phone. As I hesitated to answer, I suddenly remembered that I had only returned from a flight that morning. This, coupled with the fact that I had just spent my afternoon, at the behest of the company, giving an interview to the press. I felt that it was safe to answer my own phone. It was probably my in-laws checking to see if we had left yet. And so, I picked up the phone with a simple, "Hello", a big mistake!

At first, I thought it was a practical joke. I started to laugh and told my friend Pete not to be so bloody daft. The voice on the phone assured me that he was not Pete, and that it was not a joke, and that I was being forced drafted for a trip back to Barbados tomorrow morning. I was stunned, speechless, and deeply upset. Unfortunately, I was at the time inexperienced enough in my new job to accept my bad fortune. Had the company tried such a tactic today, I would have simply refused and accepted the consequences. Having been in the company for less than a year, I accepted my fate, albeit after brief resistance, sadly futile.

And so that was that. Despite all my protestations, I would be flying back to Barbados the following day and not up North for the remainder of Christmas. Of course, Liz was devastated, and rightly so. There was no way we could even think of taking James back to Barbados, and of course, Liz could not drive for a journey of nearly five hours with a new baby.

It was a very quiet Boxing Day evening. We sat and looked at each other, not quite believing that after all we had been through and all we had done, we were going to be parted. The house was still cold. The coal-fired Aga and the ancient central heating system took at least a day to make the home warm. There was still no food in the house, and the shops were closed. We felt very sorry for ourselves as we finally retired. I had to get up very early.

The flight back to Barbados, thankfully, was without incident. Finally getting to my hotel room, I collapsed onto the bed, totally exhausted. The phone ringing next to the bed woke me up with a start. This time I answered without fear and, hoping that Liz had managed to reach me, I picked up the phone. Listening to the person on the other end of the line, once again, I really could not credit what I was hearing. I was speaking to a journalist from London. British Airways had again given out my details. They had assured him that I would be happy to give him an interview. Apparently, I had agreed to this before I left the UK. This time, despite my inexperience, I simply put the phone down.

Three days later, I finally returned home. The next day was New Year's Eve. We had missed our first Christmas together as a family of three. There would be no late-night welcoming in this New Year. I had another flight very early on

New Year's Day. I set my alarm for five o'clock in the morning and went to bed at nine. Welcome to airline flying, I thought to myself as James started crying once more.

As a footnote to this story, the interview I gave to *The Times* was picked up by national and some international papers. *The Times* reported accurately what had happened and what I had said. The other newspapers just invented phrases and facts that simply had not occurred. I could not believe what I read over the coming days. The majority of the articles were just pure fabrication. This has made me very sceptical about newspaper stories ever since; you should not always believe what you read, well, except for this book, of course.

Chapter 12

A Day Out To Remember

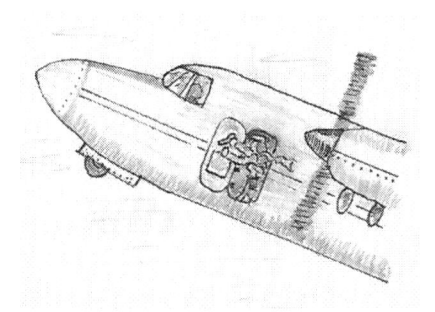

The year was now 1989; memories of the excitement and tragedy of the previous Christmas were still fresh in all our minds. On the other side of the world, a vicious and prolonged war was finally drawing to its bloody conclusion.

Early in the new year, I had an eight-day trip, Gatwick to Manchester, and then onwards to Islamabad, the capital of Pakistan.

In 1979, Russia had invaded neighbouring Afghanistan to shore up the Soviet-backed government in Kabul. Mujahideen rebel fighters opposing the invasion fought a bitter and bloody war against the invading Russian forces. Over a million people would lose their lives in the following nine years, including heavy casualties for the Russian army and the Mujahideen. Russia would finally pull out of Afghanistan, leaving the country to descend into an even more brutal civil war. This civil war allowed the Taliban to finally take control of the country in 1996. The rest, as they say, is history. The Mujahideen, by this time, had been pushed back by Soviet forces and were regrouping in Northern Pakistan. Afghanistan and Pakistan are linked by the famous Khyber Pass, one of the world's most important trade routes and strategic military locations. The Mujahideen would mount deadly nightly raids through the

Khyber Pass into Afghanistan, returning the next day to the relative safety of Pakistan.

When we touched down in Islamabad in early 1989, the war was reaching its bloody climax. Our approach into Islamabad took us over some of the most spectacular scenery anywhere in the world. We flew directly overhead Kabul, the capital of Afghanistan, before starting our descent into Islamabad. Flying directly over the Khyber Pass, the whole of the Hindu Kush was laid out before us. In the distance, we could make out Mount Everest and K2 the two highest mountains in the world. The whole scene was mesmerising. I had never seen anything quite so spectacular. The captain, Nick Rose, turned to me and asked if I fancied trying to arrange a trip to visit the Khyber Pass during our stay in Pakistan. Of course, I readily agreed. After all, what could possibly go wrong with a visit to one of the most dangerous regions in the world?

Our crew hotel was the Marriott, an excellent hotel with friendly and helpful staff. We were made very welcome, and everything was done to make our stay as comfortable as possible. Although we were well aware that this was an unstable part of the world, there were no restrictions on our movements. We played golf at the local course and then travelled to Rawalpindi, another excellent golf course. Being a Muslim country, alcohol was not widely available. However, by signing a declaration, we could order a proper drink in the international hotels. There was also a beautiful old colonial hotel in the Murree Hills just outside of Islamabad, which we visited. The barman, resplendent in his white colonial jacket and bow tie, was always delighted to welcome us. He could then legally open up his bar and serve some very drinkable Pakistani champagne. We were also regularly invited to both the British and American Embassies to enjoy a good meal with wine.

All in all, it was starting to feel more like a short holiday than a trip to one of the world's hot spots. All this was about to change. We decided to go ahead with our rash plan to arrange a visit to the Khyber Pass; what were we thinking of?

The trip, at first, appeared to be reasonably straightforward. We consulted the travel guide at our hotel who very kindly arranged everything. The plan was starting to come together. We would fly with Pakistan Airways from Islamabad to Peshawar, a flight lasting around fifty minutes. The tour guide could arrange for a minibus to take us to the Khyber Pass from Peshawar. We would spend two hours there and then back to Peshawar for the return flight to Islamabad. It would be a long day, the outward flight left at seven o'clock in the morning, and we would land back in Islamabad at around ten o'clock. The total cost, including flights and all the transfers, worked out at approximately thirty pounds each. Well, at that price, how could we possibly say no? That evening we met up with the rest of the crew and described our plans for the next day's expedition. Knowing that there were potential risks involved, we had decided not to ask if anyone would like to join the three of us. To our amazement, we were suddenly faced with a barrage of requests to join us and a certain amount of abuse for not having invited them in the first place. Instead of three, we became a party of twelve, all keen to visit the Khyber Pass.

Returning quickly to the travel desk, I enquired, not with a great deal of hope if we could book a few more places on our excursion the following day. Assuring me that it should be no problem to reserve another two seats, the agent's face fell when I informed her that I needed another nine seats. Of course, this would mean that we would require a much larger bus and hopefully, there would be enough seats on the flights. I stood there whilst she made several phone calls. After ten minutes, she looked up at me with a broad smile and informed me that it was all arranged. Her expression changed when she also let me know that the price had changed due to the extra number of people. Here we go, I thought. This is not going to work out after all. "I'm so sorry, I have to change the price," were not the words

I wanted to hear. Having told everyone that the cost was just thirty pounds per person, I really did not want to be the bearer of bad news. "As there are now twelve people, the price will now be twenty-five pounds each." Now that's the sort of news I don't mind bearing. I thought happily to myself as I returned to pass on the good news. All the arrangements had been finalised. A bus was organised to pick us up from the hotel at six o'clock the following morning. As I turned my light out later that evening, I wondered what the next day would bring. Over thirty years later, I still find it difficult to believe just how extraordinary the day would prove to be.

The day started well; the bus to the airport was waiting for twelve very sleepy and slightly hungover crew members. Our flight to Peshawar was on time, and we took our seats in an ancient Fokker F27 turboprop aircraft. The inside of the plane matched the exterior. Both had seen much better days. We all looked around at each other to seek reassurance that this was still a good idea. From the look on some of the faces, especially the girls, the rashness of last night's decision to join us was coming home to roost.

Eventually, everyone was on board, and the single air hostess closed the passenger door, and we were off. The aircraft taxied at almost double the speed we were used to in the 747. There was no time for those annoying safety briefings or welcome onboard announcements. No, this flight was definitely not going to be delayed by anything so mundane. We raced across the airfield. Before we knew it, the aircraft's engine suddenly reached full power, and our taxiing speed only had to increase slightly before the aircraft became airborne.

The thing with pre-flight checks is although they can be tedious and time-consuming, they also have the convenient benefit of ensuring all is well before the aircraft takes to the sky. Today, our bold pilots had obviously decided to do without any checks. Let's get this thing into the sky before it becomes obsolete was the order of the day. Our poor air hostess was still walking back to her seat as we leapt up into the air. This was probably just as well as the door next to her empty seat had not been closed properly and flew open as we climbed away.

Being a pilot, one always notices what is going on around you when you fly. This is true even if you are only a passenger. It's just ingrained into a pilot's DNA. I had felt very uneasy about the whole departure process, from the lack of security in the airport, to the state of the aircraft, to the absence of any kind of passenger safety demonstrations. Therefore, I was not totally surprised when the aircraft door opened as we took off. However, I was astonished by how much dust and debris an open door can create in such an old aircraft. I was also surprised by just how loud our crew members could scream. I looked at the door and realised it had only opened as far as the gust lock, although it was indeed open. This lock is used on the ground to prevent the door from being swung open in windy weather. Well, it was undoubtedly windy now. The door was being held by this lock. If the lock failed, the door would open fully. If this occurred, the door would easily have been ripped from its hinges. Had the door separated from the aircraft, it would have hit either the wing or tailplane. In turn, this would have caused the plane to lose control and crash, a fact I was well aware of. Unfortunately, everyone else on the aircraft, except one person, had also come to the same conclusion and joined the screaming started by our crew. The only person on the plane who seemed totally unaware of the danger we were in was our colleague, the captain. I looked across at him, and his eyes were closed. He was fast asleep. Unbelievable!

We were all in a very precarious situation. The aircraft needed to be back on the ground as quickly as possible. Had I been flying the aeroplane, I would have climbed to a safe altitude, kept the speed as low as possible and carried out the emergency checklist. Our pilots, however, were made of much sterner stuff. We levelled at five hundred feet and immediately turned towards the airport. Interesting, but so far so good. The landing gear had been lowered, and the flaps were set to their landing position. We would land back on the runway we had just taken off from, except now in the opposite direction. Less than five minutes after we had taken off, we had landed safely, quite an achievement. We would taxi back to the terminal to disembark. Our day trip to the Khyber Pass had finished before it had really begun, which was a huge disappointment. On the bright side, everyone was safe, if a little shaken.

The aircraft slowed and began a turn at the end of the runway before coming to a stop. The captain appeared from the flight deck and, grasping the errant door, pulled it closed with a loud click. He ensured it was in the fully locked position, something the stewardess had obviously not done earlier. He then quickly returned to the flight deck. I thought that was a very sensible decision, securing the door before returning to the terminal.

If a similar situation had occurred in the UK, the crew would have been suspended whilst an investigation was carried out. There would be mountains of paperwork to complete. The aircraft would have been taken out of service for a thorough check before being released to fly again.

Things were obviously done a little differently here in Pakistan. Having satisfied that the door was securely shut, the captain simply returned to the flight deck, applied full power and before any of us realised what was happening, we were once again airborne and on our way to Peshawar. Everyone was too stunned to say anything at all. Our captain, Nick, finally opened his eyes and asked if we were there yet. I have had more exciting flights, but luckily not many.

The rest of the flight to Peshawar, thankfully, went without incident. I looked around at our crew, who were all showing signs of shock. I'm sure that whoever was looking at me thought the same. It was only Captain Nick, who had now slept off his hangover, who looked totally relaxed.

The captain stood by the door as we left the aircraft, thanking everyone for flying with Pakistan Airways. I would have borrowed some civilian clothing and left the aircraft pretending to be a passenger if that had been me. Our captain was obviously made of much sterner stuff. Maybe it was a common occurrence and no big deal. Safely back on the ground, we all began to feel a little calmer. Some even started joking about our close shave with death. We made our way through the small terminal and found the two minibuses that would take us on the next part of our journey. We decided it would be safer if we had at least one flight crew member in each bus if we became separated, so I went on one bus and Captain Nick on the other. Our crew on this trip mainly consisted of female cabin crew, and women in Pakistan were not treated with the same respect afforded to men. The drivers both spoke perfect English and asked us if we would like to visit a school on the way to Peshawar. They explained that the children would love to meet us, as they rarely had the chance to meet any foreigners. Of course, we agreed as long as we had time, which the drivers assured us that we would. We set off into the countryside, the likes of which I had not seen before. Everywhere was a barren brownish grey. The buildings, the road, the background all seemed to merge into one. It was a very unwelcoming landscape, only the mountains in the distance giving any real sense of scale. We drove on bumpy roads until we turned off onto a single lane track which apparently led to the school. I started to feel slightly uneasy. We were in a lawless part of the world and being driven by two people we had only just met to an unknown destination. I suddenly realised just how ill-thought-out this whole trip was. The worst part of it was that we had brought eight young women with us into a very unpredictable and dangerous part of the world. If we were being driven into a trap, there was nothing we could do about it now. I cursed myself and my stupidity at agreeing to the whole ridiculous idea. And then we turned a sharp corner, and I could hardly believe the scene in front of me.

Instead of a trap, there directly in front of us was a public school. This beautiful building could have been relocated directly from England rather than rural Pakistan. This was more Eton or Harrow College than Peshawar. As we approached, we could see the students walking around in striped jackets and boater hats, straight out of Tom Brown's schooldays. We were immediately transported back to Victorian England. As we stepped down from the buses, we were met by the headmaster. He had obviously been forewarned of our arrival. The welcome we received was overwhelming. Everyone we were introduced to had numerous questions, mostly about cricket and our Royal Family. We were then invited to have breakfast in the pavilion whilst watching a cricket match. The whole visit was totally surreal; we were surrounded by beautifully maintained playing fields and buildings that would have looked at home in any county in England. Finally, the headmaster explained that the school was run by the military and was based on colonial lines referencing the British educational system. We informed him that the way the school was run was sadly not how the educational system was now in Britain. His face fell until we elaborated that his school was of a much higher standard than many in the UK. I think we made his day.

We were all reluctant to leave this oasis of tranquillity. The children, all aged from eleven to eighteen, stood to wave us goodbye. They were all immaculate in their school uniforms. It was a sight to behold, and we all felt privileged to have been in their company, even for such a short period of time.

A tragic footnote to this visit came when I watched the news in 2014. Pictures of this beautiful school filled our television screens. The Taliban had attacked the school leaving one hundred and forty-one children and teachers dead. How anyone could carry out such a shocking act on young, innocent children is beyond comprehension.

We left the school and continued our drive to Peshawar itself. Here was the real Pakistan. Stopping at an outdoor market to buy drinks, we looked around at the seemingly chaotic scene. Anything you can imagine was available to purchase. There were thousands of cages containing livestock, from reptiles to chickens, to dogs and cats to cattle. There were also clothes, food, machine parts and anything else you could think of. Nothing was thrown away. Everything was recycled and sold again. We wandered around, taking in the sounds and smells. Yes, there were lots of smells. Eventually, we were rounded up by our drivers and shepherded back towards our buses. One of the crew stopped to look at the chickens in cages. There was a particularly lovely looking white chicken with its head pushed through the wire mesh at the front of the cage, looking around at its surroundings. Our crew member pointed to the chicken. Before anyone could stop him, the vendor produced a knife and swiftly decapitated the bird. He proceeded to hand the head to our poor girl, who was now screaming for the second time that day. By pointing to the chicken, she had inadvertently bought it and sealed its fate. We had to pay for the chicken, although we declined to take what remained of it away with us. Her pointing had cost that chicken its life and me about ten pence. We hastily reboarded the buses and set off for the last leg to the Khyber Pass.

Chapter 13

Meeting the Mujahideen

Before leaving the hotel in Islamabad, we were advised to take a photocopy of our British passports. We were also advised to take American dollars with us in case the Mujahideen offered us anything to buy. They only wanted dollars, and to refuse a man with an AK47, would not lead to a long and healthy life. This seemed somewhat strange as we could not imagine what guerrilla fighters would have for sale. The last and most bizarre piece of advice was that if we were offered anything personal from the soldiers, we should buy it and then return it to them as a gift. It all seemed very odd until the hotel's guide reminded us that we were entering a lawless state at our own risk once we had left Peshawar. There were no rules or regulations here and no police force to protect us. In this part of the world, the Mujahideen were the law.

As we drove along the dusty track, leaving Peshawar behind us, the mood on the bus began to change. Again, the folly of taking young women away from civilisation into a war zone seemed more ludicrous with each mile. We would be totally at the mercy of the fighters. If they decided to shoot us, rob us or do anything they wanted to, we would be powerless to stop them. As I was the only male in our group, I decided to check if everyone still wanted to carry on. Standing up and facing the crew, I asked if there was anyone who had changed their minds.

If so, I assured them that there was no disgrace in being cautious and sensible. I had to admit that I would have been delighted to turn around and spend the day in Peshawar. Unfortunately for me, the crew were made of far sterner stuff, so we continued on our way.

As we left the dusty plain behind us, we started a slow climb into the Spin Ghar range of mountains. The scenery began to resemble a lunar landscape rather than anything I had seen on earth. We were entering the lawless zone, and my goodness, it certainly did look like it. A short while later, we pulled over to the side of the road and began to drive down a small track. Questioning our driver as to why we were leaving the road, he simply informed me that I should wait and see. A short while later, we stopped at what looked like some kind of shrine or burial ground. Our driver jumped down and asked us to follow him.

We entered what was now clearly a graveyard. There was row upon row of small headstones. Eventually, I found a legible one. It was the grave of a nineteen-year-old British soldier, killed in January 1842. The driver then explained that this was the site that marked the catastrophic British retreat from the war in Afghanistan. The British had lost approximately sixteen thousand five hundred soldiers and civilians in just three days. I sat and looked at all the graves and wondered just what these poor people went through. This place was the most inhospitable part of the world I had ever visited. In 1840, most people often travelled less than ten miles from where they were born. To bring young men to this place must have been the modern-day equivalent of me going to fight a war on the moon. I found the whole experience profoundly moving and upsetting. Our driver then reminded us that we would meet the descendants of these fighters who had inflicted such slaughter on the British Army. In this war, however, it was the Russians' turn to feel the wrath of these warriors. And with this sobering thought, we climbed back onto the bus and set off to meet our old enemy.

The start of the Khyber Pass itself is marked by a large archway which we passed through on our way to the beginning of the Pass itself. The driver reminded us once again to agree to anything we were told by the Mujahideen. They were honourable fighters, he told us, but they were very intolerant. The women were all handed hijabs to cover their heads. Also, they were appropriately dressed as previously advised by our hotel tour guide. We were ready to meet some of the most dangerous people on the planet.

The tactics employed by the Mujahideen were relatively simple. They based themselves in Pakistan, where the Russian forces could not attack them. Each night, they would form raiding parties and enter Afghanistan through the Khyber Pass. There they would ambush and attack the occupying Russian forces before returning back through the Pass. Although they were in Pakistan, the Mujahideen controlled the entire area with an iron fist.

We pulled off the road into a large area of scrubland and parked next to a group of men sitting around a large campfire. Finally, we were going to meet the people we had been warned about. Stepping down from the bus, I followed our driver, who would make the introductions. The women wisely stayed on the bus. It was a surreal feeling standing in front of a group of men, any one of whom could raise his gun and fire. And they had lots and lots of guns. They could shoot me without a second thought or any consequences; I was totally at their mercy. This realisation must have shown itself on my face because one of the fighters stood and welcomed me in perfect English. I am not sure what I had expected but being greeted in such a welcoming manner seemed at odds with everything I could see around me. I shook his hand and thanked him for his hospitality. I asked if it would be acceptable for the rest of the crew to leave the bus, and my request was granted. There could be no cameras as photography was totally forbidden; any transgressions would be severely punished. He pointed to his AK 47 machine gun to emphasise his point. If anyone had a camera, nobody admitted or used it.

Our host then asked if we would like to buy a souvenir of our visit. The way the question was phrased, it seemed impolite or just downright dangerous to decline. Beckoning me to follow him, he walked over to a tarpaulin and, with a theatrical gesture, threw the cover to reveal the spoils of war.

Now I wasn't quite sure what to expect, maybe a few trinkets or local clothing. What I most certainly was not expecting was a collection of objects taken from the Russian Army. In front of me, there was a massive collection of military paraphernalia. Gesturing to examine the items, I bent down and picked up a fur hat complete with the Russian insignia. It was huge, and I guessed it was made out of rabbit fur. As I had actually picked it up, it became my first purchase, although, at the time, I had not realised that was how it worked. I then picked up a military jacket and examined it closely. It was obviously an officer's jacket resplendent with gold braiding. There were also several holes in the front, with dark brown stains surrounding each hole. Immediately dropping the coat, I suddenly realised that my hands literally had blood on them. I stood back up and tried my best to resist the urge to turn around and run back to the bus and get the hell out of there.

Instead, I congratulated our hosts on such an outstanding collection of trophies. I was again invited to examine more items. Of course, I had little option but to crouch down and continue my morbid examination of the things laid out in front of me. This time, I was determined to avoid anything that could have blood on it, so I picked up a few huge Russian watches. I then lifted a large pair of night-vision goggles, and after being loudly encouraged, I tried them on. This caused great hilarity amongst our hosts. I must have looked quite a sight. Turning to see if the crew approved of my new look, I realised that they were all either on the bus or standing very close to it, sensibly. Even my flight deck colleagues were hanging back, looking very nervous and uncomfortable. It was time to leave. My only problem was how to do this without insulting my hosts.

As I turned back to thank everyone for showing me their collection and apologise for having to leave, I noticed a small pile of objects had been placed by my feet. I now realised that to touch was to buy, and worryingly for me, I had touched quite a few objects. I now had a choice: I could refuse to accept any of these gruesome artefacts. I could barter and try to get a better price. Or I could simply reach into my pocket and produce the asking price in American dollars. When faced by a group of guerrilla fighters armed to the teeth, the choice quickly became apparent. I paid precisely what they were asking.

I was now firmly in their good books, and I was handed an AK47 machine gun and asked if I would like to try it out. Well, this really was a once in a lifetime opportunity. Of course, I wanted to have a go. I took the gun and examined it. It was lighter than I had imagined and felt strangely comfortable in my hands. This was a weapon of war and had been used very recently to kill young men on the other side of the mountains. Somewhere in Russia, a family would be heartbroken at losing a son, or a wife would have lost her husband and father to her children in this wild and dangerous place. I felt something akin to an electric shock run from the gun's handle through my body at this realisation. I turned and tried to hand the weapon back. Instead, I was handed a magazine of bullets and told to aim at a line of old oil drums in the distance. As instructed, I handed over more dollars to cover the cost of the bullets.

Following vociferous instructions given by my new friends, I flicked off the safety catch aimed at the drums and pulled the trigger.

If you have ever fired a shotgun or similar weapon, you will have felt a hefty kickback as the weapon fires. With the AK47, multiply this several times, and you will start to appreciate just how powerful these weapons are. I held on like grim death holding the barrel as tightly as possible and keeping it pointing towards the drums. The noise and smell, as the bullets roared towards their target, was overpowering. The most shocking thing was the damage inflicted on the target. The drums flew apart, rolling backwards from the onslaught. I am embarrassed to admit that I felt a massive rush of adrenalin and euphoria. The power generated and the destruction caused gave me a feeling of invincibility. I was enjoying myself.

Apparently, I had done very well, and to show their approval, a group of the fighters took up their weapons and joined me. Unfortunately, they decided that they would show off their skills by firing above the heads of my crew standing by the two busses.

Well, that was that as far as the crew was concerned. The crew all turned screaming and scrambled as quickly as they could back into the busses, and that was just the men. The girls followed closely behind them.

And that left me, by myself, standing next to the Mujahideen who were firing their weapons in all directions. How the hell had I got myself into this position and far more importantly, how the hell was I going to get out of this alive.

The first thing was to stop firing my own weapon. Maybe, that would encourage the others to do likewise. I felt a slight deflation as I handed the now hot gun back to its owner. I hated to admit it, but I had really enjoyed firing this weapon. Luckily, the others began to either run out of ammunition or enthusiasm. The silence was deafening after the cacophony of so many guns being fired. I looked around and realised that only one bus remained; the other was probably halfway back to Peshawar.

Thanking my hosts for what I hoped would be the final time, I made a hasty retreat towards my now departing bus. The Mujahideen still had one last surprise for me. I was handed a brick sized lump of what looked like brown tar. I was assured it was of the highest quality and would be worth many times the asking price on the streets of London. I handed over my last twenty dollar note and boarded the bus as quickly as I could.

And with a final wave goodbye, we sped off, kicking up clouds of brown dust as we made our hasty retreat.

I had gone from a law-abiding citizen to an armed and dangerous drug dealer in a short space of time. What would my mother think of my new career?

It was an eerily quiet bus drive back to the airport that evening. The crew were still in shock at being fired at. I tried my best to assure the crew that I had not been involved in firing above their heads, but it still took a while for them to forgive me. The bus driver, on the other hand, seemed very pleased with me. It's not often I have a large block of hashish to hand over as a tip. I must try that the next time I get an Uber, but there again, maybe not.

I did, however, take my other purchases home with me, minus the blood-soaked jacket, even I drew the line at that. Somewhere, in a dark and dusty corner of my loft, I still have the watches and goggles. The fur hat made an excellent present for my mother-in-law, and it kept out the cold of many Northern England winters. Unsurprisingly, nobody else on the Wirral had anything even remotely similar.

As a footnote to this episode, the Mujahideen had been supported financially by the British government in their fight against the Russian forces. This was why we, as a British Airways crew, were allowed access to the fighters. I discovered, much later, that a certain Osama Bin Laden was a Mujahideen fighter based in the Khyber Pass at the time of our visit. There is a high degree of probability he was one of the fighters we met. Later that year, the Russian forces withdrew from Afghanistan. In 1996, the Mujahideen became even more radicalised and evolved into the Taliban. Many years later, this group would return to haunt me. This would result in my beloved aircraft and myself becoming obsolete. Our crew hotel, the Marriott, where we had stayed for the past ten years, became like a second home. The staff got to know many of us by name and would always welcome us back with open arms. The Taliban destroyed the hotel with a loss of over fifty lives, including many of the staff. The world as we knew it was starting to change forever.

Chapter 14

A Merger, and a New Start

As the 1980s drew to a close, I found myself flying to new destinations as our network at Gatwick expanded. In late 1988, British Caledonian Airways, or BCAL, as it was affectionately known, merged with British Airways into one large airline. BCAL flew from Gatwick; it was effectively integrated with British Airtours, the company I now flew for. We suddenly went from flying just one 747 to flying an entire fleet of eight aircraft. As is always the case when two companies merge, there are winners and losers. It was sad to see such an excellent airline as BCAL cease to exist. They had a long and proud history. Their tartan-clad cabin crew were probably the best in the world, or maybe I was prejudiced, as my wife Liz was, of course, a BCAL hostess. I personally lost over one hundred and fifty seniority places which, at the time, seemed unfair. Still, in the fullness of time, the merger turned out to benefit more people than it harmed.

The BCAL 747 aircraft were different variants to our 747s. The BCAL aircraft had different instruments and a different navigational system. Before we could fly these new aircraft, we had to attend a two-day difference course. The BCAL pilots, in turn, had to participate in a similar approach to fly our aircraft. Until all Gatwick pilots had qualified on both variants, two separate fleets were formed. The 'B' Fleet for BCAL pilots and the 'K' Fleet for the Airtours crew. No pilot could fly for the other fleet until all pilots had become dual qualified.

Whilst all of this was being organised, I was sitting at home on standby. Once a year, we would be rostered for a month of home standby duty. We could be called out to operate from either Gatwick or Heathrow to cover any last-minute absence or assignment change. The rule was that you had to report within two hours of being called out. Gatwick, for me, was a twenty-minute drive.

On the other hand, Heathrow was an hour and a half's drive, tight but still possible. We had to sit near the house phone in those days with our bags packed and uniform at the ready. There were, of course, no mobile phones back then.

The phone rang. It was Operation Control. Could I be at Heathrow within the hour? Well, this was obviously a non-starter, and I started to protest. I was interrupted by the Ops controller, who advised me to listen before I refused. "Nick, we have a 747 in Los Angeles with no one to fly it home. We have booked three seats on this afternoon's Concorde service to New York and have booked you in First Class from New York to Los Angeles. You will have a day's rest in LA and then bring the 747 home."

I was halfway out of the door before he had finished the sentence. It's surprising just how quickly you can get to Heathrow if you really put your foot down.

Despite my best efforts, the motorway traffic played its normal part in extending my commute time. I arrived with literally seconds to spare, the last door about to be closed, as I ran down the jetty towards the only aircraft that was arguably more iconic than my beloved 747.

Concorde sat gracefully, her cernuous nose the first thing you notice, as she awaited this final door to be shut. The moment I was on board, the aircraft was being pushed back. Nothing, especially a tardy pilot, would delay Concorde's scheduled departure. I was shown to my seat, luckily at the front of the aircraft. As I was preparing to put my small case into the overhead locker, I was asked to follow the stewardess to the front galley. Maybe, I had no seat; it looked like I would be sitting on a crew jump seat after all. I was not particularly concerned; just to fly on Concorde made this trip worthwhile. To my surprise and delight, instead, I was ushered into the flight deck and asked if I would like to sit in the observer's seat for the flight duration. I made a show of thinking about it, the delight on my face making a mockery of my pretence.

The odd thing about the flight deck of Concorde was that it seemed strangely familiar. At first, I could not quite put my finger on why. Looking around, I could immediately identify the majority of the dials and switches. It was, after all, a four-engined aircraft not that dissimilar to the one I flew. Of course, there were some very unfamiliar switches. One was the reheat controls used to add extra power for take-off or transitioning to supersonic flight. Flames pouring from the back of the engine was an indication that reheat was being used. On a 747, this would be interesting, as would a mechanism for raising and lowering the aircraft's droop snoot nose. As we taxied out for take-off, I suddenly realised why I felt so at home. The control column in front of each pilot was a very unique design known as ram horns. Most aircraft have a very different design. The only other aircraft with this identical control column was also designed and built by the same company that had been heavily involved in designing Concorde. The HS 125 business jet that I was so familiar with was built by the British Aircraft Corporation. Of course, Concorde was designed by the same company. Feeling very at home, I sat back and watched as we were cleared to enter the runway.

All pretence that this was a typical aircraft was quickly dispelled as we lined up with the runway. We were cleared for take-off, counting down from three, two, one, engines were set to full reheat, which caused the familiar flame out of the back of the engine, and away we went.

My thoughts drifted back to my first jet take off on the HS 125. At the time, I could not believe the power and speed of this beautiful aircraft after regularly flying much slower propeller aircraft. This was like taking yet another giant step forward. The power produced by those four Olympus engines took my breath away. The noise was quite impressive as well. Much has been written about Concorde, and I am unqualified to add to what has already been written.

The only comments I can make are of a personal nature from my perspective, as both a pilot and a passenger. On a typical flight, the aircraft climbs to a cruising altitude and stays there. Not so with Concorde, which just climbs continuously until it's time to descend. On this flight, we reached sixty thousand feet, nearly twice the cruise height for the 747. On normal aircraft, if you look out of the window during the cruise, it appears as if the plane is stationary. There is little to judge your speed against. Even clouds only appear to drift by. This is not the case at twice the speed of sound. Everything moves past very quickly indeed.

Three hours later, when I would typically expect to be in mid-Atlantic, we were approaching New York. Being Concorde, we were given a priority approach, and shortly after that, we were parking on our stand. Thanking the crew for a flight to remember, I joined my two colleagues and thanked them for allowing me on the flight deck. Sadly, that was the one, and only time I flew on that majestic aircraft. Many years later, I actually applied to fly Concorde. Still, the tragic Air France crash at Paris spelt the end for Concorde before I could even begin to fulfil my dream. We made our way to the United Airlines Terminal and boarded our DC10 flight to Los Angeles. It took us twice as long to fly to LA as it had to fly from London.

The following day, checking out of our hotel, we set off to fly our 747 home. It had been in LA for a few days due to a technical fault which had now been repaired. As there were no passengers or crew to worry about, we were driven directly to the aircraft parked on the maintenance pad. We were still chatting about our flight. None of us noticed our surroundings until we pulled up in front of our aircraft. As we left the bus, the three of us just stood and stared at the sight that met our eyes. Our engineer was the first one to speak, who just said, "Right lads, let's go to the pub."

There, in front of us, stood a beautiful Boeing 747. The morning sunshine silhouetted the aircraft giving it a majestic appearance. The ground personnel were ready to hand over the paperwork and ask how much fuel we would require. The three of us just stared at the jumbo in front of us. It was a British Caledonian aircraft, resplendent with the famous golden lion on its tail. We, of course, were not a BCAL crew. We were a British Airtours or 'K' Fleet crew. We were not qualified to fly this aircraft. It might as well have been Concorde sitting there in front of us. There was absolutely no way we could legally fly this aircraft back home. Our engineer was already walking back to the bus. The bars were opening soon.

After a few frantic telephone calls to London, we were asked to return to the hotel and await the next 'K' Fleet aircraft to arrive, which we would then fly home. A week and quite a few bars later, the captain thought he had better touch base with London once again as every aircraft that had arrived into LAX had been a 'B' Fleet 747. Operations queried what we were doing in Los Angeles? Apparently, there had been a complete communications breakdown, and we had been totally forgotten about. Nobody was aware that a flight crew was waiting in Los Angeles to fly a non-existent 747 home. We were asked to go home on the next available flight, which of course, we did. I arrived home eight days after my race to Heathrow, having not flown at all. I was also paid an overtime premium as we were very late returning from what should have been a three-day trip, an extremely satisfactory outcome as far as I was concerned. I had also experienced an unforgettable flight on Concorde. There were, of course, many other occasions when I was not so lucky on standby. At least I could always think back to my Concorde flight as I rushed around the M25 motorway on the two hours call out.

Around this time, a new concept was being introduced into aviation, Crew Resource Management, known as CRM. There was worldwide concern that tragic accidents involving aircraft were due in no small part to lack of crew coordination and teamwork. Some captains were operating in an arrogant, individualistic manner, literally like a one-man band. They refused to listen to their more junior colleagues, even when apparent mistakes were being made. First officers were made to feel they lacked the skill and knowledge to act appropriately, unable to intervene, even when the aircraft was in danger. Something needed to be done that stopped this trend and empowered the whole crew to intervene when and if it ever became necessary. This behaviour was more apparent in some airlines than others. I was proud to say that such attitudes rarely existed in my airline, especially at Gatwick.

However, each and every pilot was required to attend a three-day residential course. This would equip them with the skills necessary to embody a new pattern of cooperation and participation on the flight deck. I was duly rostered for my course. Although sceptical, I was looking forward to a few days in the Surrey countryside. The night before the course, I answered my phone. It was the course co-ordinator. I was asked if I would be prepared to delay my class as they had a pilot who needed to complete the course before taking six months off flying duties. I agreed and was offered a flight instead. I put the CRM course out of my mind. They would contact me again with a new date.

Six months later, whilst I was on leave, I received an irate call from a flight manager. Apparently, the CRM course was finishing that week and was I aware that I had not completed the course? He was rude and began to blame me for my oversight. Before he went any further, I reminded him that as I was on leave, I did not even need to be talking to him, let alone be lectured by him. I then politely informed him that I had given up my place to help the company and a fellow pilot. It certainly was not my fault that I had not been rostered before the course finished. I asked him to check his facts and call me back. Ten minutes later, the phone rang once more.

He started off with an apology. He had no idea what had actually occurred. Despite this, he told me that I would have to report to the hotel the following morning. I said no. The line went very quiet, then a booming voice asked me if I knew who I was speaking to? I replied that no, I had no idea to whom I was speaking. All I knew was that an insulting person had just interrupted my leave. I put the phone down. I was rather enjoying this. Legally, every pilot must have a certain amount of vacation each year. During this leave, the company must not contact the pilot. It is the only time that we are free of our responsibilities. This manager had no right to even call me, let alone rebuking me for something that clearly was not my fault.

The phone rang twice more before I finally picked it up. This time the manager's tone was much more conciliatory. Again, I was asked to forgo my leave and attend the course, again I politely refused. I was now thoroughly enjoying myself and his obvious discomfort. I was offered an alternative leave date. "No thank you," I replied. Had he not been so rude on his first call, I would have agreed to his requests. Finally, he asked me why I was refusing. Had I already booked a holiday? I replied that my wife was away and I was looking after our dog, Roffey. I never put him in kennels, which was true. My final concession was to attend the course, but only if I could bring my dog. He said he would check and call me back. Sure enough, five minutes later, he rang back and informed me that the hotel was dog friendly and I could take Roffey with me.

What had not been agreed upon was what to do with Roffey whilst I was in the classroom. Therefore, I turned up that first morning with Roffey in tow, taking our seats at the front of the class. The lecturers were not employed by British Airways. All eyes were on Roffey as I took my seat. Roffey settled down. I tried my best not to laugh.

I was challenged after the class by senior managers on the course. How dare I bring a dog to such an essential course. I was accused of not taking it seriously. I simply asked them to call the senior manager who had authorised Roffey's attendance. I heard nothing else from them, so I assumed they had made the call. The course lasted for three days, and I had to admit it was challenging. We were interviewed extensively; our characters were tested to their limits. At the end of the course, we were called individually into an interview room to face a panel of experts. There in front of me was a chart and graph detailing my scores and results. Apparently, some of the participating pilots had been failing this course. They had to attend a series of consultations before they were permitted to fly again. One story, not from me, I hasten to add, was of a captain who insisted his crew only entered the bus by the back door. It was precisely this type of behaviour they were trying to stamp out.

Roffey and I entered the room. There was nowhere else to leave him. My scores and results were produced. In a very sombre tone, I was told there was good and bad news. I sank a little lower in my seat. I was handed a file marked, 'Strictly confidential'. Before I could open it, I was informed that, sadly, I had failed the course. There was a pause before they continued. "However, Roffey has been outstanding, and therefore, we have combined your scores. You have both passed." I left the room with a smile on my face. Maybe, there was something beneficial to this new concept after all.

CRM changed the aviation industry forever. The type of behaviour I had been subjected to at Heathrow became a thing of the past, thank goodness. I think even Roffey benefited from his little holiday too, although he could still be a little demanding when it came time for his walks.

Chapter 15

The Kalahari Canoe Club

The 1990s were upon us. The UK economy was doing well, and people were starting to explore all of the world rather than just Europe. Our route network continued to expand, and we were now spending time in Mauritius and Seychelles and the Caribbean. Flying from Gatwick, Africa also featured on our list of destinations. Lagos, Nairobi, Harare, and Lusaka suddenly became more than just names on a map. Each destination carried its own unique challenges and idiosyncrasies. We were lucky enough, except for Lagos, to have an extended layover in each destination. This allowed us the luxury of being able to explore these beautiful cities and countries.

The world was then rocked by the First Gulf War. This had far-reaching implications for the airline industry. After years of solid growth, the travelling public had understandably become more cautious. Passenger numbers fell, and the airlines reacted by reducing our salaries while contrarily increasing our flying duties. This was only meant to be a temporary measure. However, over thirty years later, we are still waiting to return to our pre-war terms and conditions. Still, at Gatwick, we were determined not to let this affect our morale. Flying was not just a job to us. It was a way of life.

We were on our way south to Harare, the capital of Zimbabwe. The trip was scheduled to last for five days, allowing us time to relax and play golf on our two days off. During the flight, a passenger asked one of the crew if he could visit the flight deck, a widespread request at the time. Our passenger introduced himself. He was British and had moved to Harare twenty years ago to start a farm. He chatted away, and I admit I began to lose interest until he invited the whole crew to his private club.

He went on to explain that he was a member of the Kalahari Canoe Club. Apparently, they had a fabulous colonial clubhouse where you could enjoy the best food and wine. We were all invited to join him there the following evening. As well as having the best cuisine and beverages available, the club was also very reasonably priced. Well, that is always music to any crew member's ears, and the invitation was gratefully accepted. We would, of course, have to ask the rest of the crew if they would like to join us. We agreed that we would ring him later that day and confirm the number of us coming along.

As we checked into the hotel that morning, I explained to the crew that we had been invited somewhere for supper and drinks that evening. I asked for a show of hands if anyone was interested in coming along. The captain had friends in Harare and would not be joining us. The engineer also had other plans that night. So, it was just me, as far as the flight crew were concerned. Twelve hands immediately shot up, and I was relieved to see that there would be two other chaps to escort the rest of the team. Time for a few hours of sleep as we had to be at the club by five-thirty at the latest. I was not sure why, but our host insisted that it was club rules. Who was I to argue?

The hotel ran a transport service for guests, using a very old American stretch limousine, the type you see in Las Vegas or at weddings in Britain. I enquired if this vehicle was available that night, how many it could take, and the cost of hiring it for the entire evening. The reply I received was perfect. Yes, it was available, it held twelve people, and the price worked out at five pounds each. Realising that I had forgotten to include myself in the numbers, the receptionist then assured me that if I did not mind sitting up front with the driver, then all thirteen of us could fit into the limousine. The deal was done, and I went to bed feeling very pleased with myself. I hoped that if the evening went well, I would be invited back to actually do some canoeing the next day.

We all assembled in the hotel reception just after five that evening. The women had all made an incredible effort and looked stunning. I was in jeans and a T-shirt. Feeling very underdressed, I returned quickly to my room to put on a proper shirt. Hurrying back down, I joined the last of the crew as we all piled into the limousine, which had seen much better days. There was a lot of rust around the wheels and doors. Despite being painted over, the corrosion was obvious. The interior too, was much the same standard. The crew, being crew, had brought along some bottles of wine and bubbly they had purchased on the aircraft. The driver, a lovely chap, had a massive grin on his face at the sight of all this revelry. He would stay with us for the entire evening as some of the crew wanted to go to a nightclub after supper. I made a mental note to make sure he received an excellent tip at the end of the evening.

Thirty minutes later, we pulled up outside the most beautiful building, with masses of ivy and wisteria adorning the walls. The doors of the limousine were opened by the staff as soon as we came to a stop. We were welcomed and ushered through to the reception area. Obviously, our host had advised the club of our impending arrival. As we stood there, our host made his appearance with a warm welcome. We were then escorted into the club bar by waiters resplendent in white tuxedos. Naturally, we all headed straight to the bar to continue what most had already started in the limousine. The barman gave us a disapproving look and informed us that we would have to wait until the six o'clock telephone call. Not really understanding the meaning behind this call, we simply took our seats at the bar. Obviously, the local licensing laws restricted the sale of alcohol before that time. Fortunately, we had only a few minutes to wait. We attacked the large bowls of nuts and crisps instead.

I looked around at the room, clad in rich oak panelling. There were plaques and trophies in abundance, some on the walls, others carefully displayed in beautiful cabinets. There were old photographs of canoeing teams standing next to their awards. Hanging down from the high ceilings were two of these very ancient canoes. This was obviously a very proud and successful club with a long and distinguished history. I left my barstool and began to examine the exhibits more closely. I could not quite understand why the club was called the Kalahari Canoe Club. The Kalahari was just under two thousand kilometres to the south. It was also one of the hottest and driest deserts on earth. Before I could ask anyone the reason, there was a very loud boom! The head waiter had struck the large copper gong next to the bar.

The room immediately fell silent. All eyes turned towards what must have been the club captain as he rose from his seat and made his way to an old telephone sitting in the middle of the bar. Precisely as the clock struck six, the phone rang. The captain ceremoniously put on a pair of white gloves and then picked up the receiver. The anticipation was intense. There was a moment's silence, then he uttered just four words, "I see. Thank you."

He replaced the receiver with a very solemn look on his face. Obviously, there was something very wrong. We all held our breath as he turned to face his audience.

"Ladies and Gentlemen," he began, "it is with great sadness that, after speaking with our agent in the Kalahari, he tells me that there has been no rain in the desert for the past twenty-four hours."

He paused dramatically and continued. "Therefore, it is with deep regret that I have to inform you that the river is still dry and all canoeing is cancelled. You may partake of alcohol."

And with that, everyone cheered.

Our drinks came thick and fast, and as promised, they were excellent. Understandably, the club members crowded around our crew. Nothing to do with me; everything to do with our stunningly attired young ladies.

I managed to chat to our host, who was kind enough to explain what had just occurred. The club had been set up many decades before by a group of British farmers. They had no interest in sport but every interest in drinking. Not wanting their families to discover they were forming a drinking club; they invented the ruse of the Kalahari Canoe Club. As it seldom rains in the Kalahari, there was no water to canoe in. The tradition of the telephone call was started a few years later. The actual call was made by an employee upstairs. No one was allowed to start drinking until the canoeing had been officially cancelled, as it was every night, by the club captain.

A wonderfully eccentric institution that only the British could have invented. I enquired about all the pictures, trophies and plaques adorning the walls. He asked me to follow him, and we stood in front of the trophy cabinet. I was then asked to read the inscriptions on the trophies. Looking closely, I read aloud the name of each crew, the date and name of the competition. I was told to take a closer look. After each inscription in brackets, the words, 'Cancelled due to lack of rain', were etched into the trophy. Sure enough, on every plaque and trophy, the same bracketed sentence appeared. Laughing, I looked inquiringly at the two canoes hanging from the ceiling. Apparently, they were bought from a local market and hung up on display to further enhance the deception.

The rest of the evening went very well. Much alcohol and food were consumed. Far too quickly, the shutters were being closed. The club was closing. It seemed early, not much after nine o'clock. Apparently, there was no way they could explain night canoeing. Our limousine drew up outside the club, and we literally poured ourselves back into it, thanking our hosts profusely for an entertaining night.

As it was still relatively early, everyone wanted to go to the nightclub mentioned earlier. I was pretty happy to go back to the hotel, but I could hardly insist as I was outnumbered twelve to one. Promising our driver an even larger tip, he readily agreed to take us there and then wait for us. The club was only twenty minutes out of our way, so a thrilled and slightly drunk crew set off for the next part of our evening. No one could have possibly guessed that shortly one of our numbers would be dead. The majority of the others would be in the intensive care unit of a local hospital. How I wish that I could have outvoted the twelve on this occasion, and we'd returned directly back to our hotel. Instead, we set off for the nightclub. Our fate was awaiting us.

In Harare, in the early 1990s, there was a severe drug problem. Armed gangs roamed the streets selling narcotics. Anyone who got in their way would be brutally dealt with. There was no compassion on these streets. The police also operated in an equally uncompromising fashion and employed the same tactics as the gangs. If you were caught selling drugs, you were very harshly dealt with. Unbeknownst to us, our route would take us through the Badlands of Harare. We were entering one of the most dangerous places in Southern Africa. In the limousine, there were ten young women, three males and our driver. We were driving along the main road at a sedate pace. There was laughter coming from the passengers in the rear. Champagne was being drunk in ever-increasing amounts. In the front, which was separated from the main seating area by privacy glass, I talked to our friendly driver, all seemed well with the world.

Sometimes in life, a sixth sense can warn you that something is wrong or that something is about to happen. Tonight, luckily for me, was one of those times. Out of the corner of my eye, I saw bright lights coming towards us at high speed as I turned to face the driver. I was not wearing a seatbelt and just braced myself against the dashboard.

There was an almighty crash, and I was thrown sideways with great force, hitting the door with an impact that took my breath away. I could hear frantic screaming, and I realised that I was no longer inside the limousine. I was lying on the road, covered in blood. The shock I felt was intense as I tried to comprehend what on earth had just happened. There were screams and shouts and flashing lights. I knew I had to move away quickly. I could smell petrol and could see it streaming towards me. As quickly as I could manage, I dragged myself into a sitting position and tried to move my legs. There were just a few streetlights to illuminate the road. It looked like I had been severely injured as there was a hell of a lot of blood all down one side of my body. I managed to stand up and look around me. The dreadful scene that met my eyes was more like a plane crash than a car accident. Our limousine had been hit side-on by a large pickup truck with bull bars. I later discovered that the truck was being pursued by a police car. This car had crashed into the back of the pickup truck.

The impact had literally snapped our limousine into two separate halves. Most of the seats had been ejected into the road with their passengers, our crew, still strapped into them. Realising that the petrol was in danger of combusting, I went to try to help as best I could. Although I was bleeding heavily, I felt no pain. I could worry about my injuries later. The crew, who had been thrown clear of the wreckage, were not in immediate danger. I went to check both halves of what had been our limousine. Three people were still stuck in their seats, unable to free themselves. I managed to untangle some of the wreckage, enough for them to get out. The other half of the limousine appeared empty. I then went to check on the crew, who had been thrown clear.

There were a lot of injuries, although nothing I could see that was immediately life-threatening. I got the crew together at the side of the road and did a headcount. We were missing one of the crew. Looking around, I could see no sign of her. She had to still be somewhere inside the stricken limousine. I had no real choice, and at the time, I wasn't thinking of anything. I just reacted as most people would. I went back to find her. Looking into each half of the limousine, I still could not see her. Then I heard a soft but desperate crying sound coming from beneath the large bench seat. After a struggle, I managed to pull the seat free. I found her lying there, holding the side of her head. She had a rear-facing seat and had been thrown under the bench seat by the impact of the truck hitting us. I tried to move her; she gave an agonised cry. Her head, or rather her ear, had been pierced by part of the seat, and she was held fast. The petrol fumes by now were overwhelming. We could soon be trapped in an inferno. Despite her protests, l leaned forward and pulled her ear free. In doing so, this almost detached her ear from her head. Holding her badly damaged ear against her head, I coaxed her out of the wreckage towards safety. We now had everyone accounted for. All thirteen of us were sitting on the side of the road looking very sorry for ourselves.

Suddenly, it occurred that there should have been fourteen of us. I had forgotten all about our friendly driver. I rushed back to the front of the car and peered in. The driver stared back at me; his eyes wide open. His body was at an unusual angle. As I tried to move him, I knew at once that he was past any kind of help. I found out later that the blood I was covered in was his, not mine. I went back to the crew. To my astonishment, they were being led away to private vehicles. Shouting, I ran after them to find out what was going on.

If you take a patient to a private hospital in Zimbabwe, you will receive a monetary reward. The crew were being rounded up by scavengers eager to make money out of our predicament. I was furious and pushed these vultures away. Had any of them resisted, I think I would have really lost my temper.

The police, who were also badly shaken by the crash, had called for help. The licenced ambulances were now beginning to arrive. We were all taken to the local hospital, where our injuries were tended to. A few hours later, I rounded up the walking wounded who were well enough to return to the hotel with me. Five of the crew had been seriously injured and required further attention and operations.

At around five that morning, we arrived back at the hotel. We must have looked a terrible sight, covered in torn, bloody clothing. The reception staff rushed towards us to offer their help. The clerk who had arranged the limousine service just looked at me. Her partner was our driver. Sadly, I shook my head. I could see the tears in her eyes as she simply turned and walked away.

Despite the hour, I had to let British Airways know what had happened. There was no way that we could operate home in two days. They promised to have a replacement crew sent down that evening. The last thing I did before collapsing in bed was to put a note under the captain's and engineer's doors. That done, I fell into a short and nightmare-filled sleep. Three hours later, I was jolted awake by my phone ringing.

After explaining the previous night's terrible events to the captain and to British Airways, it was agreed that an entirely new crew would fly out to take our flight home. Sure enough, the replacement crew arrived the following day. At least, our flight home the next day would not be delayed or cancelled. The following evening, my phone rang again. It was my wake-up call for the journey home, or so I thought. In actual fact, it was crew control calling from London. The newly arrived replacement first officer had food poisoning, and could I please operate home?

The captain and engineer sat in First Class and enjoyed the wine and food. Despite not being involved in the crash, they settled back to enjoy the flight home. I sat on the flight deck, trying to disguise my black eye and my aching back. Sometimes, we complain that life seems so unfair. When this happens, I remember this accident and how my colleagues and I survived, unlike our poor, amiable and friendly, limousine driver.

Chapter 16

Nyumbani and the Old Oak Tree

In the early 1990s, AIDS was destroying lives and communities. If you were HIV positive, it was a death sentence. There was nothing that science or medicine could do to help you.

In Africa, the situation was desperate. All communities were affected, and of course, those who suffered the most were the poor and the very young. In Kenya, on the streets of the capital, Nairobi, young children were utterly abandoned. These poor little souls ranged in age from a few weeks old upwards. Many were orphans whose parents had died of AIDS, and they had no one and nowhere to go. Many children had simply been left to die by their desperate parents. There was a massive stigma against people who were HIV positive in African communities. The lack of medical facilities meant certain death, and children were helpless against the fear and ostracisation, tragically being left to suffer alone. The world was in crisis, which was amplified, as disasters often are, in Africa.

My first visit to Nairobi occurred at this time. Nairobi itself was an interesting destination from a flying point of view. The airport itself is five thousand and five-hundred feet above sea level. This fact alone means that the air is thinner, and consequently, the aircraft's ground speed is greater on take-off and landing. Flying a Boeing 747 into Nairobi requires the pilots to allow for this increase and to slow the plane down much sooner than they usually would. Also, arriving from London, we would fly over the Ngong Hills before turning into the valley where the airport was situated. This requires the aircraft to be higher than it would typically be for an approach into an airfield such as Heathrow. Added to this, was the possibility that terrorists would sit on the Ngong Hills and occasionally fire rocket-launched grenades at the low flying aircraft. We had to alter our approach on arrival to prevent, or at least reduce, the chance of such an attack.

The film, *Out of Africa,* featured the Ngong Hills, where Karen Blixen (Meryl Streep) met and fell in love with Denys (Robert Redford). Denys was killed when his Tiger Moth aircraft crashed, and a memorial sits at the very point where we turn onto the final approach on the north-easterly runway. By the time you have accomplished a successful approach and landing, you really feel you have earned your beer that night.

With my first landing in Nairobi and the evening out of the way, I set off the following day from the hotel to explore the city itself. Our hotel was in the middle of the noisy, overcrowded centre. As a keen runner, I usually explore a city by running through it, not a viable option today. The pavements were a mass of people buying and selling anything and everything under the sun. Instead, I just wandered aimlessly, taking in all the sounds, smells and sights of this vibrant city. On this first walk, I was approached time and time again by street children begging for money and food. I could not believe just how young some of these children were; some were barely old enough to walk. I was shocked and distressed by the level of poverty I was witnessing. Why on earth were they alone on the dangerous streets? It was just appalling; I had never seen anything like it before. Returning to the hotel, I asked one of the porters about these street children; it was from him that I learned that these children were HIV positive orphans. It seemed that society had abandoned these innocent souls to live and tragically, in most cases, quickly die on Nairobi's filthy streets.

One of the great things about British Airways crews was that our people genuinely cared about the places they visited. Nairobi was no different. Our crew briefing sheet was a long and detailed article about the very children I had just seen on the streets outside of our hotel.

There was an orphanage situated about thirty minutes outside of the city. This had been set up a year before by an American priest, Father D'Agostino. The orphanage took in these street children and relied purely on donations. The Kenyan government refused to acknowledge that a problem of such apparent magnitude existed, let alone help fund an orphanage. The name of this wonderful place was Nyumbani, a name I was to become very familiar with over the years. The article mentioned that apart from the money required to run the orphanage, they were desperate for volunteers to visit and interact with the children. They were also critically short of medical supplies. Anything we could donate would be very gratefully received.

We had two days off on this trip, so I decided to visit Nyumbani the next day. I put my plan to the rest of the crew that evening and was delighted when the majority volunteered to join me. The plan was finalised after a quick call to the orphanage and our hotel's concierge desk to arrange transport.

The drive the following day took longer than expected. Although the orphanage was only fifteen miles away, the last five miles was along a very bumpy track. The minivan was not designed to withstand such punishment. After a late-night, some of the crew were also looking very fragile. Therefore, it was with great relief that we finally pulled up outside a few wooden huts in the middle of nowhere. There were ten of us that first morning. As we stepped down from the van, we were surrounded by a gaggle of young children all clamouring for our attention. The group were silenced by one call from a Catholic nun who appeared, as if by magic. The children obediently lined up in two straight lines and waited for further instructions.

The nun introduced herself and asked us to follow her into the largest of the wooden huts. Leaving the children waiting patiently outside, we were given a detailed history of Nyumbani. On one wall was a large picture of the founder, Father D'Agostino, shaking hands with the then President of the United States, Bill Clinton. That was not something I was expecting to see. We were told that every one of the children at the orphanage was HIV positive and that the average life expectancy did not extend much beyond thirteen. A lot of the children would never even make it that far. Looking at how happy and healthy the children who had met us seemed, it was difficult to comprehend what we had just been told.

We were then asked if we were prepared to play with the children. They craved adult interaction. There were obviously risks, as at this time, HIV was quite literally a death sentence. One fundamental question was asked: did any of us have any cuts or open wounds? Fortunately, we were all free of any injuries. Had anyone been affected, they would not be allowed near the children.

We were then warned that the children we had just met were healthier and that many other children were not so fortunate. There apparently were three classifications, and the children were divided accordingly. We were asked which of us would like to visit the children who were not so well and those who would like to visit the seriously ill children. Only three of us volunteered to visit all the children.

Now the immediate formalities were over, we all had to sign a disclaimer and provide our contact details. We were free to see the children again. As soon as we emerged from the hut, the two lines of waiting children dissolved, and we were again surrounded by laughing children. About thirty children with ages ranging from around three to eleven-years-of-age surrounded us. They all wanted our individual attention. I decided that a game of football would be a great idea. That way, all the children could join in. When I was at school, we chose two captains who would then select their team, calling them out one by one. Two of the crew volunteered to be the captains, and so with the help of the nuns, we selected the two teams. There were shouts of laughter as all the children jumped up and down, desperate to be the next one chosen. This also allowed us to learn the children's names. Eventually, we had two teams ready for kick-off. We made two goals with abandoned cardboard boxes as the goalposts. I was made the referee, and the game was on with a blow of my imaginary whistle.

Football is a universally loved game. Everyone was having a great time, except for one very lonely looking boy I had noticed sitting by himself watching the game. Handing over my refereeing duties, I walked over and sat next to the solitary little figure. As I did so, I was intercepted by one of the nuns. She explained that the little boy had only just arrived. His mother had died only a few weeks previously, and his brother had also passed away. His name was Viktor. He was seven years old. He rarely spoke and never joined in with the other children. Thanking the nun, I went and sat next to Viktor. I sat quietly for a few minutes and then asked Viktor if he liked football. All I got was silence. Viktor just stared straight ahead. Not wanting to intrude on his grief, I stood up and wandered off, noticing that Viktor turned to see where I had gone. Five minutes later, I returned with another football I had been given by the nuns. Sitting a few feet from Viktor, I simply rolled the ball to him. As the ball stopped by his arm, I held out my arms to encourage him to roll it back. He merely stared at the ball, and so I retrieved it and tried again. This time he rolled the ball back to me. Progress, I thought to myself. We ended up just rolling the ball to each other whilst the other football game continued in front of us.

Suddenly, there was a loud bell, and all the children stopped playing and immediately formed two lines again. It was lunchtime. Viktor stood up and joined the back of the queue. I left them to enjoy their lunch and was led away by a nun to see the other children.

So far, our visit had been full of fun and laughter. It was almost impossible to believe that these children were terminally ill. They were so full of life. As we entered the next wooden hut, all that joy disappeared. Here were the children who were showing signs of AIDS. It was heart-breaking to see the hollowed faces and staring eyes. Row after row of young children lying motionless on very basic wooden beds, literally waiting to die. There was very little I could say or do. I had never had to witness such utter hopelessness. It was a daunting and terribly upsetting experience. We only stayed a few minutes. The children did not have enough energy to even acknowledge our presence. The final hut housed the very young babies who were showing signs of the disease. The nun explained that they desperately need incubators to look after these babies and make their very short lives more comfortable. We left to return to the main group. It was nearly time to leave.

The children, on the other hand, had different ideas. They wanted to show us around the rest of the orphanage. As I followed the excited group, I felt a small hand slip into mine and tightly held on. I looked down, and there was Viktor at my side, staring down at his feet. Not wanting to dispel this magical moment, I simply walked with Viktor holding my hand. No words were spoken between us.

It really was now time to leave, but before we left, I asked the sister in charge what we could do to help. She explained that medicines were the most desperately needed commodities. Any medicine would help. They had nothing to treat, even the most basic of the children's problems. The next thing they required was bedding and clothing. Both were in very short supply. Their final wish was an impossible dream. They needed incubators for the babies. As we left Nyumbani on that first visit, there was a feeling of hope amongst us, rather than desperation. The atmosphere in the orphanage was one of hope and optimism rather than doom, despite such human tragedy. We all vowed that we would return, bringing as much help as we could.

The route to Nairobi had moved from Heathrow to Gatwick, which meant that over the next few years, I regularly visited Nyumbani. Our crews were fantastic, and on every flight to Nairobi, there were bags and bags of clothing, bedding and toys that had been donated. We took these gifts to the orphanage, and on each visit, I was slowly able to get closer to my little friend, Viktor. I managed to get my son's local school involved. The children wrote letters to the children at Nyumbani, which I took with me, and the children at Nyumbani wrote back to them. I took pictures of my two young sons (my youngest son, Robert had now arrived, making us a family of four) to show Viktor, and he immediately referred to them as his brothers. He had adopted us.

We held a fashion show in a local hotel to raise money and had hundreds of T-shirts made with the Nyumbani orphanage logo on the front. We sold these to add to the funds we raised for the orphanage. One of our flight engineers, unbelievably, managed to secure five old incubators from the National Health Service. They were old but fully functional. We managed to get permission to put them in the aircraft hold on my next flight to Nairobi. We were so excited and could not wait to deliver them to the orphanage when we landed. The crew helped us carry the incubators from the aircraft into the terminal building. We intended to take them onto the bus and deliver them the next day. We were stopped at customs, where despite our protests, the incubators were confiscated. We were then told that we would have to pay a five-thousand-pound import fee. Of course, this was impossible, and so we never saw the incubators again.

My friendship with Viktor grew on each visit. We helped the children build rabbit hutches where they could look after their own pets. Viktor introduced me to Flopsy, a beautiful rabbit that he obviously adored. On my next visit, I asked Viktor where Flopsy was. Viktor looked up at me with a quizzical expression. As he rubbed his tummy, he explained that he had eaten him last week. He had tasted as good as he had looked. He then proceeded to show me his new bunny, tenderly stroking its ears. Viktor went on to boast that as soon as he had put on some weight, Viktor would enjoy eating him as well. How different things were in Africa. In Britain, not many children spend months fattening up their pets to eat them.

As the years passed, the money British Airways crews raised helped build new accommodation blocks and donate much needed medical supplies. I visited as often as I could. Viktor was always the first child to meet the bus.

Sadly, the Nairobi route was eventually moved back to Heathrow, which meant we could no longer visit the orphanage. We passed all the information we had to the crews at Heathrow, and they carried on our excellent work. After a while, the route was again returned to Gatwick. I made sure that I was on the first flight. The next day our bus stopped outside the orphanage. I jumped out of the bus to greet Viktor; it had been over a year since I last saw him. I stood looking around. The children, as always, were jumping up and down in excitement. The head sister whom I had met on my first visit beckoned me to follow her. We made our way to a solitary oak tree standing at the bottom of the grounds. At the base of the tree were many small white crosses, each with a name written on them. She pointed to one such cross, and there was the name, Viktor. He had died three months before I could return to see him. I was heartbroken. The sister told me that he was always talking about his English family and how I would return and take him to meet his brothers one day. He had always carried their pictures with him. I do not often cry in public, but my tears fell unashamedly for the young boy who had asked for so little in his short life.

The orphanage is still in existence to this day and still only cares for HIV positive children. Whilst AIDS is no longer a death sentence, in rich countries, the drugs used to combat this terrible disease are way beyond the means of those living in the poorest countries. There, nothing has changed, and it is still a death sentence. The Nairobi route returned to Heathrow for the final time shortly after my visit. To my utter horror and disgust, it emerged that one of the pilots who had visited Nyumbani during this period was prosecuted for sexually abusing the children. This revolting individual killed himself shortly afterwards. It was one of those rare moments that I actually believed the existence of the death penalty was warranted. There is so much that is good in humanity and in our world. It only takes a few warped individuals to undo all the good that the majority of us strive for. Thank God, Viktor had passed away before this vile man arrived at Nyumbani. Rest In Peace, my African son. Sleep well. You are still loved and missed.

Chapter 17

Characters

At this stage of my career, I had been flying the 747 for eight years, and I was, once again, starting to feel that I needed a new challenge. Although I simply loved flying the jumbo, I really missed being the person who made all the real decisions. Ultimately, I wanted my command back.

The vast majority of captains I flew with were excellent, and when it was the co-pilot's sector, they left you to get on with it, knowing you had the skills to do so. To fly with these captains was always a pleasure. Unfortunately, there was also the other type of captain. They would continually overrule any decisions you made for no real reason. Consequently, the whole trip then became unpleasant. At least when I had been the captain, I always knew what type of day I would have. My workday now depended on the whims of someone else. Occasionally, I found it very difficult to hold my tongue.

One such occasion was a trip to Entebbe in Uganda. It had been a long trip, we had flown a shuttle to Harare and another to Lusaka, and we had one flight left, returning back to Gatwick. On every sector, the captain had been unpleasant, not only to me but to the rest of the crew too. Also, he was dismissive to the local ground staff, almost to the point of making himself appear racist.

The hotel in Entebbe was undergoing refurbishment, and the captain had been complaining loudly about the work being undertaken. I was sitting by an empty swimming pool enjoying the warm African sun before our flight home the next day. The entire pool area was being renovated, even the diving board was being replaced. Reading my book, I looked up and suddenly noticed the captain striding across the lawn towards the unfortunate workmen. He started waving his arms around, pointing at the diving board and then back at the pool. What on earth was he complaining about now, I wondered. But as long as he kept well away from me, I really did not care what he did.

The following day, we were sitting on the flight deck completing our final checks before our flight home. I could not wait for this particular trip to end. The sooner I saw the back of this man, the better. The station manager, a lovely Ugandan I had met on previous flights, came onto the flight deck. He looked nervous and worried, not his usual cheerful self. He started to apologise profusely to the captain. Suddenly, all became clear. The captain had purchased the diving board from the hotel. Unbeknownst to us, they had arranged for it to be loaded onto the aircraft. Apparently, he had a swimming pool at home.

The manager explained to the captain that he could not fit the diving board onto our flight due to an exceptionally high freight load. He added that tomorrow's flight had space. He would personally make sure the diving board would be on that flight. The captain swung around and completely lost his temper. Any semblance of respect I had left for him was also lost. He swore and shouted at the station manager and used the sort of racist language that today would have resulted, quite rightly, in instant dismissal and probably prosecution. He demanded that his diving board be loaded immediately and until it was, the flight was going nowhere. With these hostile roars ringing in his ears, the poor man left as quickly as he could.

At this point in our woeful relationship, I could not hold my tongue any longer. Turning to the captain, I informed him in no uncertain terms that he had no right to speak to anyone in that manner. Unless he apologised, I would not be flying the aircraft home with him. The look on his face said it all. He was just about to explode again when the flight engineer agreed with me and threatened to walk away unless an apology to the station manager was forthcoming.

There was a deathly hush, the situation had come to a head, and the atmosphere on our flight deck was toxic. Just as the captain was about to speak, or probably shout, the station manager came back into the flight deck. He politely informed the captain that his diving board was now on the aircraft, and he was about to close the last door. Without waiting for a reply, he simply turned around and left.

Well, this situation was awkward. Indeed, I had threatened to get off the aircraft unless the captain apologised. The captain now had no chance to apologise. What to do? Of course, I had no other choice but to continue with our pre-flight checks. As you can imagine, the flight home was not the greatest time I have ever had on an aircraft.

We landed on a cold and wet afternoon at Gatwick. As usual, after the passengers had disembarked, we went down the aircraft steps and walked to the back of the aircraft, where the crew bus would meet us. We could watch as our crew bags were unloaded and placed on the bus. We were all very interested to see the infamous diving board. Of course, the crew had all learned of the furore before we departed.

The captain stood with the rest of us as each bag came down from the aircraft's hold on the conveyor belt one by one. You could see the captain's face grow redder and angrier as each bag appeared. There was no sign of his precious board. The last bags were loaded on the crew bus as the captain stood in the rain staring at an empty conveyor belt. He started swearing again and using hugely offensive language about being lied to by the station manager. It was at this point that his diving board finally appeared from the hold. The station manager had not lied. He had got the diving board onto the aircraft after all. As the board finally appeared, it became apparent how he had managed to get the entire board onto the aircraft. The board was now in two separate sections. The loading crew had simply cut the board in half. The whole crew burst out laughing and clapping, well, the entire team except one furious captain. Karma had paid a most deserved appearance.

This episode served to convince me that it was time for me to think about moving off the 747 and bid for my own command on a smaller aircraft. Over the previous eight years, I had enjoyed some unforgettable moments. My first approach and landing in Hong Kong were right up there on my most memorable flights list. This had been into the old Kai Tak airport, situated literally in the middle of Hong Kong. We had to fly towards a black and white marker board on a hill, and then just as it appeared, we were about to hit the mountain, we had to make a steep turn to the right to line up with the runway. The next problem to present itself were the skyscrapers between us and the runway. We literally had to fly between, rather than over, these buildings. I could actually look out of the side window and see into the apartments on the upper floors. Our engines would blow the clothes on the washing lines as we passed. It was probably the most challenging approach and landing we pilots ever had to do, and I loved it every single time.

Despite everything I loved about flying this aircraft, I needed to regain my command and secure more control over my working life. It was with a very heavy heart that in 1996, I put in my annual bid to move away from the jumbo. Each year, every pilot had a right to bid for another seat or fleet. Vacancies were awarded in strict seniority order. The 747 was the most senior fleet in British Airways, even more senior than Concorde.

However, in 1993, a new variant of the 747 was introduced at Heathrow, the 747-400 series. Although this variant looked very similar to the older 747s, the new aircraft had a stretched upper deck. More importantly, the flight engineer's presence was no longer required. It could be flown with just two pilots. This new variant immediately became the most sought-after aircraft to fly, and all the senior pilots flocked towards it. I had been with British Airways for only eight years. I had absolutely no chance of flying this aircraft, even as a co-pilot. To have any chance of becoming a captain, I would need to look elsewhere. I really did not want to fly the short-haul aircraft. Flying there and back to different destinations each day held no great appeal for me.

It was, therefore, with a lot more hope than expectation that I handed in my bid that year. My first choice was to become a Gatwick 747 captain on the older 747s, now referred to as the Classic 747. After that, I chose the Classic at Heathrow and then the much smaller Boeing 767, mid-haul aircraft. I made no bids for any other co-pilot vacancies. If I could not achieve my command, I would stay where I was for another year. I could hardly complain. Other co-pilots had been waiting over twenty-two years for a long-haul command. As soon as I had filed my bid, I began to regret my actions, true to my usual form. I loved flying from Gatwick. Why had I jeopardised this to return to Heathrow, where I had previously been desperate to leave. I knew that realistically I had no chance of becoming a 747 captain. However, there was a possibility I would achieve a 767 command. This was an aircraft that I had no desire to fly, and from an airport, I had no desire to operate from. What had I been thinking?

The next few months dragged by as I awaited the result of my rash bid. I should have been more tolerant of captains wanting to bring their diving boards home. Why, one day, I might even have a pool of my own, unlikely as it seemed at the time.

The letter finally arrived, and it was with the most tremendous trepidation that I ripped the envelope apart. The letter was short and sharp. 'Congratulations you have been awarded a course as a captain … on the … (I could barely look), … on the Boeing …767'!

Damn, I shouted to myself, this was the outcome I had dreaded. I would be leaving not only the 747, but I would be leaving Gatwick and all my friends. I felt both annoyed and sorry for myself all at the same time. I had ignored the time-honoured sage advice of only bidding for what you really wanted rather than what you thought you could achieve. I was about to embark on a command course and a type rating course running concurrently on an aircraft I had no desire to fly. All of this was entirely my own fault, which made matters even worse.

Our salaries were made up of basic pay, significantly supplemented by destination payments known as box payments. Each destination was put into a 'box', the longer the flight time to reach the destination, the different box value it attracted. Whilst a New York flight of seven hours was put into box 'A', a Narita or Hong Kong flight of over twelve hours was given a box 'E'. The further the letter was away from 'A', the more money the trip attracted. There were no extra payments for a box 'A' flight, whereas a box 'D' flight would attract three thousand pounds. As you can imagine, all the senior pilots bid for as many box 'D' flights as they could get. This unfair payment method lasted until 2007. Incredibly, senior co-pilots had been earning more than junior captains.

The new 747-400 aircraft, with their extra range, were operating the vast majority of these ultra-long-haul flights. Pilots on these aircraft were earning nearly twice the amount other pilots could expect. There was literally a stampede to get onto the 747-400.

All this excitement at the time didn't concern me. I was busy preparing for my 767 conversion, which was due to start in a matter of weeks.

Occasionally, if there were insufficient bids, then a supplementary proposal would be published for further applications. In 1996, there had been a rush for the 747-400 and all those lucrative routes. There were absolutely no ultra-long-range destinations at Gatwick. Therefore, no matter how senior you were, you could not bid for the lucrative routes. Unbelievably, Gatwick captains had actually begun bidding to fly as co-pilots on the Heathrow 747-400 fleet. Consequently, and quite unexpectedly, there were vacancies for Classic 747 captains at Gatwick.

A few days after receiving my notification of the 767 command, I answered the phone to training administration. Would I be interested in a 747 command at Gatwick? As you may imagine, the conversation was concise. It didn't take long to say yes. Unbelievably, I was still only in my thirties, and I was about to start my command course on the 747. How on earth had that happened, I thought to myself? As I replaced the receiver, I had the biggest smile on my face. All I had to do now was pass the course, not an easy proposition, not easy at all.

Chapter 18

The Youngest BA 747 Captain

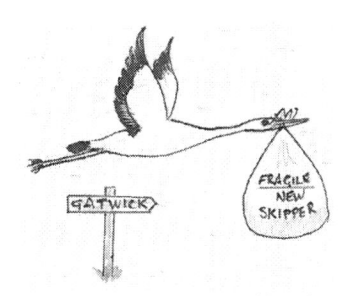

As I look back on a long career, it is difficult to comprehend that I was once the youngest 747 captain in British Airways. This is especially difficult to accept when I look in a mirror and see one of the oldest captains staring back at me. This achievement had absolutely no bearing on my ability. Once again, I had somehow managed to be in the right place at the right time. The fates or someone, somewhere, was definitely looking after me. As I took in the magnitude of just what I was about to embark on, I reflected on how lucky I was. I knew that I would be earning less than the co-pilots at Heathrow. However, it was well worth the sacrifice in salary to command a 747, even if it was a Classic version. There would be no premium routes available to me. However, before any of that could become a reality, I had a command course to pass. Unfortunately, I would have to complete this course at Heathrow. I was not looking forward to the course itself with unfamiliar routes and unknown training captains to contend with. This was especially true considering my past experiences with some of the Heathrow captains. Before I could start my course, I had to attend a week-long residential course in Surrey.

I had just over a week to prepare for my course, although I received some excellent advice over the past few months. Instead of socialising on my trips, I studied all the operation manuals. I learned or relearned all of the information I would need to hopefully, pass my course.

A week later, I presented myself again at Cranebank to start the ground school phase of the course. I was lucky that I did not have to do a conversion course at the same time as my command course. Had I gone to the Boeing 767, I would be learning how to fly a new aircraft as well as pass a command course. I considered myself very fortunate. We were tested on our knowledge of the various technical manuals. We were also grilled on the operating policies of the company. I was relaxed, had done my homework, and knew the books almost back to front. So far, so good. The following section was going to be much more challenging, the simulator course.

I had six simulator sessions, each of four hours duration, to get through. Every conceivable failure was introduced, and my ability to cope with each scenario was meticulously examined. Probably the most difficult of these was an approach, going around and landing with two engines inoperative on the same wing; it was indeed the most challenging. The Classic 747-100 series was underpowered. Even with all engines working, the older aircraft struggled at high weights, especially in hot and high-altitude destinations. Losing two of the engines made the handling of the aircraft extremely critical. Speed became paramount. It was vital not to let the speed drop even a few knots below the minimum controllable airspeed for two engines. Should this happen, managing to recover that speed became nearly impossible. The only way to increase speed was to lower the nose and descend, not something you wanted to do near the ground. If the speed continued to decrease, even with the two engines at full power, you would very quickly lose control of the aircraft.

I was also given scenarios involving various system failures, landing gear, flaps, flying controls all failed with unpredictable consequences, depending on the combination of the losses. We ran low on fuel, really low on fuel, as airports around us started to close due to the weather. We had a bomb explode whilst cruising at a high altitude. The six simulator sessions seemed to go on and on, and when they finally came to an end, I was pretty exhausted. Luckily, I had convinced the examiners that I could cope with everything they threw at me. It really helped to have a flight engineer present on the flight deck. I was grateful that I still flew the Classic 747s, even if there were no lucrative routes to be had.

The next phase was line training. I had to fly six trips with a training captain in the co-pilot's seat. I felt that I had to contend with a certain amount of scepticism during this stage of the course. There was still a definite division between Heathrow and Gatwick crews; we were seen as the poor relations, very second division to their premier league. This, of course, was nonsense. We all had to pass the same exams and checks. However, these misconceptions still existed. We had become known as the Beach Fleet. The majority of our destinations at Gatwick involved somewhere with a lovely beach, mainly the Caribbean.

We were not complaining, but the Heathrow crews were not happy, despite the premium routes being all operated from Heathrow. My first flight was to Chicago. Thankfully, the dreadful windowless reporting room had long since gone. The Heathrow crews were now housed in a sizable purpose-built building known as the Compass Centre. This bright, spacious building was a considerable improvement. The flight and cabin crew all boarded the same bus to the aircraft, a much more amicable arrangement. I was flying with the chief pilot, never a very comfortable experience. However, despite some negative remarks from, of all people, the flight engineer, the trip went well. As I had not yet passed the course, I flew from the captain's seat but still was required to wear the uniform of a first officer. Younger 747 captains were flying with airlines such as Virgin Atlantic, but I was the youngest to fly for British Airways. This appeared to be the problem with the flight engineer on this, my first trip. He was approaching retirement age and had been used to flying with captains similar in age to him. He clearly did not like flying with a captain who was over twenty-five years younger than himself. He questioned every decision I made and asked me difficult questions at inappropriate times. I was left with no doubt that he was not on my side.

Despite this, the flight there and back went as well as I could have hoped for. Flying into Chicago's O'Hare Airport is always challenging, especially as, at that time, I was not a regular visitor. Approaching over Lake Michigan, we were vectored for one runway and then given a late change of runway due to the aircraft ahead of us having slowed down too early. I was quite happy to take the autopilot out and fly a manual approach to the parallel runway. There was no time to reprogramme the aircraft's navigation system. I checked with the training captain that he was happy to continue the approach, and he replied that it was my decision. I was more than comfortable as we lined up with the new runway as we passed one thousand feet. I turned to the flight engineer to check that he was also happy to continue. His reply was not the one I wanted to hear, although it was not totally unexpected.

Loudly, the engineer informed me that he was not happy, not happy at all. He insisted that we were too low to be changing runways, and we should have flown a missed approach. Great, I thought to myself, what to do now? I was convinced that we had adhered to all the regulations and that the aircraft was in a stable approach. The training captain seemed happy, although he had not committed himself to the option I'd chosen. The runway was directly in front of the aircraft, and we were now passing eight hundred feet. Should I land or fly a missed approach? It was a Friday afternoon, and O'Hare was certainly living up to its claim to be the busiest airport in the world. There were aircraft everywhere, and the air traffic controller was shouting at everyone. It was a typical Friday at O'Hare.

Meanwhile, I was still deciding what to do. Did I continue to land with an unhappy engineer or fly a missed approach into a sky full of aircraft? At four hundred feet, I made the decision to go around. There was a possibility that I had flown an unstable approach. If there is any doubt, it is best to discuss it on the ground rather than in the air. Applying full power, I called "Go Around Flaps 20."

Flying a missed approach in the United States is always interesting, to say the least. In most other parts of the world, once you decide to go around, you follow a pre-planned route and stop your climb at a published height. This is all nicely drawn out for you already on a chart you clip to the control column. These days, the charts are all on an iPad. In the United States, although you still have your chart, you never actually follow it. Instead, the air traffic controller will issue you with a series of headings and heights, all delivered at incredible speed. You have to process this new information while trying to fly the aircraft, raise the landing gear, and set the flaps. As you can imagine, it all gets slightly busy for the pilot.

This is not how I envisaged my first sector, especially with the chief pilot sitting next to me. We levelled at two thousand feet and followed all the headings and speeds we were given. The controller's voice sounded terse. He was obviously annoyed at this British Airways aircraft playing havoc with his traffic patterns. As we were immediately positioned for another approach, we had to make time to carry out the after take-off, before descent, and approach checklists. These checklists were read out by the flight engineer, and today, my engineer was taking his time.

As we approached one thousand feet for the second time, we still had not completed the before landing checklist. After each check was completed, the checklist was put away and not produced again until I'd asked for a second time. If our checks were not completed by one thousand feet, we would have to fly another missed approach. Should this happen, we would have to declare a low fuel state. My workload was now extremely high. I was just about to ask for the landing checks for the third time when the training captain intervened with a sharp rebuke to the engineer. The checks were completed at eleven hundred feet, and we continued to a successful landing.

The debrief afterwards was interesting, to say the least. I was expecting criticism of my decision to fly a missed approach as we were fully stable and in a position to land. To my surprise, I was congratulated on going around. Apparently, he would have done the same if one member of the crew was not happy. During this debrief, the engineer sat behind us, not saying a word. When the discussion was over, I stood up to leave, expecting the other two to follow me. Instead, the training captain asked the engineer to remain in his seat for a quick chat. I left them to it and followed the cabin crew to immigration. Neither the captain nor the engineer came out for a beer that night. Strangely, on the return flight, the engineer could not have been more helpful. So, one trip down, five more to go.

The next four trips were uneventful, and I was signed off for my final line check. I felt fortunate when I found out that the trip was from Gatwick, albeit with a Heathrow-based examiner, Captain Richard (Dick) Brunyate.

The trip was from Gatwick to Orlando in Florida, just a night stop, then a return flight to Gatwick. This was my biggest test so far in a very varied career. Therefore, I presented myself in front of the man who held my future career in his hands with some trepidation. It was the first, and sadly the last time I was to fly with Dick. I prayed that he held no preconceived biased views of Gatwick crews and that my relative youth would not be a problem for him.

As I walked into the briefing area, I could see this tall, tanned captain relaxing with a coffee in hand. If you think of Roger Moore, you will get an idea of what Dick looked like with a bit of Sean Connery thrown in for good luck. I introduced myself and was slightly surprised when he didn't reply, "Bond,

James Bond." I immediately warmed to his relaxed, laid-back style, and I remember thinking that if I pass, I want to be just like Dick.

I was to fly the aircraft to Orlando, and Dick was flying us back to Gatwick. By this time, British Airways had adopted the monitored approach system. This meant that the operating pilot took off and flew the aircraft until descent. He would then hand over control to the other pilot, who would then fly the plane to one thousand feet. The operating pilot would then take control if he could see the runway. If the weather was poor, he would wait until he could see the runway before taking control or call for a go-around. Confused? I certainly was for the first few months after this system was introduced. Luckily, by the time we flew to Orlando, I had just about got the hang of this new way to operate.

Therefore, I flew the aircraft to Orlando, Dick flew an immaculate approach, and I landed in the right place. So far, so good, I thought to myself. In complete contrast to my Chicago trip, Dick insisted we all meet up in Ruby Tuesday's, a bar close to the hotel. I knew that I had to be on my best behaviour, so when Dick asked me what I would like to drink, I replied that a diet coke would be great.

Dick turned to face me, raising one eyebrow, whilst descending the other, as he did a perfect Roger Moore impersonation. He told me not to be so ridiculous and what did I really want to drink? I assumed that he had ordered a martini, shaken, not stirred. Again, I asked for a diet coke. A moment later, I was holding an ice-cold pint of lager. Dick smiled at me and assured me that the only way I could fail was to line up with the wrong runway tomorrow or not join him in a proper drink tonight. And with that, he put his eyebrows back in their right place. I think I enjoyed the rest of the evening.

The next day, I managed to get the landing runway ahead and below as I handed control of the aircraft back to Dick for one of the best landings I had ever seen. We taxied onto the stand

and shut everything down. There was silence as those big Rolls Royce engines finally stopped turning. Dick turned to me and handed me the technical log. Only a captain can sign this book, and with a massive grin on his face, he asked me to sign it. He then produced a captain's hat resplendent with a silver beaded peak. "Not bad for a youngster," was all he said.

I was now a British Airways 747 captain. Still, in my thirties, I was also the youngest jumbo captain in British Airways, a fact that I was very proud of. Dick became famous as the captain of the British Airways flight that was captured in Kuwait at the start of the first Gulf war. This occurred four years before our flight together. Dick's father had worked in Iraq years earlier, taking his family with him. Realising that his life would be in danger if he was captured by the Iraqis, Dick decided to walk out of Kuwait. His first officer and flight engineer went with him. Dick being tall and dark meant he blended in perfectly, especially after they were given traditional clothes to disguise themselves. The first officer also looked the part. The flight engineer, however, had freckles and ginger hair, not your typical Middle Eastern look. Despite this, Dick led his crew undetected for four months and eventually walked out of Kuwait. Even James Bond would have struggled to do that. Dick was indeed a real-life hero. I was proud that it was he who gave me my command. Sadly, Dick became very ill and died at the young age of just sixty years old. I tried to live up to Dick's standards throughout my career, and I based my command style on his leadership. It was a pleasure and honour to have known and flown with Dick. Rest in peace, my colleague, mentor, and friend.

Chapter 19

The Beach Fleet

I was now a fully-fledged member of the Beach Fleet at Gatwick. There were only seven jumbos based at Gatwick. We flew them relentlessly back and forth mainly to Barbados, Antigua, St Lucia and Jamaica. It was great fun and hard work. We regularly flew shuttle flights of less than an hour between these islands. Often, we would not use the autopilot and simply enjoy flying the aircraft. Our flying skills were consequently honed to a great degree, and I am proud to admit that my own flying skills were at their peak during this period. On a typical flight from Antigua to Barbados, we would fly down the west coast of Barbados and time our turn to fly directly overhead our crew hotel. Unfortunately, we occasionally woke up our Concorde colleagues on their sunbeds. We would lower the landing gear at the same time just to make sure they heard us. Well, they did fly the world's noisiest aircraft, so it was a little payback.

Flying back into Antigua later that evening, we would head for the crew hotel on Five Island Village and again, turn overhead to line up with the runway. This manoeuvre gave our colleagues, who had brought the aircraft in from Gatwick that morning, time to get our beers ready.

Flying into St Lucia was also a sheer delight. The two magnificent Piton mountains stood out and acted as the perfect beacon to guide us towards the runway. The landing aids in the Caribbean were very basic in those days and often did not work at all. We, therefore, needed our flying skills to be at their absolute best if we were going to keep the whole operation safe. With modern aircraft, you can fly a fully automatic approach without any ground facilities, a much better and safer way to fly. However, these automated approaches lacked the fun and sheer feeling of satisfaction we achieved as we flew our first-generation jumbos into these very basic airports. Amidst these halcyon days, inevitably, there were sad moments as well.

On one such memorable occasion in early 1990, I was due to fly home from Antigua in the evening. The aircraft had arrived from London, and the shuttle crew flew it on to Port of Spain. The aircraft was then scheduled for the short return flight to Antigua. We boarded the crew bus to drive to the airport, as my crew and I would fly the aircraft back to Gatwick. We arrived at Antigua's St John's Airport and awaited the arrival of the plane. We waited and waited. Our passengers were with us in the terminal building and began to ask questions about the delay. We knew that the aircraft had taxied out at Port of Spain. It was a short flight to Antigua. Something was obviously very wrong. I felt the hairs on my forearms begin to rise. Instinctively, I knew that something was very much amiss that evening.

Of course, there were no mobile phones in those days, and telephone lines in the Caribbean were not very reliable. Our operations staff at Antigua were desperately trying to contact their counterparts at Port of Spain, there was no reply. There was a strong feeling of foreboding in the terminal that an incident or, even worse, an accident had occurred, we were to be proved right.

The aircraft had pushed back normally from the stand at Port of Spain. There had been an altercation between two passengers who had boarded. This had delayed the aircraft as one of them was taken off the aircraft along with his luggage. This was far from an unusual occurrence. It was more of an inconvenience than a serious problem. What happened next, however, most certainly was not usual in any shape or form. No one could possibly have had any clue as to the tragedy that was about to unfold.

At the same time as the now delayed aircraft was slowly taxiing towards the runway, an American tourist was having an argument with his partner. After a physical altercation with his friend, he then ran towards the airfield's perimeter fence. Scaling this, he then attacked four security guards who were sitting in a Land Rover. Stealing their vehicle, he began to drive, madly chasing after the 747, eventually overtaking it. The crew, taxiing out at night in darkness, were totally unaware of this vehicle, as was the air traffic controller. The security guards had been badly beaten and had not had the chance to raise the alarm. As the Land Rover turned and faced the aircraft, the flight crew realised something dangerous was occurring. They immediately stopped the aircraft and called to notify air traffic control. While the flight crew were declaring an emergency, the Land Rover suddenly began accelerating towards the aircraft, heading directly towards the inboard engine on the right-hand side of the plane. The vehicle impacted this engine, which was still running at high speed. The resultant collision severely damaged the aircraft's engine. The hijacker, seemingly unharmed, jumped out of the vehicle and began to run away from the accident scene. Inexplicably, he then turned around and approached the aircraft again. He had thrown away his clothes and was now completely naked. The aircraft's lights were turned fully on to illuminate the scene and help the emergency services find the assailant. In full view of passengers and the crew sitting near the right-wing, the hijacker began smearing himself with grease from the stricken Land Rover. As the witnesses sat absolutely horrified at what was unfolding before them, he then climbed onto the roof of the vehicle. He launched himself into the aircraft's number three engine.

Now a two-hundred-and-fifty-pound man throwing himself into a 747's engine is never going to end well. The poor people watching from in front and behind the engine were unwilling witnesses to just what an RB 2-11 jet engine can do to a human being. I shall leave the thought there. Many of those unfortunate eyewitnesses had to undergo much-needed counselling after such a shocking incident. Although deeply traumatised, the crew's training kicked in, and they did a magnificent job of getting everyone off the aircraft, which had now become a crime scene. Of course, this flight and our subsequent return flight back to Gatwick were cancelled.

An incredible epilogue to this tragic incident took place over the next few days. The deceased hijacker was suspected of having been in a relationship with another man. This was the height of the AIDS pandemic. The local engineers at Port of Spain refused to work on the damaged engine until all the human remains had been removed and the engine thoroughly cleaned. The cleaning teams also refused to work on the engine until the remains and bodily fluids had been removed.

Now, I am not sure that I would have been brave or strong enough to volunteer, but the flight crew did just that and offered to clean the engine. The crew all deserved medals as far as I was concerned for what they did. They removed all human body parts, and thoroughly jet washed the engine the next day. The engineers then worked on the damaged engine, and eventually, the aircraft left Port of Spain. My crew and I spent a sad day in Antigua and brought the next service home.

Another heart-breaking story involved one of our lovely cabin crew. We were on a six-day trip to Barbados. She had got married on the day before we left London and had her new husband with her. They had just bought a new house and, to save money, were using the trip as their honeymoon. Luckily, we had a comfy seat for the bridegroom, and he sat on the flight deck for the approach and landing into Barbados. This was pre-9/11 when we could still invite people to join us for the landing.

As soon as we arrived at the hotel, the happy couple ran straight to the beach to swim in the beautiful Caribbean sea. There were a series of gentle waves lapping onto the golden sandy beach. The bridegroom dived straight into an oncoming wave. The beach line was very shallow, and tragically, he hit a sandbank and instantly broke his neck. He was paralysed from the neck down. We took them both home six days later.

There were, of course, many lighter moments. We often flew to Nassau, where we stayed on the aptly named Paradise Island. The hotel was on the beach and very welcoming. There was also a beautiful golf course on the island, where I often played. On one of the holes, if you wandered too far off the fairway, you met a hazard unlike any I had ever come across before. I had heard rumours of this particular hazard but did not believe the stories. After one especially wayward shot, I was about to discover that the rumours were true. I waded into the undergrowth, looking for my ball. All thoughts of this rumoured hazard were the furthest thing from my mind. Pushing back a large bush, I came face to face with what I had assumed to be just a myth. Staring straight back at me was a tiger, a huge, very much alive, tiger. As you can imagine, all thoughts of my lost golf ball quickly disappeared, something I now very much wanted to do myself. We looked at each other for a split second before he let out an enormous roar. Well, that was it as far as I was concerned. I was prepared to give him the benefit of the doubt as far as friendliness was concerned. Still, after that outburst, he had lost any chance of obtaining my friendship.

I simply turned and fled. No golf ball is that valuable. Unbelievably, this really happened. Afterwards, I learnt that the tiger was kept securely in a compound beside the golf course. He was the star in a magic show in one of the newly built gigantic American hotels. Similar hotels had begun to spring up all over Nassau. Paradise Island eventually became a building plot for Atlantis, a huge Disney-type hotel and theme park. The golf course was destroyed and replaced with artificial water features and rides. Paradise had indeed been lost and replaced by a commercial, concrete jungle. I hope one of the diggers had its blades broken by my lost golf ball.

Another favourite way to spend the day was to charter a local boat to take the entire crew to Rose Island, a thirty-minute ride away. Chuck and his wife, who were ably helped by their son, Gary, owned the boat. Eighteen of us would turn up to be warmly greeted by name. We were such regular customers. The boat would be full of beer, rum punches, wine and the most beautiful food ready to be barbecued on the white sandy beaches that awaited us. Rose Island is protected, and only local boats with a special licence were permitted to land there. The whole place is idyllic. No one is allowed to live there. Those of a certain age may remember advertisements for the Bounty chocolate bar and its taste of paradise. These were filmed on Rose Island. On calm days, we moored just off the sandy beach. On windy days, we moored in a sheltered bay on the other side of the island and walked across to the beach. This particular day was windy, and so we moored in the bay. Half of the crew decided to head straight to the beach, whilst the rest decided a little snorkelling would be fun.

The flight engineer, Geordie King, a good friend, dived in and disappeared behind a headland. Meanwhile, I decided that it would be wrong of me to allow the crew to drink the rum before I had checked that it was up to the usual standard. And so, very unselfishly, I opened the first bottle for a bit of tasting. I'm good like that. Our intrepid engineer returned a few moments later and placed some beautiful conch shells on the boat's table. Of course, the crew were enamoured, holding these beautiful objects up to the sun and receiving the most spectacular colour reflections as a result.

Well, this had definitely thrown the gauntlet down as far as I was concerned. No engineer was going to out snorkel me. And so, putting my rum down and grabbing a mask and snorkel, I set out to out-conch my friend. I slipped into the water unnoticed as the crew carried on admiring the engineer's catch. Remembering the direction, he had taken, I thought I would go around the other headland. There were bound to be better conches there, I thought to myself. The water was not deep, no more than six or seven feet, and so I swam along on the surface, looking down, hoping to see something that looked like a conch. This strategy did not seem to be working well, and I began to regret leaving my rum half drunk. The thought of that drink persuaded me to turn around and head back. I felt discouraged but was ready to concede defeat when I thought I would have one more try. Seeing a large rock formation, I swam towards it. Noticing a small overhang, I took a deep breath and dived downwards to explore what was on the other side.

When you get a terrible shock, the first thing most people do is take a sharp intake of breath ready to fuel your fight or flight reflex. This works very well on land. However, it is not such a good reflex when you are underwater holding your breath. Staring at me was a shark, not just any old shark but a Tiger shark, probably one of the deadliest sharks in the world. And he was a big devil. After swallowing a good portion of Caribbean seawater, I did my best not to panic. At least with the land tiger, I had previously met on the golf course, I was on land and could run. Here, I was in Mr Shark's territory, and there was no way I was turning my back on him and trying to outswim him. I reverted to what I was best at when faced with an insurmountable problem. I did nothing. I simply froze and floated gently to the surface, six feet above me. I kept watching him all the time. If he attacked, I had a plan to punch him in the nose. He may have got a tasty supper, but he would have a swollen nose. Once on the surface, I remained deathly still, not moving a muscle. If he had not noticed me or had just eaten a tourist for lunch, I may just get away with this, I thought to myself.

And so, I just floated, staring at my adversary. It would be either him or me. I knew where my money lay, and I wasn't feeling lucky! My mind began to drift to the old Jacques Cousteau ocean programmes that I had enjoyed so much as a child. I clearly remembered old Jacques saying that sharks had to swim to breathe. The water flowing over their gills provided the oxygen they needed to survive, which is why a shark never stops swimming. Well, my shark has definitely not been swimming for at least five minutes. Relief began to flood through me as I realised, that the beast I was looking at, was dead.

My courage returned, aided by the rum I had previously downed. I decided to dive down once again for a closer look. Down I went until I was a few feet from the shark's nose. There was not a bit of tourist but a broken fishing line hanging from the corner of his mouth. The poor shark had obviously put up one hell of a fight trying to free itself. It had succeeded but had died in the process. This was a beautiful creature, and as he was now no longer a threat, I felt sorry for him. I floated back to the surface and began to swim back to the boat. Suddenly, I stopped. I had no conch shell to show my prowess as a snorkeler, but surely a dead shark would outdo a simple conch. And so, a plan began to form in my slightly rum-affected brain.

I returned to the shark and began to drag him into shallower water. It was sad to abuse him in this way, but why waste a good shark? Now, if you have ever dragged a dead shark anywhere, you will know that its skin is incredibly abrasive, a little like a cat's tongue but much worse. A shark uses its skin to brush past potential prey to see if it bleeds. If it does, it is suppertime. Well, I had been dragging this shark for about ten minutes before I sighted our boat. Once I got close enough, I started to shout for help and began wrestling my dead opponent. Apparently, this looked incredibly realistic from the crew's point of view, especially as I was bleeding from where the shark's skin had touched mine. Whilst most of the team, including the boat's crew, simply screamed in horror, the flight engineer, Geordie, dived in and swam towards me. What bravery, what courage that man had damn him! Sadly, it was wasted on an idiot pilot. Before he could reach me, I stood up and pretended to kill the shark with a punch to its throat. By the time he reached me, the shark was dead. Well, it was dead before the fight, but I wasn't going to tell him that after all his selfless bravery. Between us, we managed to get the shark back to the boat, where I was greeted as an all-conquering hero. The conch shells were forgotten as everyone was desperate to know how I had killed the savage deep-sea monster. My wounds were carefully tended to, and I was offered more rum to soothe my nerves. I was everyone's hero. It was a wonderful feeling. I had never been anyone's hero before.

I simply could not stop myself from eventually bursting out with laughter. I admitted the whole deception whilst heaping praise on my fearless friend. There are few brave enough people to jump off a boat to help someone being attacked by a shark. After he had finished hitting me, we became friends again. The rest of the crew were now making their way back to the boat. So once again, Mr Shark and I returned to the water, unseen by the other part of the crew. Once they were safely onboard, I repeated my fake shark fight. To the utter horror of the new arrivals, half the crew simply turned their backs and said that I deserved everything I got. There were screams and panic as I appeared to be losing my life-or-death fight. Suddenly, once again, I stood up and killed the already dead beast for the second time. As the crew celebrated, Geordie simply remarked that he had wanted the shark to win. After everything was revealed for the second time, we relaxed on the boat. We made short work of the rum and fabulous food available.

A booze cruise boat set anchor next to our boat as we were packing up to leave. Suddenly, we were surrounded by snorkelers who obviously had no right to be there. So, we did what any legally licensed group of people would do; we threw a shark at them. I had never seen so many snorkels move so quickly in an absolute panic. Once again, I dived in and did my shark fight routine. This time, the rather more gullible audience was left with the impression that I had really killed a shark to save them. I simply said that we were British, and that is what any British person would do. To this day, in some tourist folklore, there are probably stories still circulating about the bravery of the British. I just hope they never read this book.

Life on the Beach Fleet continued up until the late 1990s. We were a small community compared to our Heathrow counterparts. We got to know each other, which was much more challenging to do at Heathrow. There, two pilots could be on the same fleet for over twenty years and never fly together. Each time I report for a flight at Heathrow, even to this day, it's a little like your first day at a new job. You literally could have never seen any of the twenty other crew members before. At Gatwick, things were very different, we all knew each other, and if there was a face we didn't recognise, we would do our very best to make them as welcome as possible. Flying can be a very, very lonely job. In those days, trips could last over three weeks. If a crew member did not socialise, spending that amount of time in a hotel room, week after week, trip after trip, month after month, and year after year could be dire. Life can become very lonely, especially if that crew member also lives alone. At Gatwick, we seemed somehow to innately appreciate and understand this. We did our very best to involve everyone in the activities we arranged. If someone was continually absent, another crew member would check to see if they were alright. This rarely happened at Heathrow, probably as the crews rarely flew many times together. Over the years, there, very sadly, have been occasions where crew members have taken their own lives. Flying can be a very tough career choice.

As the 1990s drew to a close and the new millennium approached, the decision was to close down the 747-Beach Fleet at Gatwick. Flights would still operate from Gatwick, but they would be flown by Heathrow crews. All Gatwick 747 pilots would become Heathrow based. We would be flying with the grown-ups from now on.

We were all devastated. Not one single pilot wanted to fly from Heathrow. We had all sacrificed the lucrative trips at Heathrow to fly with people we knew and liked. We had put so much time and effort into making Gatwick a commercial success. Now, the senior Heathrow pilots could simply bid for our routes and the premium trips they had on offer at Heathrow. Sadly, there was nothing that could be done, the decision had been made, and we were given very short notice that we would fly out of Heathrow from now on. This was particularly difficult for me personally. I was by far the most junior 747 captain in the company. Each month a list of trips was published, and like a feeding frenzy at the zoo, we all tried to gobble up the best bits. The most senior pilot in the company got every trip he wanted. The most junior, me, got what was left. This was not a problem at Gatwick as all the trips were good. I even enjoyed the occasional Lagos trip. Life would be very different from now on. I would never get the chance to fly to the most popular destinations. The Caribbean would be replaced by the Congo. Seychelles would be replaced by Chicago in the middle of winter. My halcyon days were coming to an end. Life was going to be very different from now on.

My very last flight was to position the last of our Gatwick 747s to Heathrow. Talk about rubbing it in, I thought. Even worse, a party, 'The Sunset of the Beach Fleet', was arranged at a local hotel that evening. My flight was due to depart at seven o'clock in the evening and it was unlikely I would be back in time to say goodbye to all my friends and colleagues. The flight itself took only a few minutes. No sooner had we raised the landing gear than we were lowering it again for landing. We taxied to a remote stand at Heathrow and shut the last of our Gatwick jumbos down. Even the aircraft looked sad and lonely,

I felt a little guilty at leaving an old friend all alone at a strange airport.

It was now past nine in the evening. I had been hoping to get back to the hotel before the party finished at eleven. Typically, no one was there to meet us at Heathrow, let alone drive us back to Gatwick. Eventually, we managed to flag down a passing crew bus, which took us to the main terminal. Another hour had slipped by, damn. Finally, a taxi arrived, and we were on our way to Gatwick, although sadly, it was now nearly eleven o'clock. I had missed the party. I decided to pop in any way to see if there were any guests left. I went to reception and asked where the Beach Fleet party was being held. I was told that it had now finished, but I was welcome to go and see if there was anyone left. I was still in uniform. I had no time to change. Walking down a corridor, I found the hall where the party had been held. Opening the door, I was so disappointed to see the room in darkness. Everyone had gone home. I turned to leave when suddenly every light in the room was turned on, they had waited for me! What a way to say goodbye to the Beach Fleet.

Chapter 20

The Day the World Stopped

I suddenly found myself walking the streets of Detroit rather than the golden beaches of the Caribbean. I felt slightly sorry for myself, missing the camaraderie of Gatwick. I now flew with strangers, not friends.

Reporting for the first time at Heathrow, I literally knew nobody on the crew. I was definitely the new boy. It was like the first day at a new school; I did not know where to go and what to do. I now had to allow at least two, sometimes three hours, to drive to work around the dreaded M25 motorway. The only traffic jam I had encountered on my way to Gatwick was the occasional farm tractor. That journey never took more than twenty minutes. Allowing three hours of travel time at peak periods made my working day much more arduous. The three-hour drive added to the one-hour thirty-minute pre-flight brief was a long start to the day. I could easily then have a twelve-hour flight. which meant that I would have been at work for over sixteen hours as I would make a final approach to land at my destination. As pilots, we were now flying many more hours each week, each month and each year. As I was now one of the most junior captains on the fleet, I had almost no choice of where and when I flew.

Spending Christmas at home became an impossible dream. I would endure each Christmas in Lagos or Bangladesh, away from my wife and two young sons. I knew that eventually, would make my way up the seniority ladder. However, at this moment in time, that seemed a long way off. Ultimately, common sense prevailed in the powers that be. The company realised that while some pilots were home every holiday, others never saw their families over the festive season.

Consequently, the rules were changed and each pilot was awarded a point for each Christmas he was required to work. The pilots with the highest number of points were given the first choice over subsequent Christmas periods. Sadly, for me, this was not to be applied retrospectively. By the time this rule was fully implemented, I was senior enough to be amongst those pilots at home anyway. As we all started from zero points after a couple of Christmases at home, I again found myself awaiting Santa Claus in some faraway country. Not only did my children begin to not believe in Father Christmas, but they also started to doubt my existence too.

The only saving grace for me was that I was still flying my beloved aircraft. I always felt the same thrill of excitement as we walked towards that magnificent aircraft. My working life was much more challenging now and although I knew nobody on the crew, I still had my amazing aircraft to play with.

The new millennium was fast approaching, technology was racing ahead at an almost incomprehensible speed. The new generation of 747s was being delivered at an ever-increasing rate. Their fleet size had overtaken the Classic 747 fleet. With their arrival, the best routes were being transferred to these new aircraft and their fortunate pilots. From my perspective, this meant that there was even less chance to fly to the more popular destinations. We would check in late to see the 747-400 crews preparing for their departures to exotic Cape Town, Singapore and Hong Kong. At the same time, we would be deciding how much fuel we required for Luanda, Cairo and Kano. We used to refer to the 747-400 crews as the grown-ups, and in return, they did not refer to us at all. We were yesterday's news.

I still loved to fly with a flight engineer. For me, it was the perfect set-up. If a problem occurred in flight, the co-pilot would fly the aircraft, the flight engineer would run the checklist and I, as the captain, could manage the entire operation. Happy days indeed. Despite this, I knew that the days of the Classic 747 were numbered. Technology was quickly catching up with and overtaking our version of the 747. One day in the not-too-distant future, it would make our aircraft redundant. As we prepared for our departure for Mumbai, formerly known as Bombay, nobody could have possibly guessed that today would be that day.

The flight out was uneventful. Eight hours after taking off from Heathrow, we were being vectored onto our final approach for the westerly runway at Mumbai. A ridge of hills lies close to the runway, and it is vitally important that the aircraft is fully stable as it crosses these hills. If your rate of descent is too high, you can easily set off the terrain warning system as you attempt to regain the correct flight path. The sound of the dreaded robotic words 'TERRAIN, TOO LOW, PULL UP, PULL UP', will be triggered. This ensured a go-around and a subsequent visit to the chief pilot's office. Fortunately, we made both a perfect approach and a smooth landing.

As always, when landing in India, your senses are aroused even before you touch down. Landing is always completed in poor visibility as local cooking and traffic fumes clog the air. Personally, I have always loved visiting India. There is nothing quite like it anywhere else in the world. We slowly taxied towards our gate, again the poor visibility making even this usually straightforward task a little more complicated. After leaving the aircraft, it always took ages to go through all the formalities. There were three separate books to fill out. We had to list everything we had with us, watches, cameras, jewellery, and other valuable items. This had to be entered longhand in a giant ledger. Somewhere in India, there must be massive vaults where these ledgers are kept for no reason that I can fathom out. Despite India being at the forefront of technology, we still have to fill out these forms.

Therefore, after a long drive to the hotel, we felt that we deserved a cold beer. The hotel itself was in the city centre. It provided luxurious accommodation within a sea of human deprivation. From my five-star bedroom, I would look out onto a scene of sheer poverty. Young children were playing on open sewer pipes whilst their parents prepared supper in a tent. Such a contrast from where I stood in my air-conditioned five-star luxury. The sun was setting, and the sounds, sights, and smells of India were intoxicating. As I closed my curtains, I turned and headed for the shower. After a quick drenching and a change of clothes, I was more than ready to meet my two colleagues in the club lounge for that long-awaited drink. The lounge itself was in the style of an old-fashioned Gentleman's club. Deep leather armchairs in abundance and white-coated waiters at the beck and call of guests. The three of us settled ourselves down to enjoy our Tiger beers which were served with an array of irresistible snacks. Our chairs were arranged around a small table which was constantly filled with even more delicious temptations. As Oscar Wilde once said, "I can resist everything except temptation." So, I continued to help myself to all that was on offer. Behind my head, there was a large television screen silently showing the American news channel CNN when we had entered. I was pleased the volume had been muted; I preferred to hear what my colleagues were saying rather than the usual brash voice of an American news presenter.

Suddenly, a guest from another table stood up and rushed across the room to turn the television to maximum volume. The three of us just stared at him as he began gesturing at the screen. He was joined by his friends, who all started shouting and swearing at the same time. I turned to see what all the fuss was about. They had clearly changed channels as the screen was now full of pictures from a disaster movie. There was a large skyscraper on fire with a picture of an aircraft crashing into it. It looked very realistic, but I was unsure why these people reacted so dramatically to a film.

We all just stared at the screen as the truth slowly hit us. The guests on the other table were American bankers based in the World Trade Centre. They were literally watching a terrorist attack happening in real-time next to their own offices. Fortunately, they were based in the South Tower, not the North Tower, the one showing on the screen. And then, the second aircraft hit the South Tower.

We all sat, transfixed in absolute disbelief and horror, unable to tear ourselves away from the scenes unfolding in front of us. The Americans were traumatised, and we were all in shock as we watched people jumping to their deaths from the burning buildings. We wept together as one tower and then the other collapsed. The world as we had known it had ceased to exist. Tomorrow everything was going to be very different.

We finally left our American friends to grieve as we returned to our rooms. I tried to call London for an update on our flight home the following day. Unsurprisingly, I was unable to contact anyone. The world was in crisis, and we were alone to make our own decisions.

The following day, I called the first officer, flight engineer, and our senior cabin crew member to my room to decide what to do. The flight from London had already been airborne when the attack took place and would land shortly. The question was would it be safe to take the aircraft back to London? A considerable majority of flights worldwide had been cancelled as the airlines and authorities had to make difficult decisions about what to do next. Of course, all flights to the United States had been cancelled as well as many other flights. I had eventually managed to contact London, who had advised me that they would like us to fly back that night, if possible. However, the final decision was mine alone.

The flight that night had been fully booked with over four hundred passengers. Now, with the entire world stunned and at a standstill and the possibility of more planned terrorist attacks, understandably, half of our passengers had cancelled their flight with us that night. That left us with nearly two hundred people who still needed to fly to London despite everything that had happened. One of my main concerns was the welfare of the crew. Our crew consisted of a good mix of young and older crew members. All of them had undoubtedly been affected to some degree by these events. The most essential consideration had to be the safety of the aircraft and everyone on board. Alarmingly, all the aircraft involved in the atrocities had suffered a breach of the flight deck. The hijackers had managed to enter the flight deck, overpower the flight crew, and fly the aircraft to its target. Our priority, therefore, that night was to ensure that nobody could access the flight deck except the crew. Of course, we were very fortunate that the flight deck of the 747 is on the upper deck. The only passenger cabin on the upper deck was a club class section that held about thirty passengers. We decided to close this cabin to passengers and station one of the burlier flight attendants at the base of stairs to prevent unauthorised access. We would then position another crew member at the top of the stairs to act as a second deterrent and who could alert the flight crew, should an attack occur. Finally, our flight engineer, a gentleman you would not like to come across in a dark alley, would guard the flight deck door with the aircraft's crash axe. Hopefully, this would give us a very secure way of protecting the plane. All present agreed to operate home on this basis. I found out many years later that the captain of Air Force One, another Boeing 747, had implemented precisely the same precautions. Apparently, even the President of the United States could not access the upper deck on his own aircraft.

I then called each cabin crew member individually to ask if they would volunteer to fly home that night. I allowed everyone to decline anonymously should they have any concerns or were too upset to operate. Everyone on the crew agreed to fly home.

At the airport that night, I spoke to the local duty manager and told him our plan to close the upper deck to passengers that night. He quickly became animated and informed me that this was not possible as the upper deck was fully booked. Passengers have always tried to book the upper deck on a 747 as it resembles a private jet rather than an airliner. It is the cabin of choice for most club class passengers. Again, I politely asked him to change the seats reserved upstairs to a club cabin on the lower deck. He flatly refused. I was taken aback by this attitude, especially at such a time of heightened risk. And the poignancy of the recent events only added to my dismay at his remarks. I was further shocked when he accused me of using the upper deck cabin for a crew rest area. Containing my anger as best I could, I simply turned away from him and approached the check-in desk. Without delay, I asked the agent to please call the local area manager, the most senior manager in Mumbai. After a quick discussion, I handed the phone to the squirming duty manager. The upper deck was now closed.

During the flight home, everything went according to plan. Two crew members guarded the stairs at all times. The duty manager in Mumbai had actually given me a good idea. I told the senior cabin crew member that they could take their rest periods on the upper deck rather than the crew seats at the rear of the aircraft. Our flight engineer was very subdued on the way home. He was far from his usual cheerful self.

I asked him if he was feeling well. Suddenly, I felt guilty that I had not asked him privately if he was fit to operate home. I had made the cardinal error of just assuming he was fit to fly. After a short pause, he admitted to me that this would be his last flight. I was astounded. I knew that he had many years ahead of him and that he was an excellent operator. Why then, would he give up his career? He explained that he was convinced that the Classic 747s would be grounded when we landed back in

London. No other aircraft in the British Airways fleet had flight engineers on board, and therefore, he would lose his job. As much as I tried to console him and reassure him that this was highly unlikely, his mood darkened as we approached London.

We made a standard approach and landing and taxied onto our stand on a beautiful late summer's morning. After all our passengers had disembarked, I stood up and was about to go downstairs to thank the crew when a passenger came up the stairs. This was against everything we had previously agreed on, and I tensed myself for what was to come. The look on my face must have alerted the passenger. He very quickly produced his identity card showing him to be the Heathrow duty manager. He asked me to return to the flight deck with him. The co-pilot and engineer were still performing their post-flight duties and were as surprised as I had been to see a civilian enter the flight deck. The news he brought us was devastating in its own right. All Classic 747s were to be immediately grounded before being disposed of. The flight crew were also grounded and told to go home and wait to hear from the company. No thank you, for bringing the aircraft and passengers safely home under such difficult circumstances, no apology, no reassurances as to our futures, just a curt dismissal. I saw the flight engineer's hand move towards the crash axe. I ushered the duty manager out of harm's way as quickly as I could. Our flight engineer had been correct. We were possibly all out of a job; however, he never flew again.

Chapter 21

A New World; A New Aircraft

Arriving home that morning, I entered quietly by the back door. It was still early. Despite the early hour, Liz and the boys were waiting in the kitchen for my return. Of course, they too had been deeply affected by the events of the past two days, especially as I had been away for the whole time. Very little was said as we just held each other for a few moments. The terror acts had a profound psychological effect on everyone. Even today, most people remember exactly where they were when they first heard the awful news. As the boys got ready for school, I went to bed and tried to sleep. Memories of the horrific events, the stress of flying home, the uncertainty of my own future all weighed heavily on my mind, making sleep impossible.

    I had just learned that I was a pilot on a fleet that now no longer existed within the company. Although I had been promised a course onto the 747-400 later that year, in the meanwhile, there was no longer an aircraft I could fly. My future was very much in the balance. The company could not afford to pay me to sit at home. The public demand to fly had been critically reduced to the point that the airlines were grounding aircraft and making their pilots redundant. I was still a relatively junior captain. As I was no longer qualified to fly any British Airways aircraft, I understandably felt very vulnerable if redundancies were announced. I had all the trappings of a middle-class professional. Seemingly in safe employment, I had taken out a large mortgage and had two children at a fee-paying private school. I was always just a paycheck away from bankruptcy as my monthly wage barely covered my outgoings. Things were very tight financially. The thought that I could soon be made redundant played heavily on my mind as I tried to get the sleep my body so desperately craved.

I awoke a few hours later with what I thought was a lightbulb moment. If flying was to be taken away from me, I would return to my pre-flying passion, cars. Before I started to fly, I had made a little money buying old cars at a local auction, repairing them, and selling them at the next auction. I had made a few good deals and one very poor purchase which effectively ended my car salesman career. A little bit of advice, never buy a 1970s Italian sports car. They may look fabulous. They may even seem like a fantastic purchase right up until the point you try to drive one!

The decades had eroded the disappointment of failure, and I now looked back on my short career in the automotive industry through rose-tinted spectacles. The memory of the excitement I felt, exploring row upon row of vehicles flooded back. The majority of the cars at that time, twenty odd years ago, had that heady smell of leather and wood, an intoxicating combination. As long as I stayed away from Italian sports cars, what could possibly go wrong? I was about to find out.

However, the first thing on my mind was to find a way to pay the school fees. Both the boys were at a critical stage in their education. A change of school would be devastating for them and us. A house is just a house, and although we all loved where we lived, we would downsize rather than take the boys out of school. That morning, I rang the local estate agent and organised for the house to go on the market. Once that had been done, I felt a little better, although the last time I was in a dire financial situation, I had only myself to look after. This time, I had my family to look after. I could not simply buy a car for thirty pounds and sleep in it if necessary.

I decided to go ahead with my new venture. With a good friend, I set up and registered a new company, Importacar. At this point in time, the country was established and happy to be a part of the European Union. The exchange rate between the British pound and the European currency, the euro, stood at a very healthy rate of 1/1.60 to the pound. This meant that a British buyer could buy a British, or indeed European, car cheaper in Europe than in the UK. Quite legally, you could place an order with a dealership in Europe and then import the vehicle into the UK without any tariffs. This way, you could easily save thousands of pounds on a new car. Few people actually took this option, mainly due to the complexity of ordering from a foreign dealership and the uncertainty of the exchange rates. This new company, Importacar, would take that responsibility away from the customer and deliver their new car to their doorstep for a fixed fee. Potentially, this could be a high-volume business and profitable for both the company and the client.

We went ahead and set the company up, bought all the advertising material, and opened up an office. Everything looked excellent. We spent many hours, days and weeks, setting up our website, a relatively new concept at the time. Finally, we were all set to go. Importacar would be the new kid on the automotive block. We were all ready and poised to take our first orders, and then the value of the pound collapsed. Overnight the exchange rate dropped from 1.60 euros to the pound to 1.40, then down even further to 1.20. The pound never recovered to its original value, effectively wiping out the monetary advantage of importing a car. The company struggled for a while until we decided to close it down. I should have bought an Italian sports car instead. At least, that looked nice.

And so, it was back to my day job, well, day and mostly night job. The complete termination of the Classic 747 fleet had now been confirmed. All the crews were sitting at home awaiting news of their fate. Very sadly, the flight engineers were either made redundant or offered a ground job. A very select few were offered the chance to retrain as pilots. Personally, I felt that they should have been given that opportunity. Their wealth of operational experience was invaluable. Tragically, one flight engineer and his instructor were lost during a training flight. The repercussions of 9/11 were responsible for another two lives lost.

Personally, I was now extremely concerned about my own and my family's future. Although the house was on the market, there had been little or no interest from potential buyers. The economy was still suffering the shock waves of that wicked act of terrorism. Few people felt confident enough to even consider moving home in this current climate of unease. The only option for us was to drastically reduce our monthly outgoings, which meant withdrawing our sons from their private school. Fortunately, we had already paid for the current term, which would end at Christmas. Come the New Year, they would have to start at a new school. I felt that I had let them down. Both boys had wanted to follow their friends into the comprehensive school system after finishing primary school. It had been Liz and I that had insisted they attend a private school, and now that they had both settled into their new school. We were now telling them that they would have to leave. With great regret, I made an appointment with the headmistress to arrange for them to change schools. And then the telephone rang.

I had been expecting, or more accurately, dreading, a phone call from British Airways. There could be only one reason they were calling me, and it was not to give me a flight. With the customary salutation, "This is British Airways," I waited with growing dread for the next sentence which would effectively end my career. Instead, I was asked where I was? This really wrong-footed me, and of course, I replied that I was at home in the process of arranging new schools for my children. I was then asked why was I at home when I should be attending the first day of ground school for my 747-400 conversion course? I was being given a dressing down for failing to report for a course that I had not been notified of. There had obviously been a mistake in assigning me the course in the first place.

I was about to plead my innocence when it occurred to me that if I admitted that I had not been notified, then they may realise that they had made a mistake. In what I thought was a rare flash of genius, I immediately apologised for getting my dates mixed up and assured them I would be there within the hour. Sprinting upstairs to change, I was leaving rubber on the driveway two minutes later. I have rarely driven to work at such speed. I may have even gone slightly over the speed limit once or twice. Despite being late, I managed to sign in. Breathing a massive sigh of relief, I sat down with my colleagues. For the first time in nearly fifteen years, I found myself on a conversion course. All I had to do now was pass it, and the boys could stay in school, and we could stay in our house, no pressure then.

Up until this point in my career, the term EFIS, or Electronic Flight Instrument System, had been something I had just heard about but had never seen. I was now a very latecomer to this not so new technology. Every aircraft I had flown up until this point had the old clockwork type flying instruments. We had an artificial horizon, which was very useful in keeping the aircraft the right way up when flying in clouds. We had an airspeed indicator which, well, I guess it's pretty obvious what it did. We had a vertical speed indicator that let the pilot know how quickly the aircraft was climbing or descending. Finally, we had an altimeter, which, if set correctly, would tell you how high the plane was. With these very basic instruments plus a few navigation aids, we flew our old jumbos all over the world. Now all those familiar and trusty old friends had been replaced with a television screen. My eyes were used to scanning all of the primary instruments; height, speed, attitude, all had to be carefully monitored. Concentrate on one instrument for a second too long, and the other instruments would sulk. Quickly, you would find yourself in trouble. Now, all this complex information was displayed on a single television screen. You still had to monitor all of the parameters, but it was much easier having the information in one place. Well, it was more manageable once you got the hang of it!

My other big problem with this new aircraft was that Mr Boeing had taken away my beloved colleague, the flight engineer. Not only would I now have to find the best places to have a beer down route, but I would have to read the checklist and try to diagnose any problems that occurred inflight by myself. Therefore, it was with some trepidation that after completing the ten days of ground school, I stood waiting for my first simulator session on this new technology aircraft.

We had ten four-hour simulator details to complete before being set free on the paying public. I was very pleasantly surprised at just how quickly I took to this new EFIS system. The aircraft flew in precisely the same way as my Classic jumbo. I was beginning to relax, well, I was, until the instructor started to introduce the first of many technical faults that we would have to contend with during the course.

As red warning lights flashed on the instrument panels in front of me and overhead, I simply reverted to what I knew best. Firstly, I handed over control of the aircraft to the first officer. After I was happy that he was fully in control and knew which way to fly, I turned to the flight engineer to ask him what had gone wrong and what he intended to do about it. Once these two tasks were completed, I could relax and revert to my management role, which is a euphemism for doing very little at all. Some captains simply barked orders at the flight engineer. I preferred a more sensitive human touch and always turned in my seat to make eye contact with the person sitting behind me. Putting on my best, 'please help out here' face, I turned to speak to the flight engineer. Instead of a friendly face, keen to help out, I found myself staring directly into the eyes of a very unfriendly examiner. I had completely forgotten that my engineer had been replaced by computers. These computers were causing all these red lights to flash. My slightly pathetic request for the examiner to complete the checklist for me received the disdain it deserved. Not a flicker of a smile crossed his face. This was not going well at all.

Turning back to face the brightly lit Christmas tree that used to be the instrument panel, I meekly leaned forward and produced the comprehensive book that served as the emergency checklist. Part of me still wanted to pass it back to the non-existent flight engineer, in a sort of muscle memory. Instead, I opened it and desperately tried to find the right page, a page that would both solve all our problems and save my career at the same time. I always knew that I admired the engineer's expertise in his job. I was now faced with doing that job myself, and my admiration rose at the same pace as my despair. Why were there so many pages and so much that could and would go wrong? I found myself having to run two and three separate checklists at the same time. I began to run out of fingers as I tried to keep one page open whilst referring to another page. It didn't help that I have rather large fingers, great for some things, not so good at holding the various checklists open at three different pages. All the time, I could feel the icy stare of the instructor boring into the back of my head. I was struggling to keep on top of the many system failures we were presented with.

I had lost track of at least two of the three pages I had been reading; I had to do something, or the situation could quickly get out of control. Sometimes, if things are not going well, it is best to break the cycle and start again. Deciding that this was such a time, I took back control from the first officer and asked him to look at the checklist. Maybe, he had more nimble fingers. I flew the aircraft and watched as the first officer bent down and produced a number of large, multi-coloured, plastic paper clips. I was mesmerised as I watched him go to one checklist, mark it with a paperclip and move onto the next relevant page. Within a few moments, he had everything neatly separated, and he simply moved from one page to the other with the greatest of ease. Bloody smartass, I uncharitably thought to myself, as I gave him back control and took the checklist back off him with maybe more force than necessary.

Of course, now I had everything marked for me. We completed all the required actions in double quick time. We had the aircraft back on the ground with two engines and a few other essential systems inoperative. Luckily for me, the house, and the kids, the instructor seemed not to have noticed just how close I had come to throwing my toys out of the pram. I never flew without paperclips again. I also gratefully bought my first officer a few beers that night. Luckily, the remainder of the course went smoothly. By the end, I had accepted that I would have to cope with the checklist by myself from now on. Who would have thought that a simple paper clip had managed to replace the flight engineer?

The simulator sessions finally ended. My paperclips and I had managed to convince the examiners that I could manage perfectly well without an engineer. Next, came six flights with a training captain sitting in the co-pilot's seat. All was going according to plan. I was getting good reports back from each flight, and then came the final check. Well, I should have realised it was never going to be straightforward. That never seemed to happen to me.

The trip was a delightful, well on paper, enjoyable flight, to Mauritius. We had two days off in paradise before flying back to Gatwick. I now had to do my own walk around the aircraft before each sector. This task had, of course, always been carried out by our now departed flight engineer colleague. As I looked at each part of the aircraft, the training captain asked me detailed questions. This was a bit keen, I thought, but luckily, I managed to bluff my way through. I realised I would have to be very careful with this trainer as he would not make life easy for me. The flight down was very straightforward. The approach into Mauritius is a little tricky as there is a mountain ridge that had to be considered. Best to avoid that, and fortunately, I did. As I unpacked in the hotel room, I was feeling pleased with myself. Just one more flight back to London, as long as I made no silly mistakes, I was back in business. I am sure I fell asleep with a smile on my face, a sure prelude to trouble.

The way the schedule worked was that the aircraft arrived in the early morning in Mauritius. Due to landing restrictions in London, the aircraft would sit on the tarmac in Mauritius and depart in the evening for a night flight back to Gatwick. As usual, the weather in Mauritius was beautiful; well, for the first two days, it was beautiful. The day before our flight home, the weather forecasters predicted that a typhoon, which was moving towards Africa until that point, had decided to change course and was now heading directly towards Mauritius. The flight home the next evening was now looking anything but straightforward. The latest forecast had the typhoon hitting the island the following evening, at precisely the time we were due to depart. Instead of joining the rest of the crew for an evening meal, I thought it wise to stay in my room and have a good look at the flying manual, especially the chapter describing adverse weather. There were also all the limits on wind strength and crosswinds to memorise. Not being great at the memory bit, I studiously wrote down everything I would need for the following evening's flight. Once I was satisfied that I had prepared as conscientiously as possible, I switched the lights out and tried to get some sleep. Tomorrow was going to be a long day.

Sleep was elusive. I kept thinking of all the things that had to be considered departing during a typhoon. The most critical decision that I would have to consider was, of course, would it be safe to depart at all? Everything I did and said would be put under a microscope by the examiner. There would be no help from that quarter. All decisions would be mine and mine alone. He would only intervene if he considered the safety of the aircraft was in doubt. Eventually, despite a blinking red light on the phone beside my bed, I fell asleep. Whoever had left me a message could wait until the morning. What could possibly be that important?

What seemed like just a few moments later, the phone began to ring. Sleepily, I opened one eye and peered at the phone. Who the hell was calling me in the middle of the night? I then noticed sunlight streaming in through a crack in the curtains, so not the middle of the night after all. It was probably someone asking if I wanted to go for breakfast. Best just not to answer, I thought, turning over and trying to go back to sleep. The phone rang again. Sod this, I thought, and as soon as it stopped ringing, I took it off the hook. Rolling over again, I managed to fall back into a deep sleep. Sadly, not for very long as there was suddenly a loud and persistent knocking on my door. This is ridiculous, I thought. Why can't people just go for breakfast by themselves, for goodness sake? Well, I was not going to answer the door, and I put a pillow over my head and tried once again for more sleep.

The next thing I knew, the door was being opened. What the hell was going on? And then, almost like an apparition, a figure appeared at the foot of my bed dressed in a British Airways captain's uniform. Well, this was an interesting dream, I thought to myself. What had I eaten last night to cause hallucinations like this? The vision then had the audacity to ask, in a very impolite manner, what was I doing in bed? Well, by this time, I was fully awake and ready to give as good as I got. What was my examiner doing in my room in the morning when our flight was that evening? Did he not realise that I needed as much sleep as possible? I was about to jump out of bed when I remembered that I usually slept naked. No point in making the old chap jealous as well as angry, I thought to myself. Instead, I drew the sheet up to my chin and asked him just what the hell did he think he was doing in my room?

The standoff continued for a few moments, and then he broke the spell by asking me why I was not downstairs checking out. The rest of the crew were already on the bus. This news certainly took the wind out of my sails. Why were we readying ourselves to leave twelve hours before we were due to depart? Barely containing his anger, he asked me if I had listened to the message left for me last night. His eyes were suddenly fixated on the red flashing light on my telephone, one of my running socks trying and failing to reduce its brightness. He explained that the typhoon was now due to hit the island around lunchtime. The company had brought forward the departure by ten hours. Apparently, all the crew had been notified, and the only person unaware of the change of plan was the captain, me.

Turning on his heel and marching out, he shouted over his shoulder that he would go ahead with the rest of the crew and I should pack as quickly as possible and hitch a ride with the crew bag bus. They would go on ahead without me. Slamming the door, I heard his footsteps receding down the corridor. This was far from the way I had wanted to start my final check flight.

Literally jumping out of bed, I ran around the room, trying to put everything back into my suitcase as quickly as possible. Unfortunately, I had one of those suitcases that were spring-loaded. The moment I opened the lid, the bottom of the case sprung up and deposited the entire contents of my case into every conceivable corner of the room. I am usually able to find about ninety per cent of my belongings in hotel rooms when leaving. This time in my haste, I would be lucky to retrieve fifty per cent. Over the years, I must have left enough clothes in hotel rooms to fill a charity shop.

Trailing clothes down the corridor, I checked out as quickly as possible and ran to the awaiting bag bus. The bus was actually an old truck, with just enough room to squeeze me between the driver and his helper. We set off at high speed. Well, twenty miles an hour was high speed for this vehicle. It was only then that I began to take notice of the weather. It was not raining yet. However, huge, ominous black cloud mountains were all around us, reaching far into the morning sky. The clouds began to merge into an impenetrable black mass that slowly began to obscure the sun. As we approached the airport, morning turned into night as the last rays of the sun were hidden behind this Goliath of a storm. And then it rained. This was not your common or garden old British downpour. This was its nasty, ugly, big brother. The noise the rain made as it hit the truck's roof made conversation impossible. It sounded like a million nails had been blasted on the roof. We pulled up outside the terminal building, and I made a dash for the open doorway. The distance from the truck to the building was no more than twenty feet. By the time I had made it into the safety of the entrance, I looked like I had just swum from the hotel rather than driven. Shaking myself like a dog coming out of a lake, I made my way to the briefing room to meet up with the rest of the crew. All eyes turned to meet me as I left a little puddle of water with each step I took.

Standing at the counter was my nemesis. He looked even more intimidating than the last time I had seen him at the foot of my bed. Trying to break the ice, I asked if he recognised me now with my clothes on. Not even a hint of a smile cracked his scowl. Silently, he passed me a copy of the paperwork and asked what my intentions were. I was tempted to reply, "honourable" but quickly decided against it. I put my hand into my pocket and fiddled with my paper clips. They couldn't replace my flight engineer now. I examined the printed weather conditions and put them alongside the aircraft's limits, which I had carefully written down the previous night.

Comparing the two, I announced that the conditions were outside of our limits. Taking this to mean that we would cancel the flight, the examiner informed the ground staff that there would be no flight today. Would he please inform the passengers? The station manager looked crestfallen. All the hotels were fully booked, the passengers would have to stay in the airport until the aircraft departed, whenever that might be. The examiner barked that this was not his problem and started to walk off. I quickly called him back. I had not decided to cancel the flight, I informed him. Instead, we were simply going to wait for a break in the conditions. The main problem was the strength of the wind, especially the crosswind. We could not legally or safely depart until it dropped below our limits, a sixty-five-knot gust with forty knots of crosswind. The examiner informed me, unnecessarily I thought, that the wind speed was far higher than this and I agreed that it was, but I had a plan. I decided that we could legally get everyone onboard, close the doors and wait to see if the wind dropped enough for us to depart. And despite a very disapproving look from the examiner, that's exactly what we did. I put enough fuel on the aircraft to wait on the ground for two hours. If the wind had not dropped by then, we would abandon the flight, and I personally would head straight to the nearest bar. We finally had the engines running, and once the wind dropped to sixty-five knots, we could taxi to the runway, but we could only depart when the crosswind fell below forty knots.

The examiner expressed his doubts, assuring me that the wind would increase rather than decrease. The eye of the storm had yet to arrive. There was a stony silence as we sat there on the stand. The wind strength had indeed increased. The aircraft began to rock slowly from side to side; it felt more like a boat than an aircraft, and I got seasick on boats.

The radio suddenly burst into life. The wind was now sixty knots. Would we like to taxi out to the runway despite the wind being too strong to depart? I immediately accepted their offer, and we slowly moved towards the runway. Once there, I asked if we could enter the runway and wait there, as there were no other aircraft flying that day. Permission was granted. We sat on the runway for another twenty minutes as the wind howled around us. The typhoon would be arriving at any moment. And then it happened; the wind suddenly dropped to thirty knots.

We were cleared for take-off. Seconds later, engines screaming at full power, we tore down the runway away from the approaching storm. As we climbed out, still at full power, I asked for permission to make a non-standard turn to keep me clear of the worst of the weather. The turbulence was terrible, but I had been through worse. Twenty minutes after starting our take-off run, we suddenly burst into the most brilliant sunshine. We were in the clear and on our way home. Looking over my shoulder, I caught a glimpse of the mighty storm as it reached out a huge hand and grabbed the island of Mauritius and shook it like a lion with its prey. I returned my gaze back into the flight deck and wondered if I was about to receive the same treatment.

Instead, I was met by a huge, congratulatory smile, and the examiner gave me a gentle pat on the back. Maybe, he liked me after all, or I had not pulled the bedsheets up quickly enough, and he felt sorry for me. Either way, after landing back in London, I was now a fully qualified 747-400 captain. I never managed to do things the easy way, but at least I managed to succeed in the end.

Chapter 22

Sad Times

The drama of nearly losing my job and then having to convert to a new aircraft was finally over; the difficult decisions narrowly avoided. The memories slowly faded, and I had settled down into flying the 747-400. I was beginning to appreciate just how good the aircraft really was. The original 747-100 aircraft was undoubtedly a good aircraft. However, it did have its drawbacks and quirks. When the 747-200 series came along, Boeing had listened to the pilots' concerns and had produced a much-improved aircraft. We flew both types simultaneously, depending on the routes. I was always disappointed if I had to fly the old 747-100 series. Now, with the 747-400 series, Boeing had surpassed itself. Every minor issue with the earlier series had been addressed, and the new aircraft was outstanding in every aspect. I was totally obsessed and loved every minute spent flying this new aircraft. The 747-400 was the last of the real aircraft, with the pilots still being responsible for everything the plane did. New technology was rearing its head in the aviation world, 'Fly By Wire', a terminology that sent a shiver of apprehension down my back.

The term itself was misleading as all aircraft, from the first Wright Brothers aircraft, of course, fly by wire. The control columns of all aircraft are connected to the flying surfaces by a series of cables. On the larger aircraft, the pilots would not be physically capable of moving these surfaces. For example, the rudder of a 747 is the size of a tennis court. To help the pilot, hydraulic systems aid in moving these surfaces, a little like power steering on your car.

Manufacturers like Airbus decided that their aircraft should have a new layer of protection, provided by computers. They designed their aircraft to be operated by pilots but flown by computers. Wires now carried electrical signals from the pilot's inputs and fed them into the computer. These computers then decided if the information from the pilots was safe and sensible. If they were, the computers would move the control systems in the manner the pilots desired. If the computer decided that the pilots were wrong, they would override them and fly the aircraft. This method works admirably until the point where the pilots are correct and the computer is faulty. I loved the 747 mainly because the pilot still flew the plane. The computers were there only to aid the pilots. With a simple push of a button, the computers could be disconnected.

The other real bonus of the new aircraft was that we were self-sufficient on the flight deck. Since 9/11, the flight deck door was locked from the moment we started the engines until we shut them down at the end of the flight. We had a bulletproof door with a surveillance system entry procedure. In other words, we were now completely isolated from the rest of the crew and passengers. As the flight deck was also in the upper deck, our feeling of isolation was only enhanced. We could leave the flight deck only for clearly defined reasons. On the 747-400, we had a separate bedroom with two bunk beds and a toilet on the flight deck.

On long flights, we had three or sometimes four pilots. We were rightfully christened the en-suite fleet as we had our bedroom and toilet. This was the heyday of the jumbo. Although the newer technology Boeing 777 had been introduced, we were still the dominant aircraft on the majority of the long-haul routes. Everyone wanted to be a part of the 747-400 fleet, and apart from maybe Concorde, there was nowhere else I would have rather been. The only people who were not enamoured with the jumbo were the accountants. The 747 had four very thirsty engines. The newer 777 had only two engines, which were much more efficient than our Rolls Royce RB211 engines. British Airways ceased ordering the new 747s and started to increase their orders for the 777. Still, I was convinced this was a problem for the next generation of pilots. There was no way they could stop flying the jumbo in the near or even distant future. For the first time in a long time, I felt safe and secure in my chosen profession. It was time to relax and enjoy my job. By now, I really should have known better.

I was lying by the hotel's rooftop swimming pool in Los Angeles. I had just been for a long beachside run to Santa Monica, and after a swim, I felt healthy and very relaxed. Life was good. The hotel was situated in Redondo Beach, a fabulous area, made famous by the Beach Boys in their song, *Good Vibrations*. The location was a surfers paradise, and we were in the middle of it all, a stone's throw from the beach. I was gently nodding off when my mobile phone started to ring. Answering it turned out to be one of the biggest mistakes of my life. The pain caused still haunts me every day and will continue to do so for the rest of my life.

As the ringing continued, I stretched out an arm. I tried to find the phone. I had placed it under the sunbed to prevent it from overheating on a beautiful Californian afternoon. Eventually, I held it above my head and squinted in the sunshine to see who was calling me. Using a mobile phone abroad was still very expensive. I rarely made or received calls, preferring to text instead. Something or someone was in trouble. The call was from my elderly father. I answered with a feeling of trepidation and anxiety. This could only be bad news; he was not the type of person to make unnecessary social calls.

At first, I was unsure what he was saying. The connection was poor, and all I could make out were the words, police and argument. My father was not the sort of person you would associate with such terms. What on earth had happened? The connection was getting worse, so I told my father I would call him straight back as soon as I found somewhere with better reception. Putting the phone down, I did not doubt that something was very wrong. Sitting by a crowded pool was probably not the best place to have a difficult conversation. I could just imagine people's reactions as I asked my father why he had been arrested and charged with assault. No, this was a conversation to be had in the privacy of my room. The phone kept ringing as I quickly packed up my belongings and hurried back there. I stopped to tell my co-pilot that we would have to postpone our game of tennis, due to start in a few minutes. I assured him that I would not be long. Sadly, we never played the match.

Once in my room, I checked that I had a good signal and dialled my father's number. The reception was a lot better now, and from the tone of my father's voice, I could tell that his panic had subsided somewhat. He had started to recover from whatever had upset him. However, for him to call me in the first place, whatever had occurred must be important. Listening intently, I lay on the bed as my father tried to explain what had happened. Finally, the events of the past few hours were revealed.

I had a brother, only thirteen months older than me. Still, decades rather than months, had always seemed to separate and divide us throughout our lives. We had never been close. Indeed, animosity from my older brother had just been a fact of life as we grew up together. My father was absent for most of our childhood. Long haul pilots in those days were away for weeks rather than days. We also had a much younger sister. My mother tried, but mostly failed, to bring up her three children. Sadly, she sought refuge in a bottle for her unhappiness and isolation. She spent long periods in an alcoholic institution during our childhood. Our family life was not easy.

My mother tried to restrain her drinking when my father returned home, and my brother's anger subsided. Peace returned, only to descend into chaos the moment my father departed again. I tried to explain the extent of the turmoil to my father, only for him to dismiss my concerns. My elder brother was an extremely high achiever and was destined to go to Oxford University, followed by a very successful career in finance. In his spare time, he became a professor and then qualified as a lawyer. Rightly so, he seemed to be the perfect son and was the apple of my father's eye. He could do no wrong. I could barely do anything right, but that was just the way it was, and I fully accepted it.

I was now listening to my father's voice as he broke down, once again. History was repeating itself. My brother had left it late to marry; he was in his early forties. After a short time, he was blessed with a beautiful baby daughter. Family life seemed to be agreeing with him. We occasionally spoke now. His wife was charming, and Liz and I immediately became very fond of her. Despite everything that had occurred between us, I hoped that my brother had finally found peace and happiness. Sadly, my mother was denied seeing the transformation in his life. She had died at a relatively young age. Her mind and body had been destroyed by alcohol.

I slowly managed to piece together what my father was trying to tell me through broken words and sentences. That night, the cracks in my brothers marriage were already becoming evident. There had been a huge argument, and my brother had arrived at my father's house in a very distressed state.

My father was asking me to intervene in a situation that was none of my business. Marital problems can only be resolved by those directly involved, and I tried to explain that I could do nothing to help, especially as I was over four thousand miles away. Unfortunately for everyone involved, my father convinced me to call my sister-in-law and act as an intermediary. Initially, this seemed to help. However, as with most family feuds, things can change very quickly, and oh my goodness, how quickly things did indeed change.

I managed to piece together what my father was asking of me. Would I call my brother's wife and ask her to allow my brother to return home? He explained that it seemed I was the only one she trusted within the family. She would listen to me, a fact I found hard to believe. After listening to my father's desperate pleading, I finally agreed to talk to my sister-in-law. However, I made no promises to ask her to allow my brother to return home. Instead, I would offer her support if she needed it. This was probably one of the worst decisions of my life, and its consequences nearly pulled my own family apart. I had no sense of the danger befalling us all when I made that first telephone call. I was, in my mind, simply acquiescing to an old man's heartfelt pleading.

I had always got on very well with my sister-in-law. However, I still felt a tremendous sense of trepidation as I made that fateful call. It was none of my business, and I had no right to ask her. I was hoping against hope that my call would go unanswered as it rang and rang. I was about to put the phone down and breathe a huge sigh of relief when a very faint voice answered. The situation was described with all the details. It would be inappropriate to relay them here. However, an icy chill ran through me as I was transported back to my childhood as my sister-in-law described the events of that day. Despite all I knew and against my better judgement, I reverted to being a six-year-old. I did exactly what my father had told me to do; I asked her to allow my brother to return home. In retrospect, it was a betrayal of her trust. I flew back home the next day with a very uneasy feeling in my gut. I knew that I had not done the right thing. Arriving home, I immediately called my father to check that all was now well. It most definitely was not.

My father again asked me to call my sister-in-law. There had been another argument, and my brother was once again at my father's house. There was no way I would attempt to influence my sister-in-law further. I was saddened but not surprised that my father couldn't accept that his eldest son's behaviour was indefensible. Following my refusal, tension with my father was at a breaking point. For the first time in my life, I had refused his demands. As I was about to find out, he was not a man who took lightly to being disobeyed.

Christmas was now approaching, an uncertain time of year for some families at the best of times. I now had little contact with my brother or father. We were concerned that my brother's wife and their young baby would be spending Christmas alone. After a lengthy discussion, we invited them for Christmas, and my sister would spend Christmas at my father's house. This decision would have devastating consequences as my father had forbidden contact. Christmas came and went, a welcome break from the turmoil. Hopefully, the New Year would restore some sort of peace within the family. It was a forlorn hope.

It was not long afterwards that my father discovered that my sister-in-law had spent Christmas with us. I received a threatening phone call from him. I had committed an unforgivable breach of trust, and he would do everything in his power to make me pay for disobeying him. And so began a three-year campaign of retribution against myself, my wife and my two sons. Money that had been put in trust for our children was demanded to be returned. Unspeakable threats were made against me. This was blackmail in its lowest form. Has my father lost his mind, I wondered? I intended to take the matter to the police. I was being ordered to have no contact with my sister-in-law and my niece. If I disagreed, he would try to destroy my life, along with that of my wife and sons. Before I could call the police, my sister rang and begged me not to. My father, by this time, was becoming fragile, and she convinced me that if he were arrested, it would have severe consequences for his health.

To this day, I regret being dissuaded. It was a monumental mistake.

The date for divorce proceedings approached. My brother represented himself in the High Court. What happened next stunned the legal world. During the proceedings, emails were produced that had a very detrimental effect on my brother's case. He vehemently denied having written these emails and asked for the case to be paused whilst he investigated their origins. My brother visited every internet cafe near the London courts with dogged determination. He asked the owners if they had video footage at the time and date the emails were sent. Eventually, he came across the correct cafe. Viewing the footage, he saw a motorbike rider enter the cafe and sit at a computer. Even he was astounded when the rider took off his helmet and began typing the incriminating evidence. Incredibly it, was my sister-in-law's barrister. A barrister had been outclassed by my brother in court and had taken revenge by falsifying evidence.

When the court reconvened, this new video evidence was produced. The judge halted the case, and the barrister was arrested. For the first time in eight hundred years of English legal history, a barrister was going to jail for perverting the course of justice. The case was restarted a few months later, and my brother lost his petition. He had been seeking full custody of his daughter. I was never to speak to my brother, sister and father again. As I had refused to help, I was held responsible for my brother's failure.

Later, I even had to engage a lawyer when I was threatened with false charges. My brother and my sister took my ageing father to a local solicitor to change his legal Will. As my father sat outside, a new Will was drawn up, naming just the two of them as beneficiaries. The Will was taken outside for my father to sign. I found out years later from this solicitor that he had found the whole episode disturbing. He was not even aware of my existence. He had been told that they were the only children.

Shortly afterwards, my father died, and the Will was executed. They divided his not insignificant estate between them. Myself and far more importantly, my children had been omitted from the new Will. It was never about the money. My sons had lost their grandfather. Not long after this seismic break of family ties, my brother was in his newly acquired Manor House. The building was magnificent, and he was happy to be the lord of that manor. Very sadly, shortly after settling into his new home, he suffered a fatal heart attack and died. He was only in his middle fifties. The worst period of my life was at an end. Both my antagonists had now passed away and could no longer harm myself or my family. I could never have expected my relationship with my father to end in such a catastrophic way. Only a few years earlier, he had been not just a father but a friend. We had flown together numerous times. He had accompanied me on many of my 747 trips. And yet the only time I had disobeyed him had resulted in us becoming mortal enemies.

Of all the chapters I have written about my career, this has been the most difficult to articulate. I thought long and hard about whether I should write about this period of my career. The deciding factor was that this is the story of my pathway in aviation. My father had a huge impact on my career. From my very first flight in 1974, through all the adventures and excitement, he had been an ever-present influence. All that had now ended in total anarchy. This episode of my life had a dramatic effect on my family and me. It also proved a huge distraction in my career. The ability to lose myself in the sheer pleasure of flying the 747 helped me through the most challenging period of my life.

I have not spoken to my sister since, and because of her ultimate betrayal, I never will.

Chapter 23

A Time To Reflect

One of the things that had sustained me throughout this dreadful episode was the distraction of flying the 747. I actually looked forward to the six-monthly simulator sessions. I spent even more time than usual making sure that my flying skills and technical knowledge were at the highest possible standard. Hours spent with my head in the books were hours distracting me from the feelings of hurt and betrayal. I immersed myself in my work, and in return, I received the highest marks and the best scores of my career. Things could have gone very differently if I had allowed the distractions to interfere with my flying career.

Now that this nightmare was finally over, although it still haunts me to this day. I started to settle down and once more began to enjoy life. It was also a time for reflection, a time to look back, and a time to look forward. Time, as they say, stands still for no-one. I was now approaching my fifties, in a different era. This would signal the start of the end of my career. Pilots up until this time had to retire from British Airways on their fifty-fifth birthday. This was a company but not a legal requirement. It seemed strange that pilots being forced to retire joined our competitors and flew for another ten years. We were simply supplying the market with the most highly skilled pilots. How the other airlines, especially the newer or start-up airlines, must have rubbed their hands in glee at this steady flow of highly experienced aviators. These airlines had little or no seniority systems that were embedded in the older airlines. Without the seniority system, pilots could join these competitors as direct entry captains. Everyone was a winner, except the co-pilots in these airlines and of course, British Airways itself. Something clearly had to change and change it did.

By 2006, it was finally accepted that British Airways needed to change how it paid its pilots. It had a very detrimental effect on junior pilots and positively impacted the more senior ones. Something had to be done to address this inequality. Senior co-pilots flying to ultra-long-haul destinations were paid more than junior captains flying to some demanding airports. By this time, having been a captain for nearly ten years, I found myself somewhere in the middle of this pay scale. The halcyon days of my being the youngest 747 captain had long since passed, and the junior captains probably looked at me as part of the problem, not the solution.

A new pay structure was introduced. This raised everyone's basic salary while removing destination payments. This made the whole framework of our working lives fairer and removed numerous anomalies in pay. Everyone could now bid for where they wanted to go rather than where the most money could be earned. Even the most senior pilots realised that they no longer had to fly to Narita three times a month. They could now enjoy the previously less lucrative routes. At the same time, British Airways realised they supplied their competitors with a fully trained crew who still had ten years until their legal retirement dates. They raised the retirement age to sixty, and they promptly raised it again to sixty-five. Our competitors' loss was our gain. Personally, I now had the opportunity to fly for another fifteen years instead of five. I felt sorry for the co-pilots who were waiting for the older captains to retire. They now had another ten years to await the next batch of retirements before obtaining their own commands.

And so, my working life settled down once again. The next few months and years seemed to rush past at such a rate that I tried to slow down the process by reflecting on past experiences and learning from them. Since converting onto the 747-400, I'd had some unforgettable trips, worthy of note. In no particular order, I recount the more interesting ones.

We were ready to push back for a long flight to Chennai in India. There was only the main door left to close. The ground staff had informed us that a club passenger had failed to make the flight. As we were not allowed to fly if a passenger's bag had been loaded onto the aircraft and they subsequently failed to show up, we had no choice but to locate their bag and remove it. This is much easier said than done. There are five cargo holds on the 747 where bags are stored within containers. The first trick is to decide which is the correct hold. Once identified correctly, the hold then has to be emptied of all the containers. Each container is emptied one by one until the right bag is identified and removed. The process is not unlike roulette. Some days you are lucky, and the first container opened reveals the bag. Other days it's the last container, or even worse, the bag is in a different hold altogether. That is why it is challenging to give passengers an accurate time frame when offloading bags. If there is the slightest possibility that the errant passenger can be found, it is sometimes better to wait. Once the process has been started, it is the policy to continue to its ultimate conclusion. On this flight, I decided to wait a few more minutes.

Just as I was asking for the baggage offload to begin, a breathless ground staff member entered the flight deck. The passenger had been found, and they had both run to the aircraft. I made a light-hearted remark about who had won the race before thanking the ground crew. Finally, the last door was closed, and we requested our pushback from the stand. I released the brakes, and nearly four hundred tonnes of aircraft slowly backed away from the airport terminal. We asked the tug driver and his assistant for permission to start two of our engines. Once they were running, we would ask to start the remaining two engines. Fuel was introduced into the start cycle at the appropriate moment, and both engines roared into life. This is quite an important part of our day. Get it wrong, and you can quickly write off five million pounds worth of Rolls Royce's finest engine. Cabin crew are forbidden to call or enter the flight deck during engine start. Imagine our surprise when a breathless cabin crew member requested admittance to the flight deck. It had to be an emergency. Immediately, I asked the tug crew to stop the pushback and hold off on starting the remaining engines.

Once the aircraft was safe, park brake set and air traffic informed, I asked what the problem was. Apparently, our late passenger really had sprinted to the aircraft. He had taken his seat only to suffer a massive heart attack only moments afterwards. The flight was completely full, and our poor passenger was lying on the floor. There was pandemonium in the cabin. As there was an extra pilot present due to the length of the flight, I asked her to go downstairs and assess the situation. At the same time, I asked the co-pilot to request a return to stand and call the emergency services. We shut down the two engines as we set the parking brake. It was the shortest sector I had operated. Our third pilot returned, visibly upset that she had not been allowed down the stairs to see what was happening. As I was completing the checklist, I asked her to inform the cabin crew that she was acting under my instructions. As she departed again, we completed the remainder of the checklist. No sooner had we put the checklist away than she once again returned. Apparently, the CSD (cabin services director) had sent out a command that nobody was allowed into the club cabin. I thought this could be interesting, as I got out of my seat and went to the top of the stairs.

The stairs are at the back of the upper deck club cabin, and all eyes were on me as I made my way towards them. As I was about to descend the stairs, a burly steward put his arm across the stairs. He informed me that I was not permitted downstairs until the CSD had authorised it. We stood staring at each other for a moment's impasse. I think my expression gave the game away, and he stood aside without the need for me to speak. The scene that met my eyes on entering the downstairs cabin was complete chaos. Everyone was standing up, blocking the aisles as they tried to see what was happening. It took a few loud demands before passengers started to sit down. There, on the floor, was our poor casualty, looking every inch the heart attack victim.

Around this time, the company was introducing defibrillators onto the aircraft. During each annual check, crews were being trained in their use. I asked for the defibrillator to be brought to the passenger. Unfortunately, none of the crew had been trained in its use. Therefore, it remained in the medical kit. Despite protests, I opened the kit and followed the instructions. After connecting the device, it clearly told me to shock the patient, which I did. His body rose and fell but there was still no sign of life. I tried again, still nothing. On the third attempt, the passenger coughed and started to move. A short while later, he was conscious and coherent. I looked around for the paramedics. They should be here by now. Satisfied that the patient was now breathing normally, I went to find out where the ambulance crew were. To my dismay, they were knocking on an unattended door. Letting them in as quickly as possible, I followed them back into the cabin. To my amazement, the passenger was now sitting up and asking what all the fuss was about. He even wanted to continue with the flight. This was obviously not going to happen, and the paramedics took him to the hospital.

We were now back at square one. His bag now had to be offloaded. Of course, it was in the last container in the final hold.

We were now very late. Some of the cabin crew had requested not to fly due to the stress of the incident. On arrival at the hotel in Chennai, the station staff met the cabin crew and offered support and a free meal with all drinks included. As flight crew, we were ignored, which seemed to be the way of the world at that time. Of course, this was in no way the fault of the cabin crew themselves. They just had a far superior management team looking after their interests. Our executive management was virtually non-existent. Personally, I was not particularly worried, and I much preferred to self-manage. However, a free meal and drink would have been nice or at least some acknowledgement of our involvement in resuscitating the passenger.

The next day, we boarded the aircraft for the return flight to London. I had done a little shopping and was now the proud owner of two bronze herons which I thought would make a good addition to the pond at home. I also hoped that they may scare off the real things using the pond as a fast-food outlet. On arrival in London, I thought that I had better check that my prized purchases were being treated with the care and respect they deserved. After shutting the aircraft down, I went outside to see if they had yet been unloaded. As I walked under the right-wing, I suddenly heard cries of agony and screams of panic. Rushing to discover the source of the screams, the scene that met me was shocking. One of the loading team had been caught under the wheels of a baggage trolly. The whole weight of the trolley was crushing his chest. Misguidedly, his colleagues were trying to pull him free, making the situation even worse. Asking them to stop, we then disconnected the trolley at the front and back from the line of similar trolleys.

Six of us then lifted the trolley off the poor loader. I knelt down to assess his injuries while asking his colleagues to call the emergency services. The accident victim was in a very bad way. He was bleeding heavily from his mouth and drifting in and out of consciousness. His chest was severely crushed, and his pulse was almost non-existent. I was handed the phone connected to the emergency services. After describing the injuries, it was agreed that an air ambulance was required to take the victim to the hospital. There was very little I could do except to attempt to keep the victim conscious and his airway clear.

Next to him, I noticed his mobile phone had fallen onto the ground. Fortunately, it was not locked, and I checked his last message from his wife. I was losing the battle to keep him conscious. He had little interest in talking to me. On impulse, I dialled his wife's number. I explained to her that her husband had been in an accident and needed her help to keep him awake. He would soon be on his way to the hospital, and it was vital he remained conscious until the air ambulance arrived. I gently held the phone to his ear. His eyes were closed. We were losing him. I then heard his wife as she began to shout at her husband. His eyes suddenly shot open as he was told in no uncertain terms not to be so bloody selfish and to stay awake. She went on to say to him that she was on her way, and if he had gone to sleep before she got there, she would kill him. He lay there listening to the threats from his wife until the noise from the air ambulance made conversation impossible.

Watching the departing helicopter, I began to wipe the blood from my hands and clothes. As I looked around the remainder of the loading crew, they each shook my hand. Nothing was said. Nothing needed saying. I then enquired about my herons, and amazingly there they were. In the weeks and months that followed, I kept a check on the victim's progress. Thankfully, he made a full recovery, although he may have suffered some permanent damage to his hearing from the verbal abuse he had suffered from his wife.

Of course, both incidents had to be reported to the relevant authorities. I duly filled out an air safety report for each of the two flights. I heard nothing back. Imagine my surprise when weeks later I picked up a copy of the company newspaper only to see a picture of my cabin crew under the headline of 'Hero

Crew'. The article went on to describe how they had saved the lives of two people on one trip. They had all been given a free holiday. I could not help but smile. At least I knew the truth. Six months later, I received a letter thanking me for my actions and offering me a holiday in Dubai. I wrote back, mentioning that a bit of support or recognition at the time may have been more appropriate. I refused the offer. My next flight was to Dubai anyway.

Chapter 24

Singapore Sling

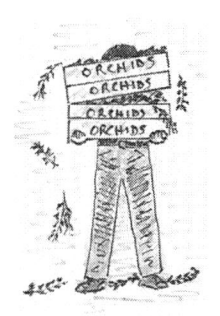

We had just started our descent into Singapore. The flight so far had lasted thirteen hours; we still had at least another hour before we would be landing. It was a busy time. As the thrust levers slowly came back to idle, there was an unusual vibration. Something was not right. Looking at the engine instruments, initially, everything appeared to be normal. However, when I tried to increase the power, there was a definite rumble from one of the engines on the left wing. Very shortly afterwards, a number of lights illuminated, together with a series of messages on our computer screens. Number one engine, the outboard engine on the left wing, was not feeling at all well. Following the checklists, we shut the engine down. On the jumbo, with its four engines, losing one is not a massive problem. The aircraft will fly quite happily on three engines. Indeed, it is not even considered an emergency. After securing the engine and trimming the plane to fly with two engines on one side and just the one on the other side, we continued with our approach. We informed air traffic control and advised them that we did not need any assistance. We could carry out a standard approach and landing. After a quick chat with the cabin crew leader, we confirmed that nobody had noticed the engine had been shut down. I asked him to brief the crew of the situation and advised him that no special procedures would be necessary.

After a quick reassessment of the situation, we briefed as necessary to cover all eventualities. Although we practise landing on three engines every six months in the simulator, the company policy was to carry out an automatic landing when an engine fails, if possible. The aircraft behaved perfectly, and thirty minutes later, we literally kissed the runway, as the jumbo performed a perfect landing.

After the passengers had left the aircraft, we went to have a look at our unhappy engine. It was immediately apparent why we had the vibration and warnings. One of the blades at the front of the engine was severely twisted and distorted. There was no way this engine could be repaired. It would have to go back to Rolls Royce for a complete overhaul. Well, it was no longer my problem. I now had two days off in Singapore, so off to the hotel for some well-deserved rest, and maybe, just maybe, a Singapore Sling in the world-famous Raffles Hotel. Well, that was the plan.

The following day, there was a red flashing light on the bedside phone. Having learned my lesson from the Mauritius flight, I thought I had better check my messages this time. I had to listen to the message twice before realising what I was being asked to do began to sink in. Would I be prepared to fly the aircraft back to London? At first, I thought, wow, they fixed that engine quickly. After listening to the message again, I realised that I was being asked to fly the aircraft home on three, not four, engines. Of course, there would be no passengers or indeed cabin crew, just the pilots. This is an approved procedure as long as one of the captains had been trained in the technique of a three-engine take off. I politely pointed out that I had not received the required training. Apparently, they were way ahead of me. A fully trained pilot was already on his way. He and I would bring the aircraft back to London. Why me, I asked? Only to receive a light-hearted answer, "because you broke it in the first place." I had to smile. There was no pressure to accept the flight, but I accepted the assignment when I found out that the other captain was a good friend. It would be fun, well, at least I thought it would be fun.

The next evening, instead of joining the rest of my crew for a meal at the wonderful Fatty's restaurant, I was on my way to the airport for the flight home. I had spent an interesting couple of hours being briefed on our take off that evening. There were many stringent restrictions on a three-engined take-off. The most critical of these was that the maximum take-off weight was drastically restricted. As with every take-off, the calculations considered that you may lose an engine just as you leave the ground. Of course, with a four-engined take off the aircraft will happily climb away on three engines. Tonight, we were taking off with three engines, and we had to calculate our performance on two engines. It was not great. We quickly decided that we could not load enough fuel to fly directly to London and still be within our allowed take-off weight. Apart from heading straight to Fatty's, the only option that was looking more and more attractive to me was to fly to Dubai, where we would refuel and carry on. I have never been that good at mathematics, but I quickly realised that this would mean not one three engines take off, but two. This was certainly not what I had signed up for. I could almost taste the fantastic food on offer at one of my favourite restaurants.

However, my partner was made of much sterner stuff. Either that or he did not like Chinese food. After a quick discussion with our two co-pilots, the decision was made to continue with this plan. All thoughts of delicious food and the cold beer disappeared as quickly as they had arisen. We were going to Dubai and then onwards to London.

I watched the demanding take off with a feeling of admiration at my colleague's skill, and I have to admit a sense of slight unease. We lined up on the longest runway available. As we had a failed outboard engine, the two inboard engines were slowly increased to full power, the brakes were released, and we slowly moved down the runway. We could not immediately apply full power on all three available engines as we would lose directional control. At eighty knots, a speed at which the rudder could effectively control the sideways force of two engines on one wing and only one on the other wing, power was slowly increased on the third engine. It seemed to take forever for this last engine to reach full power. The end of the runway now seemed much closer than usual. Finally, all three engines were at their maximum capacity, trying to compensate for their absent friend. The airspeed was increasing but at a much slower rate than I was used to. The end of the runway was now uncomfortably close. And then the nose of the aircraft gently lifted into the night sky. A moment later, all eighteen of our wheels lifted off the runway; we were finally airborne. I thought to myself, what an aircraft, what a pilot, as we began a gentle turn to bring the plane around and point it towards Dubai. As we reached our cruising height, my colleague handed the aircraft over to me and went for a well-deserved rest. In six hours, we would need him to do it all again on departure from Dubai.

The 747 really did fly well on three engines. The main problem was to keep the fuel balanced. With two operating engines on one side and only one on the other side, we continuously moved the fuel around. I set the alarm on my watch to remind me every thirty minutes to monitor the fuel. After turning pumps on and off, we kept ourselves in balance all the way to Dubai. The landing was straightforward. All pilots were trained in this manoeuvre. Of course, I had carried out a three-engined landing the day before.

An hour after landing, we were on our way once more, accelerating drunkenly down the runway at Dubai. After this take off, my colleague retired once again for another well-deserved rest. Balancing our fuel continuously through the night skies, we touched gently down at London eighteen hours after leaving Singapore. It was a job well done by everyone, especially my expert colleague. That night, Liz and I went out for a Chinese meal, not quite Fatty's, but just as enjoyable.

Fast forward a few months, and I was on my way home from Singapore once again, happily this time with all four engines behaving themselves. The next day, I was attending the wedding of Laura, the daughter of very close friends, Sue and Paul Casey. I had offered to bring home ten boxes of beautiful orchid flowers. Singapore had some of the finest orchids in the world. Very kindly, some of the crew had offered to help me carry these large boxes from the aircraft to my car. These boxes were safely stowed in our flight deck bunks. Due to the flight time, we had four pilots, two captains and two co-pilots. I had flown the aircraft to Singapore, and my co-pilot and I were the 'heavy' crew on the return flight. This meant that the other pilots performed the take-off and landing. We took over whilst they had their rest and handed back control for them to land the aircraft.

We were due to land at four-thirty in the morning, one of the very few flights allowed to land before Heathrow officially opened at six o'clock. Everything went very smoothly, a beautifully flown approach and a landing I could only dream of completing. Exiting the runway, we were cleared to taxi to our stand. I was sitting directly behind the operating captain whilst my co-pilot sat between the two pilots. As we turned a sharp corner, the technical log, a large ring binder book we completed on every flight, fell from the small table behind me. As it hit the floor, the rings opened, and all the pages fell onto the floor. Cursing under my breath, I stooped down to pick them up. Collecting them, I turned back and was startled to see that we had nearly parked.

On each stand at Heathrow, there is an electronic parking system. The ground crew selects the type of parking aircraft, and the system then tells the pilots to turn either left or right to keep them on the centreline. As the aircraft nears its final stopping place, the system counts down the distance to go until it tells the pilot to stop. Pilots are not allowed to self-park. If the system is not operating, a marshaller has to be called to guide the aircraft onto the stand.

As I retrieved the last page of the technical log, I looked up, and I instantly realised that we were too close to the terminal building. Immediately, I called out a warning to stop the aircraft.

After such a peremptory warning, the captain immediately applied the brakes, as all good pilots would have done. He informed me that the parking system was working normally but had not warned him to stop. I suggested that there was clearly something wrong, and we should request assistance from a marshaller. Before we could make such a request, we were informed that the aircraft had impacted a loading trolley. We had been involved in an accident, and the police had been informed. Not a good way to finish a flight. After a short delay, the passengers disembarked. None were aware of our problem. The impact had been very slight, and there was no damage to either the aircraft or the baggage trolly.

Had this incident been in the car, both parties would have looked at their vehicles, accepted there was no damage and simply carried on with their day. Bumping a 747 into something, however slightly, was not an incident to be treated so lightly. After the cabin crew had departed, the four of us were interviewed by the police. After they were satisfied with our explanation, we were driven to an interview room back at the crew report centre in a small minibus. We were just about to set off from the aircraft when I suddenly remembered the ten boxes of orchids still languishing in the bunk area. Rushing back up the stairs to retrieve them took much longer than expected. I could only carry three boxes at a time. We squeezed into the minibus surrounded by boxes of orchids. We looked like something out of the keystones cops rather than four pilots on their way to a very demanding and unpleasant interview, conducted by the aircraft accident branch of the Civil Aviation Authority.

Balancing my precious cargo as best I could, I made my way unsteadily up a flight of stairs, my three colleagues following me with their boxes of orchids. We made a very incongruous sight. Whatever happened, I was determined that Laura was going to her orchids for her big day. We were seated in a room and had the coffee we had just purchased taken away. Apparently, we were to be drug and alcohol tested. Fortunately, I called our pilots' trade union, and they sent a representative to assist us. It was all starting to get very serious. We were held in that room for several hours, unable to use our phones or have a drink, whilst we awaited the various incident teams to arrive. Eventually, after individual interviews, my co-pilot and I were informed that we were cleared to leave. No blame was attached to either of us. Indeed, I was praised for my swift response. Of course, we refused to leave our colleagues as we were in this together. Anyway, I couldn't manage my orchids without their help. So, we stayed and waited. The whole process took most of the morning, not ideal after flying all night. Eventually, we were allowed to leave, and four fatigued pilots, balancing boxes of orchids, made their sorry exit.

Initially, we had been accused of taxiing onto the stand without guidance. It was subsequently established that the ground staff had not correctly entered our aircraft's details into the guidance system. As a result, the computer could not decide when to advise us to stop as it didn't know the length of our aircraft. We were exonerated of all blame. However, it had been a very unpleasant experience that left its mark on the operating pilots. On the bright side, I managed to deliver the ten boxes of orchids to Sue and Paul for their daughter's big day. As the happy couple made their way down the aisle, they passed the bunches of orchids tied to the church pews. The whole effect was beautiful. Luckily, at the time, they had no idea how close they had come to walking down a very bare aisle.

Chapter 25

Send Three and Fourpence

We were waiting at Miami airport. The inbound flight from London had been delayed due to a technical issue with one of the engines. Nothing particularly untoward about that. Technical issues were unusual but not uncommon. One of the truly remarkable things about British Airways was its approach to safety. Not only was safety the airline's first priority, it was also their second and third priority. As captains, we were at the frontline of safety. We were there to ensure the highest standards were observed and maintained to safeguard our passengers and crews. If we were not happy about anything, we had the total authority to delay or cancel a flight. There was never any pressure put on us to keep the show on the road. If we said no, then no, it was. I realise that this is not the case in all airlines, so I have always been so grateful and proud to work for British Airways. Over the four decades I have worked for the airline, many things have changed, not all of them for the better. However, the one thing that has never changed or ever been in question is the absolute priority to passengers, crew, and aircraft safety.

Secure in this knowledge, I waited as the bulbous nose of our aircraft started to fill the panoramic windows of the terminal building as it taxied to the stand. As the four massive engines slowly ran down, we waved at the pilots on the aircraft. They were on the same level as us due to the height of the flight deck.

After the passengers had departed, we made our way up to the flight deck to determine the cause of the delay. Chatting to the incoming crew, we discovered that one of the engines had been using more oil than was usual. The ground engineers had done a thorough examination at London and had changed an oil filter. They had then signed the aircraft off as fit to fly. All well and good, and I would have done exactly as the crew had done and flown to Miami. The problem was that the same engine had again used far more oil than the other three engines. The Miami engineers were busy topping up the oils, so I went to chat with them. The engine covers were open when I arrived, and three engineers stood there literally scratching their heads. I was a regular visitor to Miami and knew the chief engineer well, a lovely chap. He could find no reason for the high rate of oil consumption, except for the fact that this particular engine was due for a major service in the next few weeks. Oil seals did occasionally leak, and they would all be replaced anyway at this check.

I was not overly keen on this explanation, and so we came to a compromise. After talking with our operations in London, we decided to do a full power run on the engine and check immediately afterwards for any leaks.

We had over three hundred passengers waiting in the terminal for their flight home. They were already delayed for over two hours. Rather than leave it to the ground staff, I went into the departure lounge and explained what was going on using the public address system. I have always believed that if you are honest with your passengers, they will generally understand. Try to bluff or, even worse, lie to your passengers, then you deserve everything you get.

And so, just the two of us pilots and the ground engineer closed the aircraft up and requested permission to taxi to the far side of the airport to perform our full power run. I had never done one of these before, and it was very enlightening to see and experience the aircraft's reaction. Making sure that the brakes were fully set, I slowly increased the power on the suspect engine. There have been severe incidents on other airlines where the aircraft had moved forward during these runs, causing severe damage and injury. My feet were firmly covering the brakes should any unexpected movement occur. As we increased the power, the aircraft began to shake, it was not used to having one engine at full power whilst the other three were idling the day away. I could feel the aircraft wanting to move sideways. I tightened my grip on the brakes. We could only run the engine at full power for five minutes. That was the limit set by the manufacturer. I must admit that I felt relieved as I slowly reduced the power to the normal idling power. We taxied back to the terminal and shut the aircraft down. Moments later, the covers were again removed from the engine, and four engineers were shining their torches into every corner.

Twenty minutes later, the chief engineer declared that no leak could be found, and he was happy to sign the engine off. He was happy, but I was not. My reasoning was that the leak, or high consumption, would not become apparent on such a short five-minute run. The problem really was the high oil usage over many hours, not minutes. Therefore, I very politely declined the offer to fly the aircraft back to London that evening. I knew that I was disappointing many people, but I thought back to a very early piece of advice I had received when I first started to fly....

"It's much better to be on the ground wishing you were flying than to be flying wishing you were on the ground."

With that thought in my mind, the flight was cancelled, and we went back to the hotel. I rang our operations department in London to explain my decision. As expected, it was accepted without question. However, there was a problem. The aircraft could not be three engines ferried as I had done on a previous occasion from Singapore. The local authorities at Miami prohibited this due to the sizeable built-up area surrounding the airport. Another option was to fly a new engine to Miami. However, this would take time, and the aircraft was needed at the height of the summer season. This option was quickly dismissed. Suddenly, I had a plan, not a great plan as it turned out but a plan, nevertheless. I was happy to take off on four engines and shut the problem engine down at the top of the climb. Just before descent, we could restart the engine and complete a normal landing. Of course, there would be no passengers or cabin crew on the aircraft. This cunning plan was put to our flight management team, a few hours later, it was approved by Captain Doug Diss. We went to bed early. Tomorrow was going to be an interesting day.

The following day, we were taxiing out for our four-engined take off. An empty jumbo is a lonely place to be. Its sheer size seems to be further exaggerated when it is devoid of passengers and cabin crew. Carefully monitoring the engines, we set take-off power and accelerated down the runway. At precisely the right moment, the nose of the enormous aircraft lifted into the bright morning sky. We were safely on our way.

The plan that had been agreed was to climb to the most efficient altitude calculated for a three-engine cruise and then to shut down the engine with the high oil consumption. Before we began our descent into London, that engine would be restarted and a normal four-engine landing completed. As we approached our cruising height, the little printer between the two pilots began to type out a message. We used this device, known as ACARS, to request weather information and send and receive notifications. The co-pilot reached down and tore off the long message. Reading it, he then handed the note to me. This was a direct order from London which read, 'Captain Doug Diss (our Fleet Manager) disagrees with shutting the engine down, please continue on all four engines'.

This was the exact opposite of what had been previously agreed. I would not have agreed to the flight with this scenario in place, especially as the weather in London precluded an automatic landing due to high winds. I had a choice now, either return to Miami or continue the flight on four engines. We had a lengthy discussion between ourselves. Looking at the oil quantity, the engine appeared to be behaving itself. Maybe, the engineers at Miami had been correct after all about that full power run. After a short while, we decided that we could not justify returning to Miami. So, we continued across the Atlantic Ocean. London was seven hours away.

We had received our Ocean crossing clearance at the height we had requested when we expected to be flying on three engines. As we were now not shutting an engine down, we could ask for a higher level. However, something in the back of my mind advised me not to go for a higher level but to stay at our original height. Although this would require a little more fuel, it meant that if we did have to shut the engine down, we could stay at our current height. We had plenty of fuel, and if the worst happened, it would make life a little easier. If you had to make an unexpected descent over the ocean, where there was no direct air traffic control, you had to turn away from your route in case there was another aircraft below you. Happy in our decision making, we slowly painted a four-engine contrail across the morning sky.

Four hours later, things were not looking quite so rosy. We had been making hourly observations on the oil consumption of our suspect engine. As I had feared, the oil level was dropping with each mile of our journey. At the present rate, we calculated that the engine would run extremely low on oil an hour before we were due to land. We started to recalculate our options. We were now past our point of no return. In other words, it was quicker to continue rather than return. To preserve our dwindling oil supply, we brought the engine back to idle thrust, re-trimmed the aircraft and reduced our speed. Looking at the weather all over the UK and Northern Europe, all were experiencing low clouds and high winds. If we had to land on three engines, I would have to land the aircraft as the wind was outside the automatic landing limits. I quietly swore to myself and cursed Captain Diss. We should be thinking of restarting the engine at this point, not shutting it down. My thoughts and curses were rudely interrupted by a sudden cacophony of bells and red flashing lights. We had run out of oil.

Immediately, we went through our well-rehearsed actions for an engine failure. We practised every six months in the simulator, hoping we would not have to use these skills in real life. In anticipation of events, we had completed several touch drills to make sure we were on top of our game. Fortunately, we were way ahead of the game. We were at the correct height and had the aircraft trimmed out. After a simple memory drill and a follow up with the printed checklist, we were fully prepared for our approach and landing, well, all apart from the awful weather waiting for us.

In the simulator, we flew an approach on three engines in relatively smooth conditions. Although we had to manually land the aircraft on three engines at the maximum permitted crosswind, the simulator did not reproduce the turbulence we experienced on that approach. We bumped our way down through the clouds, the aircraft struggling with the power adjustments due to the turbulence. Eventually, the runway appeared out of the side window. We were flying at an angle to allow for the strength of the wind from the left-hand side. Over the runway, close the thrust lever, kick off the drift and allow for the failed engine, and bump, we were down.

Now all pilots are perfectly capable of these types of landings, exciting but not overly challenging. What annoyed me was that all of this could have been avoided if we had been allowed to shut down and restart our engine. I wanted a strong word with Captain Diss. I asked to be put through to the man who had caused me so many problems. Picking up the phone, he immediately denied sending any such message. In fact, he had asked for a message to be sent explicitly agreeing with the plan we had submitted. I read out the message I had received inflight. There was a pause. A moment later, he read out his version of the message, 'Captain Doug Diss agrees with the procedure'. This had been interpreted as 'disagrees', Even I had to laugh. It was a classic case of the famous military command 'Send reinforcements; I am going to advance' being delivered as 'Send three and fourpence; I am going to a dance'. I went home a wiser and more cautious man. Don't believe everything you read.

Chapter 26

Unexpected Consequences

It was due to be a routine trip to Lagos, the capital city of Nigeria in West Africa. I had been flying there since the late 1980s, nearly a quarter of a century before. How quickly time and life passes. Whilst not everyone's favourite destination, I had always quite liked the trip. The flight was relatively short, at six hours in length. The route to Lagos was a daylight flight. The views down through France, across the Pyrenees, past Barcelona, and then the Balearic Islands were a visual treat. Many years previously, I had suffered my first, and hopefully last, mid-air collision on this route. You do not usually read a pilot's personal account of a mid-air collision. You read about the subsequent accident and the number of deaths. Luckily for me and everyone else on that 747, we all survived. I was admiring the stunning views as we crossed the Pyrenees mountain range. As the weather was crystal clear, I could make out the city of Barcelona and the coastline in the far distance. As I always did on such days, I felt highly privileged to do the job I did. Life and everything else felt good. Well, it did, until I saw a huge object suddenly filling the windscreen.

Most people who have been in a car accident will testify that time seems to slow down, almost to a standstill in the moments before the impact. Precisely the same thing happened to me on this occasion. One second, I was looking at a clear blue sky. The next second, an object was about to impact the aircraft's windscreen directly in front of me. I would love to say that I reacted instantly, disconnected the autopilot and saved three hundred and fifty lives by my heroic actions. The reality was I had hardly got the words, "what the heck is that?" out before there was an almighty bang as the object collided with the front windscreen. Even more frightening was the fact that the thing was far more extensive than I had at first thought. Parts of it trailing along the side of the aircraft, and then just as quickly as it had appeared, it was gone.

There was a stunned silence. Well, it would have been silent if the poor co-pilot, whose attention at the time had been directed inside the aircraft, had not been swearing so loudly. We looked at each other in amazement. The co-pilot had seen part of the object as it made its way down my side windows, but he had not seen the actual impact. After checking that we were still alive and not in some transitory nether region between heaven and earth, we became pilots again.

We carefully scanned all of the instruments, everything seemed to be normal. I was especially interested in the engines on the left wing. Whatever we had hit, or had hit us, had made its way towards those engines. They were both apparently operating normally. After a few moments of intensive investigation, we were happy that there was nothing immediately wrong with the aircraft. The cabin interphone started to ring. A number of our cabin crew had heard or seen an object on the aircraft's left side. Naturally, they wanted to know what had happened. My reply that, "so did we," probably did not do a lot to reassure them.

We reported the incident to the Spanish air traffic controller. We had to repeat ourselves three times before making him understand that we had suffered a mid-air collision. Understandably, it was his first time as well. After discussions with our operations unit in London, we agreed that we could continue to Lagos as there was no apparent damage. It was only after landing that the object was finally identified. A weather balloon used to collect data from high altitude had broken loose. We had hit the balloon and its instruments. There were scratch marks along the left side of the aircraft, and pieces of the balloon were still attached to parts of our fuselage. Still, astoundingly, that was the only evidence of our encounter. My beer tasted all the better that night as I toasted Mr Boeing for manufacturing such a remarkable and robust aircraft.

A few months later, I was once again reporting for a trip to Nigeria. Lagos always seemed to throw up unusual incidents, and today would prove to be no exception. After the usual delays with passenger bags, we finally closed the doors and requested push back. Although it was only a six-hour flight, we had loaded as much fuel as we could. This was known as tankering. We used this process when the availability or cost of fuel at our destination was in doubt. We slowly taxied towards the runway; we were a very heavy aircraft on a very warm morning. As we approached the runway, I heard the distinct sound of an electrical relay clicking in and out. We stopped the aircraft and tried to identify the source of the noise. There were no warning lights and no other clue except a faint click every few moments. After a short discussion with the company engineers, we decided to return to our stand for further investigation.

Twenty minutes later, a swarm of engineers flooded into the flight deck. They spent the next hour taking panel after panel off to discover the cause of the mystery clicking. Relays were changed, and finally, we were declared fit to fly. Once again, we pushed back and started to move towards the runway. Again, I began to hear the faint but unmistakable sounds of clicking. Stopping the aircraft once more, we looked at each other. What to do now? Another call to engineering was made. We decided that the engineers would come to us rather than returning to the terminal. Another two hours went by, with the engineers still scratching their heads. All the while, our passengers, understandably, were getting very nervous and irate. I made numerous announcements over the public address system, their effectiveness reducing with each hour that passed.

Finally, there was a eureka moment as the engineers discovered the cause of the mysterious noise. There was a faulty relay in one of the flap motors. Of course, this only presented itself when the flaps, the parts of the wing that move up and down on take-off and landing, were extended. Whilst we were on the stand, of course, the flaps were up, and the relay was not in use. A quick change of parts, and we were finally ready to go.

Just as we requested permission to continue taxiing, we received a call from the cabin. Despite my reassuring announcements, there were a large number of passengers demanding to get off the aircraft. They no longer wanted to fly to Lagos. I decided that the best thing to do was to go downstairs and reassure the passengers personally. I even put my captain's cap on, something I never usually did inside the aircraft. Hopefully, I would appear more authoritative and convincing, I thought, as I descended into the main cabin. As I walked down the stairs, I was surprised at the apparent anger and fear in a number of our passengers. I approached the leading group of about twenty people. I began my speech about how British Airways always put safety first. I even tried the old and trusted method to calm nervous passengers. I assured them that as there was a VIP on the aircraft today, we would be taking even more care than usual. Inevitably, someone would ask who the VIP, or very important person, was. I would then tell them that it was me. This had always received a few smiles and had done the trick in the past. However, today, the atmosphere was very different. All I received for my attempted reassurances was a sea of very distraught faces. Amid all the shouting and arm-waving, I noticed that there seemed to be a leader of the group, a woman the others turned to for approval. I asked her to accompany me to the galley where we could hear each other speak. I once again started to explain that the aircraft was totally safe and fit to fly.

She quickly interrupted me, "No, no, captain, they are not worried about the aircraft. They are worried about Lagos."

Well, this certainly was a turn up for the books and had me completely perplexed. Why on earth were they worried about going to Lagos? They, after all, were on a flight to that very city. As patiently as she could, this lovely lady explained about life in Lagos. The city and the area around the airport were unsafe after nightfall. The flights were arranged purposely to land in daylight, enabling the passengers who used public transport time to reach their destinations during the hours of safety. We were now over three hours late, meaning that many passengers would have to travel during the period they considered to be unsafe. Well, this was news to me. I had mistakenly thought that the unrest was due to our technical problems. How wrong could I be? She explained that the majority of the passengers wanted to get off and wait for tomorrow's flight, and quite honestly, I could not blame them. As there was absolutely no way I was taking people to what they considered a danger zone, I informed her and the rest of the passengers that we were delaying the flight until the following day. It is not often that I am cheered by the passengers, which makes it especially pleasant when it does happen.

We called up for permission to return to our stand once again. We had all been on the aircraft for over four hours without actually going anywhere. It was definitely time to get off. As we started to move, there was another distressed call from the cabin. Passengers were reporting that fuel was pouring out of our wings. What next? I thought to myself as I brought the aircraft to an immediate stop. A quick check confirmed that, yes, fuel was pouring from our wings. It seemed like a good idea to shut the engines down as four great heat sources next to a large fuel spillage did not seem to be a prudent position to be in. We also needed immediate assistance from the fire services, so we called up to announce our emergency. We were summarily informed that there was another, more significant emergency on the other side of the airport. The fire services were on their way to attend to that one. This really was not turning out to be my day. Despite the other emergency, we were still in need of immediate assistance. I asked the nature of the other aircraft's problem and a time frame to expect help. I was very reluctant to evacuate our passengers, especially as there were pools of fuel all around the plane. However, if we could expect to receive no prompt assistance, this may be the only solution.

Imagine my surprise when I was told that the aircraft in trouble was a British Airways 747 flight number BA075 to Lagos. I could also hear the controller's disbelief when I informed him that we were the BA075, and I could see a fleet of fire engines heading away from, not towards us. A few seconds later, I saw blue smoke from the fire engines as they slammed on their brakes, did a very impressive turn and came racing towards us.

Twenty minutes later, the wonderful firemen had treated the fuel spillage and confirmed that the aircraft was now safe. A tractor was eventually attached to the plane, and we were towed, once again, back to our stand. As we finally applied the parking brake, I breathed a sigh of relief. That was enough excitement for one day.

The subsequent inquiry revealed two facts that I could not have foreseen. The fuel spillage was caused by the flap motors running for an extended period whilst the relay problem was investigated. Typically, these motors run only for short periods whilst the flaps are moving. Having them continually running the heat from the motors had caused the fuel in the already full tanks to expand and vent overboard, hence the apparent leak. Another aircraft had seen our predicament but had misidentified us to air traffic control. They, in turn, had sent the fire services to the wrong aircraft. All very simple, in hindsight.

We stayed overnight in London in the same hotel as our passengers. The following day, I stood by the aircraft door and personally welcomed everyone back on board. I was greeted like a long-lost friend. Thankfully, the flight to Lagos was utterly uneventful. I even managed to avoid the balloons this time.

As we entered the baggage reclaim area in the terminal at Lagos, we were treated as heroes. All our passengers began clapping simultaneously and rushed towards us to thank us for getting them to Lagos safely and in daylight hours. The fact that they were twenty-four hours late did not seem to worry them at all. I now knew why Lagos had always held a soft spot in my heart. It was the people.

252

Chapter 27

Busy Going Nowhere

It was midwinter, a snowstorm was forecast to arrive the following day. I was scheduled to fly to Miami roughly as the snow was expected to start falling in the London area. From past experience, I knew that we would be in for a long day. The English are not the best equipped when it comes to dealing with snow. After spending an hour refreshing my knowledge of all the cold weather procedures that we would probably need the next day, I was about to turn in for an early night. That's when the phone rang. By now, I really should have learned my lesson and ignored it.

I have always been of the mindset that if you can help someone and it is within your powers to do so, then help you should. What happened in this instance made me seriously reconsider this approach to life in the future. It was another captain calling to ask me if I would consider swapping trips with him. He had friends on my flight to Miami, so would I take his flight to Nairobi instead? I like Miami, the hotel is good, and I could do a long run adjacent to the ocean, one of my favourite routes. It also provides a great break from the worst of the winter weather. I usually bid for these Miami flights, and now that I was relatively senior, I was usually successful. So, my first reaction was to say no, thank you. Then my mantra kicked in, and I managed to catch myself from automatically refusing his request. Feeling very noble, I agreed to the swap. I was now off to Nairobi in the morning. Well, that was the new plan anyway.

The alarm pulled me reluctantly from the depths of my slumber, out from a warm bed into an icy, dark, and forbidding morning. The time was half-past five. As it was mid-winter, it would not be light for a few more hours. Venturing outside, I was met by a huge ice cube where my car had been parked last night. Twenty minutes later, I managed to get the car doors open, and the engine started. Whilst the whole thing warmed up, I went back indoors to thaw myself out. The snow had yet to arrive. Maybe the freezing temperature had scared it away. Driving to the airport, dawn slowly tried to make its presence felt. Small, weak strips of light did their best to break through the dark, forbidding clouds. As night slowly turned into a bleak imitation of day, I wondered if we would get away before the threatened snowstorm arrived.

Long-haul aircraft typically spend the majority of their time in the air. Unlike their short-haul counterparts, which usually spend the night at the airport, the big boys fly throughout the night to reach the earth's far corners. They return to London mainly in the very early mornings, like a vast swarm of worker bees returning to their hive. The sky around London is filled with these aircraft circling whilst awaiting their turn to land. Once on the ground, the aircraft are rapidly descended upon by teams of ground staff. They immediately begin to prepare for the next departure, usually within three hours of landing. This leaves little time for snow and ice to accumulate on exposed surfaces. Aircraft these days have very advanced systems to prevent icing in flight. Once on the ground, however, the aircraft is unprotected and highly vulnerable to the elements. Hopefully, my aircraft had recently landed, and we could take off before the storm arrived. If that was the case, we would not have to start the long and complicated process of de-icing the aircraft. It was, as it turned out, a very forlorn hope. I made it to the briefing area to be greeted by a very grateful captain who was preparing to take my Miami flight out. It was a nice touch to thank me personally, and I appreciated the gesture. We were due to depart within twenty minutes of each other, and pleasantries completed, we bade each other farewell and safe flying.

To business then, after greeting my two co-pilots and briefing the cabin crew, we set about deciding how much fuel we would be taking. Delays are almost inevitable on days like these, so it is always a good idea to have extra fuel, one less thing to worry about. This morning, our only concern was that the runway at Nairobi was scheduled to close to allow for essential maintenance work. However, that work was not due to start until six hours after our expected arrival, so it was not particularly relevant. Everything seemed set. The snow was holding off. The crew had been asked to keep a close eye on the aircraft's exterior if the snow arrived before we departed. Having an extra eighteen pairs of eyes checking through the windows for the deadly ice always seemed like a good idea to me.

As we started to board our passengers, a few small snowflakes fluttered idly past our windscreen, like small white butterflies seeking their next flower. They looked so innocent and beautiful as they began to settle on our side windows before melting and running down the window. As beautiful as they were, I immediately knew that it would be a long day. In my wildest imagination, I could never have dreamt just how long a day it would turn out to be.

The snow was now getting heavier. It was settling like a vast blanket over our aircraft. Consequently, we would be going nowhere fast. Trying to get ahead of the game, we called up and requested the de-icing trucks to come to our stand at the first sign of snow. This request was met by a laconic reply, "you and everyone else." We were added to the queue and told to expect a three-hour delay, a great way to start the day.

After explaining the situation to our very understanding passengers, we settled down to await the de-icing teams. The 747, being such a large aircraft, needs at least two rigs to treat it. These rigs are not dissimilar to a fire engine as it sprays a burning building, only this time, snow and ice are the enemies. Eventually, our trucks arrived, and after speaking to their team leader, we shut off the aircraft's air conditioning system. This prevents the fumes from the icing fluids from being drawn into the cabin. Once we were secure, they began spraying the aircraft. Maybe, it would not be such a bad day after all. For aircraft now requesting treatment, the delays were over five hours.

The whole de-icing process from start to finish takes about thirty minutes. There was a lot of aeroplane to treat. Therefore, I was surprised to hear from the team leader when he called up after only ten minutes. It was impossible to treat a 747 that quickly. I was correct. He was calling to inform us that one of the trucks had broken down. They were arranging for a replacement. It should only take another hour before it would arrive. Only an hour! What planet is this guy on, was my immediate thought, one which prudently I kept to myself. There was no point in the other truck continuing as both sides of the aircraft had to be treated simultaneously. It was pointless having a clean plane on one side and a snowy one on the other. Also, the de-icing fluid only lasts for a certain amount of time before its potency begins to decline. There was nothing else for it but to wait. Finally, the replacement truck arrived, and the whole process started again from the beginning. Imagine my exasperation when ten minutes later, the team leader calls up again.

"Please don't tell me the truck has broken down again," was my heartfelt plea.

"No, of course not", was the reassuring reply. "This time, it's run out of de-icing fluid." These were not the words I wanted to hear.

Another hour dragged by as a new truck, full of fluid, finally arrived. We had now been on the aircraft for over four hours, and we still had an eight-hour flight ahead of us. It really was turning out to be a long day. My mood was not lightened when I heard the Miami flight call up for permission to taxi. What on earth had possessed me to swap? Still, the second new truck had now arrived, and the pair of them were busy blasting away at the tremendous amount of snow that had built up on the aircraft. Finally, they finished their task. We turned the air conditioning back on and called up to request our push back and start. Finally, we were on our way. Surely nothing else could go wrong, could it?

As we prepared to start our last two engines, there was a call from the cabin. This was never good news at such a critical moment. And as predicted, good news it most certainly was not. A passenger who had been taken unwell, very unwell, wanted to get off the aircraft. After unsuccessfully persuading the cabin crew to lock him away in a toilet and pretend to discover him after take-off, we asked for permission to be towed back onto the stand. The dying whine of the two engines we had managed to start perfectly reflected my mood in the proceedings. Would we ever getaway today?

Another hour later, the unfortunate passenger and his bag were taken off the aircraft. We again requested the de-icing trucks to return. Five hours and counting, and we had only managed to move less than one hundred metres. My new best friend, the team leader, eventually came back onto the headset and asked if I had missed him. I assured him that if I had something to throw at him, I most certainly would not miss him. Banter over, he assured me that they would complete their task as quickly as possible.

We were now six hours behind our schedule. The passengers, the crew, and I were just plain fed up. We also now faced the problem that the runway in Nairobi may be closed. We asked our operations department to call Nairobi and request an extension that would allow us to land. They came back and assured me that the authorities in Nairobi would approve the extension. So once again, we requested push back and started-up. I held my breath as we finally started to move under our own power. It was now the middle of the afternoon in London. Already, what remaining daylight was beginning to fade away. The snow had turned the airport into a winter wonderland. We taxied very slowly, the ice on the taxiways making our progress very precarious. We had all of our anti-icing systems working flat out. Our crew were constantly checking the wings for any sign of ice or snow. Returning to stand for further treatment was no longer an option. We would be out of crew duty hours, and I'm not sure any of us could face those de-icing rigs again.

Finally, it was our turn to line up on the runway. The conditions were truly appalling. Snow was being swept across the runway by near blizzard conditions. We were in the middle of the storm's fury, and I, for one, wanted to get out of it as quickly as possible. We waited as the aircraft ahead of us immediately disappeared into the grey overcast the moment it raised its nose. The clouds of snow were just about at ground level now. I briefly thought of my Miami flight which was now heading into a beautiful Florida sunset. Once again, I swore quietly under my breath. We were given our take-off clearance, running the engines up on the runway to clear any last remnants of ice. I released the brakes just as the engines reached full power. Tonight, was not the time for reduced power take-off. The aircraft slowly accelerated down the runway. I had the controls crossed to help keep the plane straight as a strong crosswind did its best to blow us sideways. It was a difficult take-off, and I certainly had my hands full. Just as we reached eighty knots, the speed at which we would only abandon the take-off for a significant problem, I heard something I had never heard before in all my years of flying, "Speedbird 69, STOP. I say again, STOP."

Now when you are trying to keep a 747 going in a straight line on a windy, snowy night, you are pretty much fully occupied. No time for idle thoughts, no time to appreciate the beauty of the snow rushing past the cockpit. Nope, you are entirely concentrated on the task at hand. And then some controller in his nice warm tower goes and spoils your day by calling stop. Of course, there is no time to politely inquire why you are being told to stop. No, you just slam the thrust levers closed and apply all the braking you can. We were below eighty knots, so we did not need to use reverse thrust to slow the aircraft. The brakes did a splendid job all by themselves.

We were asked to vacate the runway at the next available exit and call our company. What on earth had we done wrong to justify such drastic measures? A quick call to the operations department soon clarified the reason. The authorities at Nairobi had decided not to extend our landing permission, and their runway would definitely be closed at the time of our arrival. All in all, it had been a good decision to stop us before we got airborne. At least our problems were now over, and we could all go to a hotel or home. How wrong can one person be?

Naturally, the first thing we asked was for permission to return to our stand or any stand for that matter. There was a definite pause before we were informed that there were no stands available. Every stand had an aircraft on it awaiting de-icing. Fair enough, I thought. Okay, could we go and park on some remote part of the airport and wait for a fleet of buses to take us to the terminal? There was another, even more, noticeable pause. "Sorry, there is nowhere for you to park. All inbound aircraft are being diverted. There is no room for any more aircraft," came the next piece of information I did not want to hear.

This was another first for me, air traffic control telling me to stop and ground control now telling me I could not park anywhere. My Miami flight, at this time, would just be touching down. The crew would soon be sitting outside a bar sipping an ice-cold beer in the sultry evening sunshine. I, on the other hand, was sitting forlornly on my aircraft in the ice-cold.

And so, we waited, engines running on a snowy taxiway, unable to find anywhere where we could shut the engines down and get the now, very unhappy passengers, off the aircraft. We had now been on the plane for eight hours and counting. Something had to be done and done quickly. My pleas fell on deaf ears. We would have to wait for one aircraft to move before we could take its place. An hour later, we finally turned onto the remotest of remote stands in a part of the airfield I hardly knew existed. As the four engines eventually wound down to welcome silence, our problems were far from over. Yes, we now had somewhere to park, but there were no buses to ferry our passengers back to the terminal. Another hour passed, and still, we waited. Finally, a solitary bus appeared out of the snowstorm. It pulled up at the bottom of the stairs that had been placed up against the aircraft. Only thirty passengers at a time could be taken to the terminal, a thirty-minute round journey. The crew performed miracles keeping the passengers from storming the bus each time it returned. Tempers were frayed, and feelings ran high.

By this time, the three of us had joined our cabin crew colleagues in trying to restore and maintain some sort of order in the cabin. The number of passengers slowly dwindled until finally only the crew and one passenger remained. Sitting quietly, our passenger had waited until everyone else had disembarked before explaining his difficulty. He had been carried into the aircraft as he was totally dependent on his specially adapted wheelchair, which was in the aircraft's hold. Sadly, without this wheelchair, he was unable to move.

To make matters worse, he could not speak without the aid of a vocal box, also part of his wheelchair. He was communicating by writing down what he needed to say. He had been looked after by one of the crew. He was due to be met in Nairobi by his fiancé. They were getting married in two days.

We had now been on the aircraft for nearly twelve hours, and we were all exhausted. Of course, we could not leave our very special passenger alone on the plane. On the other hand, I could not expect the crew to remain on the aircraft indefinitely. As much as I was tempted to jump on the bus, I volunteered to stay and allow the rest of the crew to go home. Incredibly, one of the co-pilots volunteered to stay and help me. The three of us waved goodbye as the last bus made its way through the snow towards the terminal.

As the astronauts once said, "Houston, we have a problem," only in this case, it was, "Heathrow, we have a problem." We needed a loading team to open the hold and retrieve the wheelchair. We then needed a bus to take us to the terminal, and then we needed a hotel room that was wheelchair friendly. None of these necessities were available as the snow had now shut down the airport. Every hotel was now full of stranded passengers. Things were not looking good at all. Of course, it was impossible to contact anyone in operations. Everyone was working flat out to deal with the chaos caused by the weather.

Two hours later, a single loader arrived to unload the wheelchair. Clearly, this was beyond the capability of one man, and so myself, my co-pilot, and our new loader friend managed to retrieve the wheelchair from the vast belly of the jumbo. One problem had now been solved. Just the transport and hotel hurdles remained.

I rarely have good ideas. My mediocre ones are things to be cherished. Tonight, however, I exceeded my own low expectations. From the corner of my memory, I dredged up a hotel nearby where we stayed many years ago in my executive flying days. After a quick Google search, I had their number. Yes, they had a room that was suitable for a guest in a wheelchair. They would only hold the room with a prepayment. Not having a company credit card, I used my own card. Hopefully, I could reclaim the money later.

Looking into the gloom, two small headlights began to appear. We were in business as a small minibus made its way out of the snowy landscape. We managed to get our passenger onboard, and we set off for the drive across the airport. Over fifteen hours after leaving the terminal this morning, we were finally back. It was now two in the morning, and the arrivals hall was packed with stranded passengers. Up until that moment, there was nobody else around wearing a uniform. I had unwittingly entered the lion's den. Suddenly, I was surrounded by a sea of faces, all waving tickets or passports in my face. I could do very little except offer words of sympathy or comfort. It was not their fault that they had no idea of the abysmal day I was having. With our new friend fully restored to his wheelchair, we could finally communicate. His story was extraordinary, and he was very stoic about his predicament. Clearing customs, we made our way to the main arrival level. We now faced the new problem of how to get our friend to his hotel. His wheelchair was very large, far too big for my small car. After numerous calls, it became apparent that we could not secure suitable transport to the hotel.

Of course, we could not leave him alone, especially after all we had been through together. Instead, we all made our way to the departure lounge to await the arrival of the morning shift, due at five o'clock. We sat chatting until our colleagues arrived. They took our passenger under their wing and promised to look after him until his rescheduled flight later that morning. Finally, precisely twenty hours after my alarm clock woke me up, it was time to go home. We only had to wait thirty minutes to get a bus to the crew car park. Blinking away my fatigue, I drove away from the airport. Imagine my reaction when the motorway closed due to the snowfall. An hour's drive turned into a three-hour marathon. I walked back through my own front door some twenty-four hours after closing it behind me. As I made my way upstairs, my mobile phone rang. It was the operations department. Could I take the delayed Nairobi flight out at midday? I think I managed to reply without swearing, although I could not guarantee that fact. I am now much more careful before I blithely agree to a trip swap.

Chapter 28

Life Changes Forever

I was now moving into my fourth decade of flying the 747. The years and life's events had slipped past without me really noticing. I would leave on a trip only to return and discover that our two baby sons had started primary school. I would return from another trip and find out they had started secondary education. On the next trip, one of them was missing. Apparently, he had started university. Life was swiftly passing me by as I flew my jumbo to the far-flung corners of the world. The idea that I had once been the youngest 747 captain now seemed absurd as I passed what looked like teenagers wearing captains' uniforms. Where had the months, years and decades gone? I was definitely an analogue pilot in an ever-increasingly digital world.

  British Airways announced that they would be retiring the entire Boeing 747 fleet in 2024. Using my fingers as a calculator, I figured that both the jumbo and me would be retiring at approximately the same time, give or take a year. This seemed entirely appropriate. We would both disappear over the horizon into a setting sun. I had under five years left until we were both destined to be assigned to the annals of history. I was determined to wring every ounce out of these last few years. Everything that I had in the past put off until I next visited a country now became a must-do on my list. Time was running out. Retirement, once an unthinkable event, was now very much a reality. As a young pilot, I would stand at various bars worldwide and listen to what I thought of as ancient captains discussing their pensions. I had found the whole subject very alien and boring. I now found myself actively engaged in such discussions. I was now keenly interested in cash equivalent transfer values and additional voluntary contributions. Pension pots and equity values now held real meaning for me. I had, without really noticing it, become an ancient captain. My co-pilots were now giving me that bored look I had so regularly used on those poor captains many years before.

Shaking myself from my reflections like a dog emerging from a muddy lake, I vowed that I would be different. Ghosts from the past would not slowly draw me towards old age. No, I was going to go out kicking and screaming. And so, I took up kitesurfing. I had always been active. I ran for pleasure most days, and over the years, I found myself in various predicaments as I pounded the streets of cities all over the world. Now though, I needed a new challenge, something to keep me away from any discussions involving pensions.

The idea had been sparked off by a birthday present from my younger son, Robert. He had bought me a kitesurfing lesson. Years before, I had enjoyed windsurfing on my many Caribbean trips. Warm seas, warm weather, and gentle breezes had made the whole experience a pleasure. Falling off, a trick I mastered very quickly, had never deterred me. Apart from the occasional jellyfish, being immersed in the Caribbean Sea was hardly a problem. Once the jumbo had been withdrawn from these routes, the delights of windsurfing became less attractive. Trying to keep warm, fully dressed in a wetsuit, gloves, and head protector was just not the same. As lovely as it may be, the English Channel is not where I would choose to be for most of the year. Slowly, I fell out of love with windsurfing, at roughly the same rate I kept falling off my board.

Now, however, I had a new sport to try. The even better news was that I could enjoy my new sport in Cape Town, a destination I visited every month. The only problem with Cape Town was that the sea temperatures were freezing, much, much worse than the English Channel. After my introductory lesson, I was hooked. I bought my own kite and board and happily accepted the sea temperatures as I practised on the beach, close to the airport at Shoreham, where my career had started all those decades ago. Once again, I was taking to the Sussex skies, albeit now with a kite. I was mostly out of control, a little like my first solo flight in 1979. I was keen to try out my new sport in the warmer climate of Cape Town. My first attempt ended in abject humiliation. Packing borrowed gear in the hire car, I set off on the relatively short drive to Sunset Beach. I had been advised that this was a popular kitesurfing area. Just thirty minutes after setting off, I pulled up into the beach car park. I carefully unpacked all my gear and squeezed it into a slightly too small wetsuit. Feeling that I looked the part, I sucked in my tummy as best I could and strode towards the beach. Had this been back in the 1970s, I would have easily blended into the cool crowd clustered along the shoreline. Unfortunately for me, I was now forty years too late to look cool. Still, I was confident that I could hold my own with these youngsters. After the English Channel, the Atlantic Ocean held no fears for me. Well, it didn't until I read a sign next to the water.

It had taken me about twenty minutes to inflate my kite, check my harness, and secure my safety lines. With the kite flying high above my head, I slowly made my way to the water's edge. Other kite surfers flashed past, many performing aerial tricks. Everyone seemed way above my skill level. Still, I was sure that once I was in the water, all would be well. And that's when I saw the warning sign. The gist of the warning was that sharks were present in the area. If you were menstruating, then you were warned not to go into the water. I had to reread the sign a few times before the meaning sunk in. Suddenly, the allure of kitesurfing vanished. All I wanted to do was get back in my car and get away as quickly and hopefully, as quietly as possible. Other kite surfers were looking at me as they awaited their turn to enter the water. What to do? Did I risk the shark-infested waters or turn around and perform the walk of shame back up the beach with my elementary skills? Being British and an intrepid aviator to boot, I, of course, did the only thing possible, I fled.

It was a long, lonely walk back to the car as I dragged my half-inflated kite and ego behind me. With as much dignity as I could muster, I peeled off my wetsuit and let my stomach return to its normal shape. With a final look at the fearless kite surfers, I started the engine and headed back to the hotel. I consoled myself with the thought that these were not just any old sharks. This was the home of the great white shark. Who was I to dress up to make myself look like a giant seal and enter his domain? Leave it to the experts.

I did manage to find an incredible inland lagoon at Langebaan, a very cool seaside town two hours to the north. There, I spent many happy days kitesurfing with people of my standard. I was safe in the knowledge that no sharks were waiting for me as I frequently tumbled from my board. The local instructors were terrific. I would have a lesson in the morning and would practise in the afternoon. Life seemed good, up until the moment my favourite instructor came off his board. The safety line failed to deflate his kite, and he was dragged, unconscious, into deeper water. By the time the rescue boat reached him, he was dead. If such a professional surfer could suffer a horrendous fate, I knew that my chances of avoiding serious injury or worse were relatively high. My passion for the sport was on the decline. I rarely kitesurf these days.

Despite my attempts to hold back the years, I knew that Father Time was hot on my heels. Despite running every day, I could not keep ahead for much longer. The finishing line was in sight for both myself and my beloved 747. The only good thing was that we both had a few years left in us before the inevitable finishing line. And then, after a trip to China, one of my co-pilots mentioned that there were reports of a virus spreading rapidly throughout the region of Wuhan. I was not unduly worried. Although we did fly to China on the 747, it was not a place I chose to visit if I could avoid it. My aircraft and I were safe. This, of course, turned out to be the greatest misjudgement of my career.

Just a few months later, I was preparing for our departure from Miami. Wisely, I had managed to avoid swapping this trip. A friend I had known for a long time, the station engineer, came onto the flight deck looking very downhearted. He usually greeted me with a smile and a joke. Tonight, he could barely manage a sentence. He handed me the technical log to sign without so much as a word of greeting. This was so out of character for him. A few months previously, he had been laughing uncontrollably as we taxied onto the stand. At the time, we had the Miami station manager on board. He was retiring after a forty-year career at Miami Airport. Air traffic control asked us to stop on the taxiway. The airport fire services were going to spray an archway for us to taxi under as a mark of respect for the manager. We waited for ten minutes, but despite all their best efforts, all they had managed to do was spray the aircraft and scare our passengers. It took a long time for him to wipe away the uproarious tears of laughter.

Tonight, he was very different. Clearly, something was terribly wrong. After a few moments of hesitation, the whole story came out. He had heard rumours that this new virus had become a worldwide pandemic, and the world as we knew it was changing forever. He predicted that he would be made redundant along with the majority of the staff at Miami. He looked me directly in the eye and stuck his hand out. This was a hardened career engineer, the salt of the earth, the best of the best. I had never seen anything even remotely bother him. He took life as it came and smiled at adversity. This time, there were tears in his eyes as he shook my hand, holding on much longer than was usually comfortable. By the time he let my hand go, there were tears on his cheeks. His last words to me were to wish me luck. He doubted we would ever meet again. Tragically, he was correct. As we climbed into the night sky, I had a strange feeling that something was ending. I never flew a 747 to America again. As we touched down in London, the world had indeed changed. We were in something called lockdown, whatever that was.

Chapter 29

They Think It's All Over

I was lucky enough to play golf on a number of occasions with the legendary Kenneth Wolstenholme, the BBC commentator who so famously uttered the words in this chapter's title. Ken was a bomber pilot in the Second World War, a fellow aviator as well as a thoroughly decent human being, sadly, no longer with us. I hope that he would approve the use of his famous line that I have chosen to mark the end of my Boeing 747 career.

After landing from Miami after the sad farewell, I returned home to a different world. We were all in lockdown and all British Airways aircraft were grounded.

Initially, we were assured that the 747 would be making a comeback as soon as conditions allowed it. In the meanwhile, we were all put on indefinite leave, which as the months passed became known as a furlough.

As professional pilots, we had to fly an aircraft or a simulator every twenty-eight days to remain current. This period could be extended by a few days if really necessary. Thirty days was the absolute limit. Lockdown started in March 2020. Nobody was flying and we all sat at home wondering what would become of our industry. Having aircraft sitting around doing nothing is eye wateringly expensive. Aircraft have to fly to earn their keep. The cost of the finance on each and every aircraft was still being paid out. The cost of maintenance still had to be met. Simple parking charges can be thousands of pounds a day, that is, if you can find somewhere to park the aircraft. On top of all this, aircraft hate to sit around doing nothing. Leave a serviceable aircraft for a week, and you can expect a few problems when you start it up again.

Against this background, I sat watching events unfold. Our 747s were being flown to provincial airports all over the country to be put into storage. It was at this point that I seriously began to doubt if I would ever get the chance to fly the Queen of the Skies again. Had I known that the last Miami flight was going to be the last time I would ever fly the jumbo, I could at least, have said a fitting goodbye. Instead, I simply got out of my seat and walked away.

There were a few 747s flying mercy missions to repatriate stranded tourists. Unfortunately, I was now out of my recency period. I was also overdue for my biannual route check. Every two years, a training captain would sit behind me checking everything I did on a flight. This usually meant that I heard a lot of tut-tuts in my right ear, but so far, I had managed to pass all of my check flights. There was, therefore, little or no chance that I would get to fly anytime soon. And then the phone rang.

Would I be prepared to do a simulator check at six o'clock tomorrow morning? This was at the beginning of June. I had not flown since early March, quite a long time and very short notice, but what the heck. I readily agreed.

The session went as well as could be expected. I was a little rusty at first but after a surprisingly short time, I was back in the groove. I almost landed the simulator properly, something I rarely did on checks. Luckily for me, the real aircraft was much easier to land. I drove home that morning feeling pleased that I was now once again 'in check'. This feeling of achievement lasted until I remembered that I was also due a route check. Well, there was no chance of that happening in the current circumstances. And then the phone rang, again.

Would I be prepared to fly to Cape Town the next day? Let me think about that for a millisecond was my immediate reply. I was then told to wait to hear about the trip before agreeing so readily. This was no ordinary flight. Would I be prepared to fly the aircraft to Cape Town whilst being route checked by a training captain? I would then stay on the aircraft and fly directly back to London but as a passenger. This meant being on the aircraft for a total of just under thirty hours. I was informed that I was perfectly within my rights to decline their kind offer.

This time it took me a little longer to agree. Being on a route check is always stressful, not most people's idea of a fun day out. I had hardly flown in the preceding three months, a couple of trips to get nicely back into the swing of things first would have been nice. Of course, at this point, that was a luxury I would never have. I had been given a golden opportunity to fly my aircraft one last time. There had been very credible rumours that the entire fleet of 747s were going to be grounded for good. If this was my final chance to say goodbye to my aircraft, how could I possibly refuse?

And so, I reported the next afternoon ready to fly an empty aircraft to Cape Town to pick up three hundred stranded tourists. Nothing was normal and familiar anymore. There were Covid-19 tests to endure, everyone was wearing masks, and the airport was completely empty. It felt like entering a parallel universe except that most human beings had been taken away. It was four months since I last flew an actual aircraft, and at that time, everything was almost mundane; it was so routinely normal. Today was a very, very different situation, and to top it all, I was being checked out on everything I said and did. After nearly thirty-four years of flying the 747, I suddenly felt as though it was my first day all over again. Everything was vaguely familiar, yet different. I planned to take everything very slowly and methodically. We could not afford to make even the smallest of errors on this flight.

The cabin crew would normally meet in a room to discuss the flight and at the appropriate time, the flight crew would introduce themselves. This was a great way to build teamwork and to get to know the crew. Today, of course, we were not allowed to meet together in a small space. Instead, I wandered around trying to find out who was in my crew. At the pilot's briefing, we carefully looked at all of the paperwork. The weather report at Cape Town was forecasting the small possibility of fog at the time of our arrival. I discussed this with my co-pilot and decided to take on extra fuel. I noticed the training captain making notes, not a good sign, especially before we had even really started. Then, looking at the technical notes I noticed that an outflow valve had been misbehaving. This valve allows air to leave the aircraft to protect against over pressurisation. Basically, it is fully open on the ground and as the aircraft climbs it slowly closes to allow the aircraft to pressurise. If it suddenly opens, the aircraft will lose all the precious air and the oxygen masks will drop from the aircraft's bulkhead. It can also require the pilot to make an emergency descent if it cannot be manually closed. Once on the aircraft, I decided that it would be a good idea to practise this manual closing procedure, in case it should be required. Whilst we did this, I noticed the training captain once more, scribbling away. Oh dear, not again.

Eventually, we slowly taxied towards the runway. I was acutely aware that I was under intense scrutiny. This was not at all what I'd hoped for on what may well be my final 747 flight. The departure was smooth; we were literally the only aircraft in the sky. On our way through France, Spain, Algeria, Niamey and Accra, ours was the only voice on the airwaves. It strongly reinforced the feeling once again, that we were in a parallel universe, and we were the only occupants in this strange new world.

During this quiet period in the cruise, our training captain decided to de-brief our departure process. Why had we taken extra fuel when it was company policy to disregard forecasts when the probability of fog was below thirty percent? My answer did not impress him. My local knowledge of the weather in Cape Town at this time of year apparently was not a scientific reason to carry extra fuel. I could see that he was only just warming up. Why had I gone through the touch drills of a checklist for an outflow valve? Not only was this not orthodox, but it was also unnecessary as the aircraft had flown twice since this issue had occurred and, on our departure, we had had no problems. Therefore, his view was that it was an overreaction and a waste of time. My counterargument was that we had the time to practise the drill and climbing away carrying out a difficult checklist is made much easier if we had just practised it. My explanation fell on deaf ears.

Twelve hours later, we began what was to be my final ever descent in a 747. We called the approach controller for a weather update; the airport was now covered in a dense fog with the visibility right on our limits for an automatic landing. I had hoped to be able to fly my last approach and landing without using the autopilot Now, I would have to carry out an automatic landing. I felt a wave of sadness sweep over me, quickly replaced by a feeling of relief that we had taken on extra fuel. If the conditions got any worse, we might have to wait for an hour for them to improve before diverting. There were beautiful views of the stunning beach at Noordhoek as we flew over Table Mountain. The fog bank was only sitting over the airport itself, everything else was crystal clear. We turned over False Bay and began our final descent towards an invisible runway. At five hundred feet above the ground, we entered the fog. From bright sunshine, we were immediately plunged into a dark grey world. The automatic pilot flew a faultless approach and I concentrated on trying to see the runway. Although this was an autoland, due to this airport's facilities, it meant that the pilot had to see the runway before we reached fifty feet. At Heathrow and other airports, we could land without the need to see the runway at all, always a strange experience. At the automatic callout of 'Decide', I just managed to discern three runway lights. The 747 kissed the runway. We were down. She really was the best aircraft ever made, my Queen of the Skies.

We slowly taxied towards the terminal. Visibility was still very poor but improving quickly. As I applied the brakes and shut down those magnificent Rolls Royce engines, I knew that a quite remarkable era had come to an untimely end. I sat there in silence drinking in the unique atmosphere of a 747's flight deck. This exceptional aircraft had flown the equivalent distance of flying to the moon and back many times. She had looked after her crews and passengers for over thirty years. The old lady had served us well and just performed another perfect landing. I leant forward and patted her control column, thanking her for making me look good over the years. My mood was broken by a tap on the shoulder from the training captain. I had completely forgotten all about him. Was I ready for a full debrief? Turning around I replied, "No, not really," but I knew I could not escape that easily.

The debrief itself went on for what seemed an age. I admit that I stopped paying full attention once he confirmed that I had passed. No mention was made about the extra fuel for the forecast of fog, and I for one, was not going to try to score points. I was far more interested in saying the last goodbye to my aircraft. I was about to write a note to the crew flying us home to mention the outflow valve when I was asked to leave. Apparently, the ground crews had to disinfect everything. The training captain insisted a note was not necessary as the fault had been fixed.

Three hours later, we took off for our return flight to London. The aircraft was completely full this time, and I was in my passenger seat, more than ready for hopefully a good, well-deserved sleep.

Ten minutes later there was an automatic announcement on the public address system. All the oxygen masks were about to fall from the ceiling as the aircraft depressurised. That outflow valve had not been repaired after all. I looked across at the training captain as all of the cabin lights suddenly illuminated. Maybe, just maybe, a little time spent on practising the drill had not been such a waste of time after all.

Chapter 30

Thank You and Good Night

The crew managed to close the valve manually, slightly late but still safely. The oxygen masks were put to one side, and we continued our flight home. Thirty hours after leaving London, we were home. Again, we were the only aircraft airborne. We were coming home alone.

A few weeks later, the decision was made to permanently ground all of our Boeing 747's. My route check had in fact been totally unnecessary. Never again would I fly a Jumbo. We were entering uncharted territory. My whole career appeared to have come to an abrupt end. Pilots worldwide were being made redundant, civil aviation was entering into a crisis from which it still has to recover. I was fortunate in the fact that my career was coming to a natural end. I only had two years to go before my retirement date. I felt terribly sorry for my younger colleagues. They had young families, huge mortgages, and now a very uncertain future. Aviation had changed forever, and incredibly sadly, so had the career prospects for the professional pilot.

After returning from Cape Town, the news I had been dreading but expecting finally arrived. The entire Boeing 747 fleet was being grounded with immediate effect. Not only were they grounded, but they were going to be cut up and sold for scrap. We were put on indefinite leave, all of our futures looked very bleak. There were photographs and video footage as each aircraft made its final ignominious flights to their graveyards over the following weeks and months. The Cotswolds Airport had row upon row of majestic jumbos all lined up awaiting their fate. My colleagues and I felt a tremendous sense of loss and sadness as our aircraft was literally destroyed before our very eyes; it was heart-breaking. For myself, I knew that I would soon be joining my aircraft on the aviation scrap heap. I still had two more years of flying ahead, so I accepted a transfer to the Boeing 777, a great aircraft but sadly not in the same league as the jumbo. I knew nothing could ever replace the 747 in my heart.

I started the Boeing 777 course in October 2020. Apart from my flight to Cape Town, I had not flown for nearly eight months. And so, for the first time since September 1987, I found myself reporting at Heathrow to begin a course on a brand-new type of aircraft. It felt very strange reporting that first morning. The old teaching compound at Cranebank had been sold for development. As I passed it on my way to the new Global Learning Academy, it was haunting to see this once proud building slowly decomposing. The development plans had obviously stalled, and the facilities were now falling apart without the help of any demolition company. I had seen photographs of the interior that had been posted on social media. Everything had literally been left as it was when the last class finished. There were books, manuals, equipment and all the paraphernalia used in our training. All were in place awaiting the next group of trainees, which of course, would never arrive. A shudder ran through me at the recollection of all my ground and simulator sessions. The empty buildings seemed to mock me as I made my way to the new training centre. Either that or they were trying to warn me of what lay ahead. Had I listened to those ghostly structures, my career may have had a more happy ending.

The ground school phase of the course lasted for two weeks. I had certainly not wasted the eight months that I had been grounded. I had spent at least four hours a day studying and hopefully learning all the technical manuals. The learning method was not dissimilar to the carrel system I had used all those years ago when I started on the jumbo. This system meant that we sat in front of a mock-up of the flight deck of the 777 whilst simultaneously completing a computer learning module. Back in 1987, when I first converted onto the 747, there were no computers. Instead, we listened to a recorded description of the various aircraft systems. This new way of learning was far superior. I was paired up with a terrific partner, Johnathon. He was also a 747 captain, having flown Concorde previously, so no pressure there then. I managed to keep up this time, and we both passed all the ground examinations without too much drama.

The simulator phase came next. The 777 is a modern, computer-driven, fly by wire aircraft. For the first few sessions, I made the mistake of over-controlling the plane. Muscle memory from thirty-four years of flying the jumbo was a hard habit to break. Also, I now had to start the landing flare at thirty feet instead of fifty. The ground looked far too close, as I tried to land the 777, and I would revert to flaring at fifty feet. To be fair, had I tried to flare a jumbo at thirty feet, the wheels would come up through the wings. We were given a new short conversion course, and we had little time for any repeats or practise.

Despite this, I learned to fly the 777 to a good standard and passed the course's simulator phase. I finally had a shiny new endorsement on my licence. I was a 777 pilot. I just hoped that the line of sad jumbos lined up at various airports awaiting their fate would forgive me.

The line training phase of the course came next. I was happy with my ability to fly this new aircraft. In so many ways, it was far easier to fly than the jumbo. The fly by wire technology aided the pilot to fly smoothly and accurately. Unlike the jumbo, we had the use of autothrottle for the entire flight. This meant that the computer moved the thrust levers to achieve the desired speed, even with one engine inoperative. This was a luxury we could only have dreamt of on the jumbo, or indeed any aircraft I had previously flown.

My first flight was to Bangkok, a place I had visited on many previous occasions. Once again, I was transported back to my first days in the company. This time, however, I had all the new restrictions of Covid-19 to contend with in addition to flying a new type of aircraft. We had to report at a hotel and queue up to take our Covid-19 tests. We then had a nervous hour's wait to get the results. This first flight was a freighter flight with no passengers. We were flying out to collect the vital personal protection equipment or PPE so crucial in keeping the NHS and our hospitals running. The training captain was excellent, and despite all of the new procedures, we managed to push back on time. Our third pilot carried out the checklist for securing the aircraft in its freighter configuration, which was standard.

The flight to Bangkok went smoothly, even though everything seemed somehow surreal. I was in a different aircraft for the first time in over thirty years. I had to wear a mask at all times except on the flight deck. Everything seemed familiar but somehow different. I took control of the aircraft at one thousand feet and flew a good stable approach right down to fifty feet when I flared! Damn! Still, I gently flared again, and we made a smooth touchdown well within the normal touchdown zone. Hopefully, the training captain had not noticed the slightly high flare. It was a forlorn hope. We debriefed on the aircraft. Everything had gone well. I just needed to make sure I flared or raised the aircraft's nose at thirty, not fifty feet. Still, it was a safe landing, just a little finessing required.

We were then escorted from the aircraft by people; I assumed they were people as they were dressed head to foot in white suits, so it was difficult to tell. Not a fraction of a human being could be seen. They were more like technicians from a crime scene than the ground staff at an airport. We were marched, literally marched through the airport to an adjacent hotel. Here similarly suited staff herded us to our rooms. Once there, the door was opened, and we were ushered into a small, poorly decorated room. The door slammed closed behind me, and that was the last human contact I would have until twenty-four hours later, when the whole process was repeated in reverse. Food was supplied twice, it was left outside the room, and we were only allowed to collect it when the guards stood back. If I'm ever unlucky enough to go to prison, I will be way ahead of my fellow inmates in the procedures required.

The flight home was a repeat of the way out, only this time I flared at thirty feet in London and was rewarded with a very smooth touchdown. Job done, and I went home reasonably satisfied with my performance. In other words, I was bloody pleased with myself and went home happy. I was surprised when I read my training report a few days later. Very few of the good points raised during my debrief were mentioned, but the slightly high flare in Bangkok was highlighted. Still, the overall score was good, and it was recorded as a good start to the line training phase.

My next trip was to my favourite destination, Cape Town. Again, I was due to operate both flights. The trip south went well. It was an eerie rerun of my last 747 flight. Luckily this time, there were no technical problems to contend with. I knew the route so well that I automatically selected the subsequent radio frequency before being given it. I knew all of the enroute diversion airfields. I had operated into most of them in the past. This time, the training captain was more intense and seemed more interested in finding out what I didn't know rather than what I did know. Despite this, the approach and landing went as well as I dared hope, and I flared at thirty feet for a smooth touchdown. His only comment was that I may have been striving for the perfect landing rather than putting the aircraft down earlier. I just smiled and kept my thoughts to myself.

We had two days off in which to relax and enjoy the sunshine. It was December which is early summer in Cape

Town. My plans were disrupted when the training captain arranged for two sessions of technical questions. Both of these sessions were arduous, but I managed to answer all of his questions satisfactorily. The flight home was also a little demanding. More questions were asked at inappropriate moments, not a pleasant way to pass the evening. The approach and landing were again good. I just kept saying to myself as we came over the runway, thirty feet, thirty feet. Luckily, for me, it worked.

My final flight of the year was to Dubai, again a place I knew very well. This time I knew the training captain. We had both been on the Beach Fleet many years before. We arrived in Dubai on time, in the right place, and without any hitches, job done. The return flight again went well. It was a good end to the year.

My next trip was to New York, another destination that I was more than familiar with. The weather in January can be unpredictable. As we made our way down the approach, we were rocked and buffeted by a winter storm. The conditions were challenging, with the crosswind right on the limits of the aircraft. As we taxied onto our stand, I was feeling reasonably pleased with myself. The return flight went well, and I was back on track, well for the time being anyway.

My next assignment was a four-sector flight to the Caribbean from my favourite airport, Gatwick. I had not flown from Gatwick since the 747 Beach Fleet days nearly twenty years before. A lot had changed in those years, and once again, I felt that everything was familiar yet different. I even had trouble finding the new car park and had to twice stop and ask the way to the crew reporting centre. The training captain was the same one I'd had on my Cape Town flight, so I knew it would be difficult. I had absolutely no idea just how difficult it would turn out to be.

I had arrived over an hour early to make sure that I had plenty of time to familiarise myself with the set-up at Gatwick.

Long gone were the buildings where we used to report. We were now stationed at the opposite side of the airport. Still, everyone was friendly, and I explored my new surroundings with a certain amount of optimism. It was not to last long.

I returned to the briefing area in plenty of time to prepare the paperwork before the training captain arrived. Covid-19 had taken its toll on the flight programme at Gatwick. All short-haul operations had been closed down or moved to Heathrow. The majority of the crews had either been made redundant or furloughed. The atmosphere was solemn. There were very few people in the building, which was slightly disconcerting. The training captain was waiting for me as I returned to the briefing counter. The paperwork was still not available. Instead of a friendly chat, I was met with a barrage of technical questions which were unrelated to today's flight. I managed to answer each and every question. Still, I was unsure why I was being interrogated, and I asked why he was taking such a draconian approach to the flight. It felt like I was being treated as a new pilot rather than a captain with nearly forty years of experience. I was not at all happy with his attitude, and I made my feelings clear. Unfortunately, there were just the two of us. We did not require a third pilot on the flight to Antigua. There was no respite from his unpleasant demeanour.

It was my sector, and I made the fuel decision after consultation with my not too friendly partner. We made our way out to the aircraft, where we met our cabin crew. I completed the exterior walk around the plane and returned to the flight deck to prepare for the flight. While conducting my various checks, the training captain put all of our details into the aircraft's computer. This information would then be sent to Heathrow, where our performance details would be completed. It usually took about five minutes to complete this procedure and obtain a printed message. We would then enter the results into the aircraft's computer. These details must be absolutely correct as all of our take-off and climb out speeds are derived from these calculations. To get these details wrong could result in catastrophe. To attempt a take-off with the incorrect speeds selected had resulted in accidents with other airlines.

We waited for the figures to be printed, nothing. I asked for the figures to be resent. Another ten minutes and it became evident that there was a problem. A quick phone call to Heathrow confirmed our suspicions. The primary computer system, which calculated the take-off figures for aircraft worldwide, had failed. This was such an infrequent occurrence; personally, I could not remember the last time that this had happened. There was only one thing for it, we would have to revert to the old fashion method. We would have to get the performance manuals out and do a manual calculation. I asked the training captain to complete these calculations whilst I informed the crew and passengers that there would be a slight delay to our departure. This did not go well with my colleague, who told me that he could complete the manual calculations as quickly as the computer. Personally, I was not confident that I could do likewise. There were no computers when I flew the classic 747, and we completed a manual calculation for every departure. In those days, I was fluent in their process. However, that was over twenty years ago. Today, I was going to take my time and check and then double-check everything we did.

As I completed my passenger announcement, I was handed a set of calculations from the other captain. He then asked me to read them aloud, enabling him to load them into the aircraft's flight management system. I was being rushed, and I was feeling uncomfortable with his approach to the flight. We were completing a process that I understood but that I was not fluent in. I asked for a few moments to run my own calculations. I would then compare my results with his to ensure that the two sets agreed with each other. Despite his assurances that his figures were correct, I took the time to check.

As I started the comparison, I felt an ice-cold shiver run all the way down my back. The two sets of figures were very different; there was a large discrepancy. I rechecked my figures. I must have made a fundamental error. If he discovered this error before I did, I would be in dire trouble. I could quickly fail this check. I checked my figures for a second and then a third time. Whatever mistake I had made, I could not identify it. I was in serious trouble. Whilst I continued checking, my colleague was becoming more and more impatient. The tension was mounting, and I was delaying our departure. He began writing notes, never a good sign when you are under intense scrutiny.

I began to carefully check his calculations. He had correctly used all of today's conditions, including the temperature, the wind and the air pressure. All of these factors have to be included. He had used the correct take-off weight. Why was there such a difference between the two sets of figures? It made no sense to me. And then, at the very bottom of the page, the answer jumped out and grabbed me by the throat. I froze. This could not be happening. Was this a test or a trap? Had this been done intentionally to see if I would discover the mistake. I had to make an instant decision. If for one moment I thought that this had been done deliberately, then I would simply refuse to fly with this trainer. I would stand up and go home. How I wished that I had chosen to do that.

Instead, I passed the calculations back and asked him to recalculate his figures. He snatched the form away from me and insisted that the figures were correct. I agreed with him that, indeed, his figures were accurate. They were correct, but not for the runway we were using today. He had based his figures on the wrong runway. He stared at the paper in front of him, not moving a muscle. His next move would decide if I was getting off or staying with the flight. If he admitted or indicated that this was a deliberate mistake, I would not continue with the operation. Instead, he recalculated his figures and handed them back to me. This time our calculations matched precisely. We entered these figures into the flight management system. Ten minutes later, we were airborne and on our way to Antigua.

It was a five-day trip, definitely the least enjoyable five days of my career. Nothing I did could please this individual. Every suggestion or decision I made, he countered or questioned it. Our landing in Antigua was in a tropical storm. The windscreen wipers were doing their very best to clear the deluge away from our windscreen as I took control at decision height. The runway was barely visible as we came over the threshold. I was more than happy with my landing in these extreme conditions. The next day we flew a shuttle flight to Turks and Caicos. I elected to use the recommended runway at Turks. It gave me a nice headwind. Instead, he insisted that we use the reciprocal runway as it would save time. I had to land with a ten-knot tailwind instead. On the return flight to Antigua, I completed what I considered to be a good night landing.

The following night, we took off on our return flight to Gatwick. This time, I was flying the approach for his landing. I have never been a fan of selecting the flaps and landing gear during the latter stages of the approach. I prefer to slow the aircraft down a little earlier to give myself more time and space to get the aircraft in the correct configuration for landing. This is known as a stable approach, the aircraft must be stable by one thousand feet, or a missed approach must be flown. I prefer to have the aircraft stable by two thousand feet which makes for a much less exciting landing. Excitement is something I prefer to experience in my leisure time.

After landing, we taxied to our stand and shut down. Thank goodness the ordeal was now over. I had never before wanted to get off an aircraft so much. I could just put this behind me and move on. I prepared for a critical debrief. I knew that we were very different people and that he did not like my laid-back style. He was not happy unless he was doing something. I was not happy when I had to do something. We could not have a more different style of operating an aircraft. However, I had come across his type before, and it had not been a problem. We are all different. I expected a few negative remarks, but overall,

I knew that I had done a good job. I had made three good landings and had created a good account of myself. I had picked up the error on our departure from Gatwick, an incident that had not been mentioned since. At least the flight was over, and I could move on.

The next trip was to Chicago, again a place I knew well. It was now late January, and the weather in the Windy City was brutal. Daytime temperatures were twenty-five degrees below freezing with lake effect snow forecast for our arrival. Why, oh why could I not have my check flights in the middle of summer?

We made our approach over Lake Michigan; the visibility was excellent. For once, my luck was in, and we made a visual approach at night. The landing was good, and we taxied to our stand. Leaving the terminal, the full force of the brutal temperatures became apparent. On the drive into the city, the snow arrived. By the time we reached the hotel, there were stranded vehicles blocking roads. The snow was so heavy the streets were quickly becoming unpassable. They really knew how to do a good snowstorm in Chicago. I silently breathed a massive sigh of relief that we had landed just in time. I could really, really do with luck being on my side for a while.

The following day, the scene from my window was beautiful. Everything was covered in a white blanket of crisp snow. Temperatures were still minus twenty-five degrees, and the news channels were warning people to stay indoors. So what did I do? Well, I put my shorts on and went for a run along the lakeside. I had a thermal vest, gloves, and hat, so I felt confident I wouldn't suffer hypothermia as I made my way towards the lake. Unsurprisingly there were very few people about. As I approached the lakeside pathway, barriers across the entrance warned that the running track was closed. I was confident that the warning did not apply to me personally, so I made my way around the barrier. I was rewarded with a beautiful 10K run along a deserted lake. The blanket of snow deadened all sound, and as the snow began to slowly fall once more, I entered a different universe where my normal senses were gently subdued.

There was no sound except for my breathing as I made my way into the snow. My visual references were limited to just a few yards as the snow continued to fall. There was a complete stillness to complement the scene. Not a breath of wind hindered or helped me as I continued my run. Despite the bone-chilling temperature, I felt only elation. I was running at a pace I rarely achieve, and with each kilometre, I felt more and more refreshed. I was literally running away from my troubles. God, it felt good. An hour later, I entered the hotel with a massive smile on my face. I felt cleansed. Unsurprisingly, I was met by some curious stares as I made my way across the elegant entrance hall. The abominable snowman had obviously just checked in, and he was leaving a trail of water as he waited for the lift to arrive.

The return flight to London went well. I was complimented on the trip and was finally signed off to complete the next stage of the course. Maybe that run through the snow had worked its magic. I certainly felt revitalised and ready for anything else that may get thrown at me. How wrong I was. I had no idea just what was about to come my way.

A few days later, we were on the approach to Islamabad, the capital of Pakistan. As we passed one thousand feet, I was scanning the outside world for any glimpse of a runway. There was nothing but a blanket of white clouds outside of the aircraft. We were now passing five hundred feet, and still no sign of any lights. This did not look good. We had to see the runway by two hundred feet, or we would have to fly a missed approach. The training captain was flying the approach using the autopilot. I had elected to complete an automatic landing in such poor conditions. One of the most challenging manoeuvres on landing is transitioning from an automatic approach to a visual one seconds before landing. It leaves the pilot very little chance to adapt from the autopilot flying the aircraft to manually flying it before landing. I had always used the old adage, 'let the plane take the strain' and complete an autoland in such circumstances. At precisely two hundred feet, the runway lights slowly came into view as the automated voice of the aircraft announced, 'Decide'. I was going to let the aircraft complete the landing using the autopilot, and so I announced, "Land, I have control."

At this point, I was asked to take the autopilot out and complete a manual landing. I should have refused, let the aircraft land and talk about it later. Instead, I disconnected the autopilot as we crossed the threshold of the runway. The visibility was abysmal, and I landed slightly to the left of the centreline. In a routine flight, this would not have been commented on. I had often seen similar landings in poor conditions. We landed well within the normal touchdown zone. This, however, was not a routine flight. This was probably the most challenging type of landing. I had made a very smooth touchdown. Everything had been completely safe. Yes, it was slightly off the centreline, but nothing excessive or indeed unusual. Not every landing can be perfect, but every landing has to be safe.

I was subsequently given a flight to Mumbai. I flew a good approach and landing. The training captain duly recorded the fact, and I went to the hotel both relieved and satisfied. It looked like I was back on track. My next trip was the final line check. All I had to do now was fly the aircraft back to London without falling into any traps.

The flight home was a freighter. In other words, we had no passengers or cabin crew, just cargo in the holds. The co-pilot and I waited at the hotel check out desk. The training captain was late checking out. Whilst we waited, I chatted to the co-pilot and asked him if he would carry out the pre-flight freighter checks on aircraft. He had flown the 777 for nearly fifteen years and was more than happy to make sure the cargo checklist was completed. This was the procedure I had used on my previous 777 cargo flights. Eventually, the trainer arrived, and we set off for the airport. I noticed that he had a massive suitcase with him. I commented that he would not be allowed to check his case into the hold as we were a freighter, not a passenger flight. He countered that he would be allowed. He was the captain.

Of course, once we arrived at the airport, he was informed that he would have to take his case onto the aircraft. Only freight was allowed into the aircraft holds. We queued up at the security area. The co-pilot and I placed our wheelie bags onto the conveyor belt and made our way through the scanners. Suddenly, I heard a commotion behind me. The trainer's large suitcase would not fit into the scanner. He was being asked to empty his bag and put the items contained in it through separately. He made the cardinal error of arguing with the security team. This was never going to end well. It took nearly thirty minutes for security to process the contents of his case. As they started to confiscate prohibited items such as pen knives and scissors, his anger and frustration increased. During this commotion, I had a quiet chat with the other pilot. We were now thirty minutes late, and once again, I confirmed that he was happy to complete the cabin checklist.

Eventually, we were on our way to the aircraft. The atmosphere was challenging as the other captain complained about the heavy-handed security checks. I did my best not to become distracted by his anger.

On the aircraft, I completed all my pre-flight checks. The co-pilot reported that he had completed his freighter checks. At this point, the training captain turned to me and demanded why I had not completed the freighter checks myself? Replying that I had delegated this to the co-pilot, he barked that this was totally unacceptable. Apparently, I should have done this myself. I was astonished at his remarks, explaining that I was simply following the procedures I had been taught. My answer did not satisfy him, and he stormed off the flight deck to repeat these checks. The co-pilot and I looked at each other and shrugged.

After he returned, we continued with our checks and procedures. Eventually, we came to the point where we input the take-off calculations into the flight management computer. He placed the computer-generated figures on the console between the pilots. I checked the figures were correct, and as I always do, I asked the co-pilot to check them. We were all happy they were correct, so I read the figures for the trainer to insert them into our computer. Once this was completed, the training captain turned to me and asked if I was happy that everything had been completed correctly.

From the look on his face, I knew that I was in trouble. I re-checked everything and could not identify an error. And then he carried out one of the most astonishing things I have ever had the misfortune to witness on an aircraft. He picked up the printout of the figures and, with an almost theatrical flourish, unfolded a small section at the bottom of the page. He had folded over a small sentence at the bottom of the message and had made it invisible to me and the co-pilot. Only a very few runways have a non-normal acceleration height, usually for noise abatement purposes. I was furious and astonished that a fellow pilot had deliberately hidden vital information from his colleagues. I made my feelings very clear. In retrospect, I should have walked away. Instead, I settled for an assurance that he would not do anything so unprofessional for the remainder of the flight.

Nine hours later, we were approaching a foggy Heathrow airport. I was asked to complete a manual landing. This time I refused and completed an automatic landing.

After shutting the aircraft down, he proceeded to go into a detailed debrief. This went on for nearly an hour before I held my hand up and told him to stop. I had had enough.

I made my way to my car. I sat there for what must have been thirty minutes before I could summon up the energy to drive home. My head was pounding, and I shook it to clear my thoughts. It was then that I noticed a red stain running down my shirt. For the first time in my life, I was suffering a nosebleed, a very heavy nosebleed. The pressure had gotten to me. My body was finally rebelling.

I drove slowly home; my headache was still intense. I opened my back door and walked slowly into the kitchen. I was humming the Rolling Stones tune, *This Could Be the Last Time*, as I picked up the phone. I rang my aviation doctor and reported my symptoms, as I was legally required to do. Thirty seconds later, my pilot's medical licence was suspended. My career, which had started with failing my initial medical, appeared to be drawing to a close for the same reason. Alfie, our golden retriever, came to my side. He laid his head on my lap and began to gently whimper. This was the dog that would hang his head and go quietly to his bed the moment he saw me in my uniform. Equally, the moment I stepped back into the house, he would turn himself inside out at the excitement of my return. Today, instead of the usual barking and jumping, he had simply laid his head on my lap and stared up at me. He knew something was seriously wrong, and he was doing his best to comfort me. The good news for Alfie was that he would get to see me every day for the first time in his long life. He would not have to endure the pain of my departure for the foreseeable future. Life for Alfie, at least, was about to get a whole lot better.

Epilogue

Pathway for the Modern Pilot

For the first time in my adult life, I had time to reflect on over forty years of commercial flying. Not since I was eighteen had I had more than two consecutive weeks away from flying. Having been flying long haul for my entire career, my body had experienced more jet lag than was good for it. My way of coping on a day-to-day basis has luckily served me well. The strategy I chose was running. I ran to stave off the effects of the dreaded jet lag. If I flew to the United States, I would go for a five or ten-kilometre run before bed. I would run the next day again before flying back to Heathrow. Once I arrived home, which invariably was a very early morning arrival, I would go straight to bed. Three or four hours later, my body clock would wake me. I would then go for a late morning run. By doing all this, I could more or less guarantee that I always slept well and adapted to the local time of the country I was in almost seamlessly.

The downside to this came twice a year when I took my two-week holiday. It was almost like my body had been waiting for this break in my regular routine. It would shut down for the first week, leaving me feeling tired and irritable. I rarely had to go sick when I was flying, however on my first week of leave, if there was a bug going around, I would invariably catch it. I only started to feel vaguely human towards the end of the second week, which of course, was too late. Before I could really start to enjoy my downtime, I was flying, once again.

Now, with my aircraft and myself grounded, I had time to fully recover from the rigour and demands of my job. For the first time ever, I enjoyed watching my garden mature, bloom, and die back over the seasons. Simple things that most people take for granted. For decades I had been denied these simple pleasures because of my chosen career. By far, the most significant thing I was able to do was to reflect and reflect in great detail about my career and the changing face of aviation.

My path into aviation had been a relatively unusual one. I had been one of a small group who had self-funded their training. Not for me, the luxury of two years at an approved flying school. I worked hard for every hour I spent in an aircraft. All the ground school study was completed alone using second-hand study material.

However, once I started flying for an airline, I was treated as a professional. The training was superb, and I enjoyed the benefits of some of the best training facilities in the world. I had become more and more concerned for my profession as I saw the rise of budget airlines. Whilst everyone wants air travel at the lowest possible cost, the fact is that by definition travelling by air is expensive. If you look at the cost of buying an aircraft, the cost of fuel, and the cost of maintenance, it does not take an accountant to work out that the price of a ticket has to be more than the price of a bus ticket. Yet every week I would see advertisements for flights to Europe for less than ten pounds. Even if the aircraft was packed with one hundred and fifty passengers, that worked out to revenue of one thousand five hundred pounds. This would not even cover the cost of the landing fees.

Of course, the prices began to creep up but still barely covered the enormous overheads of operating the aircraft. Something had to give, and very sadly, the accountants' eyes turned towards an easy target, the pilots. We, as a profession, were now firmly in their cross-hatched sights.

Becoming a pilot is a complicated and expensive business. Many people apply to the airlines for pilot training courses, but the vast majority fail to get accepted. These new budget airlines began to realise that prospective pilots would do anything to become qualified. They took this passion and used it to their advantage. Whereas once airlines would choose the best applicants and train them at their own cost, these new airlines saw potential pilots not as an expense but as a way of saving money. Prospective candidates would now have to pay for their own training. They would have to pay for their own type ratings on the aircraft the company wanted them to fly. They would have to pay for their own uniforms. If they wanted to eat on the aircraft, they could bring their own food or buy a sandwich. Once qualified, the new pilot would not be paid a full salary until all these debts had been repaid. Believe it or not, some airlines are not even paying their new pilots for the first few months of their contracts. These airlines were taking advantage of the passion for flying that burned deep within the souls of their pilots. The cost to the individual could be one hundred and fifty thousand pounds for the initial training and then a further thirty-five thousand pounds for the cost of training to fly a particular jet aircraft.

I felt great anger towards these companies who are taking advantage of the next generation of airline pilots. Yes, I had to do it the hard way, but it was my choice. Had the airlines trained me then, they would have accepted the cost. Today, only those with wealthy parents or those prepared to take out enormous loans can afford to become pilots. This is just wrong.

There no longer exists the pathway I took way back in the 1970s. Today, the prospective pilot has to attend a full-time training course. There will never again be a pilot who would become the ultimate self-improver, the youngest captain on the 747 and eventually, the most experienced 747 captain in the world. Changing fleets so close to my retirement date had not gone well, I missed the 747 and I hoped that it missed me. The training in British Airways is second to none. It is a world leader in ensuring a safe operation. It was unfortunate that I flew with the wrong people at the wrong time. I have no criticism of the overall standards at British Airways. As this book goes to print, I am completing the process of regaining my medical certificate. I hope to be back flying in the months ahead. Despite this testing period, I can honestly say that although I felt disappointed in how things have transpired, I will always strive to improve. I will continue to evolve in the best way I can, by still improving.

THE END - FOR NOW

One of my first students, Chris Cotterell, was on his final descent into Gatwick. It was the final hour of his final flight. Once his Boeing 777 touched down, his long and distinguished career would be over. At that precise moment, his daughter, Charlotte, was on her very first flight. She was experiencing her first hour of airline flying as a first officer. Incredibly, they managed to speak to each other as Chris's 777 flew overhead of Charlotte's 737. My generation of pilots are all on our final approach. We are passing on the baton to a new generation as they begin their take-off roll. I wish them all the best of luck; it is now their turn to continue improving.

THE FUTURE

Overtaken by a Butterfly: The Stories Behind Running the World, will be published next year. Follow me as I try to avoid catastrophe, and natural disasters whilst running in various countries all over the world. From each far-flung location, every run seems destined to end in the most unusual circumstances, often with hilarious consequences.

Photo Gallery

Life with the 747

301

The Classic 747.
Lots of dials and buttons for the flight engineer to play with.
Photograph courtesy of Olivier Cleymen.

The 747-400.
The flight engineer has been replaced
by a cup holder.
Photograph courtesy of Al Pashley.

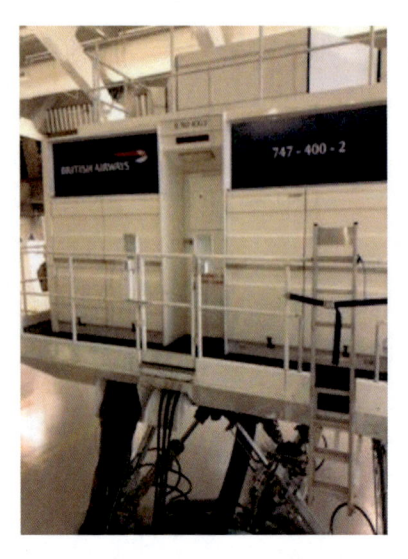

The dreaded simulator.
Eight hours of torture every six months.

Off to Cape Town, on what would turn out to be my very last flight on a 747, after a record breaking thirty-four years.

Another day; another spectacular view.

Greenland in the summer.
Not a bad view from the office window!

Final approach on my final 747 flight.
Landing into Cape Town.

Gosh, she was such a good looking 'Queen of the Skies'.

Boys on Tour. Rob, Me, and James. A road trip from Las Vegas.

Liz and the boys join me in the Grand Canyon.

About to take Robert and my niece, Amelia to New York on a visit to see James.

Passing on the baton to the next generation.
My pupil, Chris Cotterell, with his daughter, Charlotte, as she embarks on her career as a pilot.

Peter Brown and myself; best friends and business partners for over sixty years. Back to where our flying careers began. Shoreham Airport, gateway to the world. So many memories.